Critical Study of Nathaniel Hawthorne's *The Scarlet Letter*

Devaleena Das

PUBLISHERS & DISTRIBUTORS (P) LTD

Published by

PUBLISHERS & DISTRIBUTORS (P) LTD

7/22, Ansari Road, Darya Ganj, New Delhi-110002
Phones : +91-11-40775252, 23273880, 23275880, 23280451
Fax: +91-11-23285873
Web: www.atlanticbooks.com
E-mail: orders@atlanticbooks.com

Branch Office
5, Nallathambi Street, Wallajah Road, Chennai-600002
Phones : +91-44-64611085, 32413319
E-mail: chennai@atlanticbooks.com

Printed in India at Glorious Printers, A-13, D.S.I.D.C., Jhilmil Industrial Area, Delhi-110095

Dedicated to

The memory of my aunt, late Abantika Sarkar

Nothing matters but the quality
of the affection—
in the end—that has carved the trace in the mind;
dove sta memoria?

–Ezra Pound

Preface

I believe, Nathaniel Hawthorne's *The Scarlet Letter* is one of those literary masterpieces which will always remain as 'contemporary'. Rooted in the colonial history of America, the charm of the novel lies in the fact that regardless of its historical context, the novel encompasses timeless predicaments of humanity. Above all, Hawthorne's magnificent narrative playfulness has endowed the text with ceaseless magical appeal for amaranthine interpretations. As a result, even after innumerable critical reviews and analyses of the text, it seems always inadequate to get a complete grasp of this magnanimous interplay of complex human psychology, history and society. In this book, I have tried to conglomerate exhaustively all the possible and relevant critical views along with my own analysis of the text.

This book is the outcome of many years of my teaching of Hawthorne's text and my assorted papers and essays which I wrote for various conferences. Hawthorne's *The Scarlet Letter* cannot be confined simply within the boundaries of literature, and therefore, in this book I have tried to scrutinize the novel from interdisciplinary perspectives, especially from perspectives of psychology, cultural studies and history. The book contains comprehensive study of each chapter of *The Scarlet Letter* concentrating on critical analysis of minutest of details. The chapters in the book are primarily designed for the students to help them develop their critical and analytical power. This is further supported by chapters which deal with author's age, his biography, and themes merging in the novel. Originally designed for students pursuing master's degree in English Literature, the book covers chapter synopses, Hawthorne's biography, critical and theoretical approaches like feminist reading, psychoanalysis or postmodernist viewpoint. It took me more than a year to write this book primarily because of the text's unending nuances and significance. I hope I have captured the essence of Hawthorne's text and believe that the book will become a useful guide for students.

Devaleena Das

Acknowledgements

I express profound gratitude to my students who encouraged me to shape my class lectures in the form of a book. I am eternally indebted to my husband, Mr Pushkar Raj, for his silent unwavering encouragement, support and immense contribution in editing and forging the text. Numerous libraries have provided immensely helpful resources. I owe particular thanks to The American Centre Library for valuable books and journals. My parents, Kuntalika Das and Nityananda Das, have been my immutable support in their constant reassurance of their confidence and stimulation. I am indebted to them.

Devaleena Das

Contents

Preface .... *v*

Acknowledgements .... *vii*

1. Tradition and Individuality: Nathaniel Hawthorne... 1

2. History of *The Scarlet Letter* 13

3. Chapter Synopses with Critical Interpretations........ 21

4. Historical Echoes and Puritanical Ideals in *The Scarlet Letter* 171

5. *The Scarlet Letter* in the Light of Psychological Interplay 192

6. The New Eve Hester Prynne and Sexual Politics..... 206

7. The Child of Nature: Pearl 221

8. Arthur Dimmesdale: A Bundle of Contradictions.... 231

9. Chillingworth: The Black Man and His Alchemy.... 241

10. Hawthorne's Narrative Technique in *The Scarlet Letter* 252

11. The Art of Symbolism 261

12. Textual Notes and Allusions.................................. 271

13. Nathaniel Hawthorne: Biography 291

14. Chronology of Hawthorne's Life 308

15. Chronology of Hawthorne's Works 314

Bibliography 316

Chapter 1

TRADITION AND INDIVIDUALITY: NATHANIEL HAWTHORNE

The foundation of the United States is marked by violence, gunshots, insurrection, destruction, revolution and riots that provoked American writers to deliberate on the socio-political and cultural issues of America. American literature has witnessed the summit of cultural watermark in the pre-Civil War period aptly identified by F.O. Matthiessen as "American Renaissance" in his book entitled *American Renaissance: Art and Expression in the Age of Emerson and Whitman*. However, "American Renaissance" flourished at a time of national crisis, slavery, "Second Great Awakening"[1] and anxiety when the positioning of the 'self' amidst political, social, and religious tumults became crucial. The American territorial expansion, Andrew Jackson's Indian Removal Policies, Mexican War, Annexation of Texas, Manifest Destiny, and James Polk's Oregon Compromise have all contributed furore and turmoil to the history of the nation.[2] Besides, rapid development in commerce and spread of capitalism also made a strong impact in the development of America.

A pageant of literary masterpieces reflected the quintessential imaginative vitality of America. These books include *Representative Men* (1850), *The Scarlet Letter* (1850), *The House of the Seven Gables* (1851), *Moby-Dick* (1851), *Pierre* (1852), *Walden* (1854), and *Leaves of Grass* (1855). The blossoming of such artistic accomplishments happened because of perfect sporadic fusion between the writers and the reader which rarely happens in the literary history of a nation. This cross fertilization due to perfect reciprocity between readers and writers is ignited by versatile writers like Ralph Waldo Emerson, Henry David Thoreau, Nathaniel Hawthorne, Herman Melville, Alexander Poe, Walt Whitman and Emily Dickinson. Far removed from 'anxiety of influence',[3] this cluster of writers ushered in a new literary breeze fluttering the green foliage of American Literature. It has been the time when the spirit of individuality is recognised as the crucial momentum for historical progress. Nathaniel Hawthorne stands as the perfect example striking the note of national ideology of individualism. The antebellum tyrannies,[4] slavery and racism although persisted, yet Hawthorne with his romantic individualism deviated from his predecessors and arduously attempted for revolution and reform.

The spirit of Transcendentalism and mysticism started with the publication of Ralph Waldo Emerson's pamphlet *Nature* in 1836. Transcendentalism encompassed aesthetics, religion, and society and can be seen as an American form of Idealism and Romanticism. The theory of Transcendentalism cannot be reduced easily to some concrete definition because each of the individual transcendentalists propagated their philosophy differently. The primary aspect of Transcendentalism is the belief in a direct relationship with God and Nature. Emerson influenced Hawthorne and appeared like a "mystic stretching his hand out of cloud-land, in vain search for something real."[5] Hawthorne's writings reflected that though Transcendentalism is beckoning, yet it is excessively optimistic idealism which may lack element of pragmatism. Hawthorne also developed good friendship with Thoreau and appreciated his work but at the same time wondered about his principles of Transcendentalism. Yet the essence of Transcendentalism cannot be completely erased from Hawthorne's writings. Despite differences in opinions, like the transcendentalists, Hawthorne tried to explore the mystery of an interior life in the midst of outward life. Hawthorne's birthplace, Salem, was the hot spot of the germination of Transcendentalism. In the Salem Lyceum,[6] some of the greatest exponents of Transcendentalism initiated their philosophies. Regarding his quandary position of whether he supports the transcendentalists or not, Hawthorne has explained in the introduction to "Rappacicini's Daughter" the dilemma of 'to be or not to be':

> As a writer, he seems to occupy an unfortunate position between the Transcendentalists (who, under one name or another, have their share in all the current literature of the world) and the great body of pen-and-ink men who address the intellect and sympathies of the multitude. If not too refined, at all events too remote, too shadowy, and unsubstantial in his modes of development to suit the taste of the latter class, and yet too popular to satisfy the spiritual or metaphysical requisitions of the former, he must necessarily find himself without an audience, except here and there an individual or possibly an isolated clique.[7]

Idiosyncratic of Hawthornian style which never transparently asserts anything, Hawthorne neither conforms nor rejects the transcendentalists. He may not believe in the hyperbolic aestheticism but Transcendentalism has definitely instigated the spirit of individualism in him. Though popularly known as a Romance writer, Nathaniel Hawthorne is equally brilliant in dealing with the most poignant issues of his days—Puritanism and its effect, Transcendentalism and Feminism. He has been intrigued by history and its appropriation, the politics of religion and the burden of his ancestral lineage but the charm of this "man of true genius and a highly cultivated mind" remains in his subtle critical responses to the contemporary socio-political contexts. Though a shy and reclusive artist, his works reflect his internal struggle to accept the incongruences of his time. Like his own life that shows opacity and ambivalence, his literary output is always intrigued by multiplicity of meanings. He has always maintained distance with volatile controversial aspects of his time but never denied their legitimate space.

Born on July 4, 1804, in Salem, The Massachusetts Town, "the obscurest man in American letters",[8] as he called himself, Nathaniel Hawthorne was the only son of the naval officer Captain Nathaniel Hathorne and Elizabeth Clarke Manning Hathorne. The year Hawthorne was born, was significant in American history because on the same day, Thomas Jefferson was re-elected as the President of the United States. More expeditions continued in the New Found Land and New England expanded rapidly in the West. During Hawthorne's days, Salem was very popular for its harbour and proliferation of trade and industries. Both economic and cultural expansion developed across the world through sea voyages and explorations. William Hathorne from Hawthorne's family has been the first immigrant to settle in the New Found Land. This earliest autocratic forefather of Hawthorne was the founder of a theocratic society and played a crucial role in deprecating the natives of the land. He also established many offices; and had been a notorious tyrant in his ruthless enterprise of evacuation of the Indians. His son, John Hawthorne was the Judge of Salem who obediently followed the footsteps of his father. His merciless tyranny is unforgettable, especially in his role of driving away witches from the New Found Land by murdering, hanging and burning them. John confiscated properties of many innocent people, condemned them with severe punishments like burning of tongue, cutting of body parts or wearing heavy metallic alphabet on breasts.

The next Hawthorne generation however failed to achieve such high position but the Puritanical ferocity and tyranny is eternally imprinted and entwined with identity. It is interesting to note that Nathaniel Hawthorne added the "w" to his surname after his graduation that marked a difference from his ancestors. He remembered such ghastly persecution of Ann Coleman who had been subjected to trial under William Hathorne:

> Naked from the waist upward, and bound to the tail of a cart, [she] is dragged through the Main-street at the pace of a brisk wall, while the constable follows with a whip of knotted cords. A strong-armed fellows is that constable; and each time that he flourishes his lash in the air, you see a frown wrinkling and twisting his brow, and, at the same instant, a smile upon his lips. He loves his business, faithful officer that he is, and puts his soul into every stroke, zealous to fulfil the injunction of Major Hawthorne's warrant, in the spirit and to the letter. There came down a stroke that has drawn blood! Ten such stripes are to be given in Salem, ten in Boston, and ten in

> Dedham; and with those thirty stripes of blood upon her, she is to be driven into the forest.[9]

Hawthorne sometimes explicitly and sometimes implicitly reflected his guilt conscience because of his forefather's violent act. At the same time, he has been equally aware that to establish national literature of America free from the shadow of literature of England, one cannot deny the history of the birth of the New Found Land. To break free from English Literary umbrella and to achieve American literary independence, one must acknowledge his root and impartial review of the past centuries by delving deep into the socio-political history of the United States. While living in Salem after his graduation, Hawthorne occasionally visited the western side of the town known as Gallows Hill, where many natives were executed during witchcraft trials in 1692. Superstitious belief and unrealistic fear were very much in vogue despite the new secularist philosophy developed by Benjamin Franklin, Thomas Jefferson, and Thomas Paine. Hawthorne's visit to haunted places, barren lands or forbidden territories make him realise that one cannot deny the past in order to comment on American life.

Death is a common scenario in the contemporary world of the United States. Many young men have died in the course of explorations and sea voyages. In 1808, Captain Hathorne died at the age of thirty-two when he got infected with yellow fever in Dutch Guiana, South America. Captain Hathorne was a silent reserved man whose stern sombre attitude is said to have been reflected in his son. Nathaniel aged four at that time, with his mother and two sisters shifted to Mrs. Hathorne's relatives, the Mannings. The maternal lineage of Hawthorne ancestry is not much acclaimed. The Mannings shifted from England in 1679. Although Puritanical attitude has been a part of living in the ancestral blood, later it is observed that the family inclined more towards Unitarian principles. His father left little money and there was hardly any luxury in Nathaniel's life. The Mannings house on Herbert Street had been full of family members including four uncles, four aunts and grandfather Richard Manning. Child Hawthorne grew up more in the company of women and hardly any male member created strong impact in his life although his uncle, Robert Manning tried best to fill up the filial absence. Some of his biographers believed that this ambience resulted in a shy and introvert Hawthorne. Hawthorne also remained distant from his mother who had been emotionally strained after the death of her husband.

His disagreement with Puritanical sanctimonious practices and theologies germinated from a very early age. Injured in mind and body, he disliked going to school and preferred education at home. Joseph E. Worcester, a well-known lexicographer, provided Hawthorne personal guidance and Hawthorne started spending his time among books of Shakespeare, Spenser, Bunyan, and 18th century novelists. At this juncture he witnessed the battle between the American warship Chesapeake and the British Shannon. He also lost his grandparents followed by their migration in 1818 to a land owned by the Mannings near Raymond, Maine. Nathaniel's fondest memories of these days are when "I ran quite wild, and would, I doubt not, have willingly run wild till this time, fishing all day long, or shooting with an old fowling piece."[10] This idyllic life in the wilderness exerted its charm on the boy's imagination but is too short and ended abruptly in 1819, when he was admitted to the school of Samuel Archer, the man who remained as epitome of morality and discipline.

In 1821, when Hawthorne entered Bowdoin College in Brunswick, Maine under the regular guidance of Salem lawyer Benjamin L. Oliver Jr., his classmates included Henry Wadsworth Longfellow, who would become a distinguished poet and Harvard professor and Franklin Pierce, future fourteenth President of the United States and Horatio Bridge, who would publish Hawthorne's first collection of short stories. Besides these eminent figures, Calvin Stowe, a minister and a reformer, husband of the famous writer, Harriet Beecher Stowe who wrote Uncle Tom's Cabin also developed close friendship with Hawthorne. Strongly fascinated by Shakespeare, he joined college literary society called the 'Athenaean', visited concerts to watch Shakespearean plays like *King Lear* in Boston and started penning poetry. At the same time, he was fascinated by the psychological depth in Scottish Literature. Captivated by the English literary pillars,

Hawthorne was still unsure about his career, which is reflected in the letter to his mother:

> The being a Minster is of course out of Question. I should not think that even you would desire me to choose so dull a way of life...as to Lawyers there are so many of them already.... A Physician then seems to be "Hobson's Choice," but yet I should not like to live by the diseases and infirmities of my yellow Creatures.... What do you think of my becoming an Author, and relying for support on my pen. Indeed I think the illegibility of my handwriting is very authorlike. How proud you would feel to see my works praised by the reviewers.... But Authors are always poor devils, and therefore Satan may take them....[11]

At this juncture of life, he was equally perturbed by family lineage and struggle for individuality. Hawthorne had been aware of the power of tradition and natural inheritance but his artistic spirit compelled him to choose the difficult path of a writer than ascending to the ancestral role of authority. With financial instability, he still managed to publish hand-written satiric newspaper called the 'Spectator' with the aid of his sister Louisa. Behind the shy and calm stature of Nathaniel Hawthorne, one can get a glimpse of the budding revolutionary spirit wilfully rejecting the roles of his forefathers.

Hawthorne's writings have reflected his attempt to define America by reviewing and redefining the past. Hawthorne showed that no matter how uncomfortable the past is, the spirit of revolution can originate by travelling back through successive shades of time and space. Even if he wanted to severe the horrific history of the ruthless ancestors, he could not afford so. Born and brought up in the heart of Salem's maritime activity and attracted by the murmuring waves, the flashing sails of the ships in the sunlight and the bowsprits of the vessels, how can someone wipe away his orientation? The fear to conform to convention and tradition had been always in his mind and therefore in the introductory chapter of *The Scarlet Letter* he has written about "the grave, bearded, sable-cloaked...progenitor" of his family, "who came so early with his Bible and his sword". The conflict between authority, tradition, individuality, idealism, passion and career is a perennial subject in Hawthorne's life. Apart from deviating the ancestral career option, Hawthorne's courtship and marriage had been another departure from the tradition of his family. Hawthorne's secret engagement with Sophia Peabody followed by marriage was an extremely strained affair and the secret was revealed just few days before his wedding. The family members resented the concealment of the engagement and no one attended the wedding. The secret engagement is a matter of public ignominy as if the son has abandoned the women of the family who reared him in the absence of the father figure. Hawthorne always struggled to erase his embedded cultural orientation but never succeeded in blurring it. Hence, even after prolong cold distance between Hawthorne and his family, he could never abandon them and reunited at some point. For Hawthorne, therefore, tradition and history are intrinsically coexistent in present and cannot be segregated. Hawthorne's oscillation between tradition and individuality is reminiscence of what Levinas expressed in his *Totality and Infinity*: "History is worked over by the ruptures of history, in which a judgement is borne upon it."[12]

In 1849, Hawthorne wrote *The Scarlet Letter*, his most outstanding work that complemented him with hallmark of the first grade American author. Arlin Turner, one of Hawthorne's best twentieth-century biographers commented:

> for Hawthorne, the author of moral romances and studies of human character, the important consideration was not what an event or a situation was, but rather what his creative imagination conceived it to be. To him, every object, act or person, including himself and his activities, was less significant in itself than what it could be taken to represent.[13]

The Scarlet Letter is remarkably startling because it was unbelievable from shy Nathaniel Hawthorne who was ashamed of his earlier novel *Fanshawe*. He has infringed the question of morality, social convictions and the burden of shame. No one could have imagined that the same man who was suffering from prolonged embarrassment and frustration due to *Fanshawe* could even dare to think of such volatile issues like challenging the forefathers, disavowing the social and family obligations or reflecting on human relationships behind the codified social parameters. Even Hawthorne was sceptical in terms of readers' acceptance of such volatile issues. It is like a dream to discover the American genius disturbing the traditional world whose lingering roots can still be traced back in him. *The Scarlet Letter* is that phenomenal nucleus work in the history of American literature, in which the inherent controversial issues insinuate ceaseless interrogations regarding Hawthorne and America from the time of their birth.

The Scarlet Letter ushered in a new chapter in Hawthorne's life and in 1849, when the family moved to Lennox, Massachusetts, another literary personality, Herman Melville added new meaning to friendship in his life. Their strong friendship was soon evident when Melville dedicated his book, *Moby Dick*, to Hawthorne. During this time Hawthorne is said to have penned *The House of the Seven Gables*, which tragically accrues his conflict with Puritanism, added once more the legendary women figures in the chauvinist American literature whose conflicting ideologies reflect Hawthorne's own conflict with Calvinism and Transcendentalism. Though the immediate male members of the Hawthorne family have been absent in the author's life yet the aura of the male ancestors haunted him. The contraposition is reflected in his texts where Hawthorne presented some of the ever daring straight forward American femme fatal which very few contemporary authors can ever think of.

The dauntless spirit of Hawthorne may not be reflective in his reserve and reticent feature but his works suggest that his cultural insight into emergence of America and his psychological delving into human characters are unnerving even today. Like the psychologist Chillingworth of *The Scarlet Letter*, the Hawthornian discourses have disturbed the disciplinary societies and the multiple layers of the self. In his Preface to *The Scarlet Letter*, the personal essay called "The Custom House," he has both indulged in "an autobiographical impulse" and at the same time insisted that he would "keep the inmost Me behind its veil." Sauntering among villages and solitarily studying human mind, Hawthorne focused on the several boundaries that have fortified the self and the difficulties to evolve out of it. His thirst for wandering across the world is revealed when he wanted to join as an editor or as historian at a time when American government undertook a huge project that involved expedition in the South Sea. In his Preface to the third edition of *Twice-Told Tales*, he has stated that his sketches "are not the talk of a secluded man with his own mind and heart..., but his attempts...to open an intercourse with the world."[14] For him the forsaken abandoned papers in the Custom House hold immense importance than the Puritanical doctrine or the notes of the clergymen. In his Preface to *Mosses from an Old Manse*, he has explained that "It was as if I had found bits of magic-looking glass with the images of a vanished century in them."[15] No doubt, Hawthorne remained discrepant and mismatch in the group of Melville, Thoreau and Emerson. Nathaniel Hawthorne is always neoteric because he reflects on those coercive aspects of humanity like sin, power or psychosis which are relevant at any time in any culture and civilization across the globe. The Freudian clinical discourses of sexuality, conscious, unconscious and subconscious levels of the mind or the presence of the 'uncanny' are already anticipated in the Hawthornian philosophy. Hawthorne reckoned the social ramification of the anxiety of secrecy, repression and the incarnation of the evil which Sigmund Freud has theorised in his seminal article "Das Unheimliche," in 1919. Michel Foucault's power dynamics in relation to social vigilance and surveillance is reminiscent of what Hawthorne's texts served as vignette exemplifying that the horror of observation and gaze is enough to cross the line of sanity. Hawthorne's assaying of repressive discourse, guilt, indelible stain and repentance conduits from individual or personal life to American consciousness trying to unveil the hermeneutic desire within each of us.

NOTES

1. After the establishments and proliferation of the Puritanical doctrines about God and Christianity in the New England, the most significant religious revivals that profoundly shaped American Christianity are The First Great Awakening and The Second Great Awakening. The First Great Awakening occurred around 1730-40 founded by Jonathan Edward and continued till American Revolution while the Second Great Awakening happened in the first half of the

nineteenth century. The Second Great Awakening under the impact of Transcendentalism has shaped the burgeoning American culture. It is a form of unprecedented revivals that emphasised the visit of the Holy Spirit. Charles Grandison Finney is the pioneering leader of the Second Awakening. The former re-visioned the concept of sin and repentance while the latter looked for the Christian Reasons for Slavery. It directly influenced antebellum reform movements, abolitionism, prison reforms, and women's rights.

2. The American territorial expansion started in 1830s and 1840s and is justified by Manifest Destiny. In 1830, President Andrew Jackson in his Second Annual Message to Congress explained Indian Removal Policy and expanding the American territory by driving away the five predominant Indian tribes. It is one of the most significant incidents in the history of the nation. The germ of American expansionism can be traced back to its colonial roots that encouraged expansion of the national borders by forcibly seizing lands from the Native Americans and the Mexicans. The Manifest Destiny is the widely believed theory that American settlers are destined by God to expand their empire. The most influential advocate, Journalist John L. O'Sullivan, of Jacksonian democracy, in his 1839 article propounded the "*divine destiny*" of the settler Americans to expand their land. Though he did not mention the term Manifest Destiny, but propounded that Americans are chosen by God "to establish on earth the moral dignity and salvation of man". In 1845, O'Sullivan penned another essay entitled "Annexation" in which he first used the phrase 'manifest destiny'. The process of land acquisition started under such beliefs that United States is destined to spread self-advancement, civilization and democracy across the continent to the Pacific Ocean. The conflict between the United States and Mexico from 1846 to 1848 popularly known as The Mexican War further led to annexation of Texas, which Mexico considered part of its territory despite the 1836 Texas Revolution. Last but not the least, *The Oregon Treaty* between the United Kingdom and the United States signed on June 15, 1846 in Washington, D.C. is noteworthy. It settled the Oregon boundary dispute where both Britain and the U.S. claimed proprietorship.
3. See Bloom, Harold. *The Anxiety of Influence: A Theory of Poetry*. Oxford University Press: New York, 1973. It refers to the shadow of influence of the predecessor writers and explains that all literary texts are in response to earlier texts and writers whom the new present writers cannot completely avoid.
4. 'Antebellum' means existing before a war. In this context, it refers the period before American Civil War. Antebellum tyranny refers to the practice of slavery that existed before the American Civil War.

5. *Ordinary Mysteries: The Common Journal of Nathaniel and Sophia Hawthorne*. ed. Lawrence, Nicholas R & Werner, Marta L. American Philosophical Society: Philadelphia, 2005. p. 79.
6. The Salem Lyceum was the most significant hall in Salem formed in January, 1830. The first lecture was delivered by Judge Daniel A. White. The purpose of building such a hall was for intellectual discussions and lectures.
7. Hawthorne, Nathaniel. *Tales And Sketches*. New York: Literary Classics, 1982. p. 975.
8. Hawthorne, Nathaniel. *Twice-Told Tales*. New York: Hougton Mifflin Company, 1851. p. 13.
9. Hawthorne, Nathaniel. *The Snow-Image and Other Twice-Told Tales*. New York: Hougton Mifflin Company, 1851. p. 87.
10. Bloom, Harold. *Nathaniel Hawthorne*. U.S.A: Chelsea House Publisher 2003. p. 8.
11. Woodberry, E. George. *Nathaniel Hawthorne*. U.S.A: Kessinger Publishing, 2004. p. 9.
12. Levinas, Emmanuel. *Totality and Infinity*. Kluwer Academic Publisher: Netherland, 1969. p. 52.
13. Turner, Arlin. *Nathaniel Hawthorne: A Biography*. University of Michigan: Oxford University Press, 1980. pp. 88-89.
14. Hawthorne, Nathaniel. *Twice-Told Tales*. New York: Hougton Mifflin Company, 1851. p. ix.
15. Hawthorne, Nathaniel. *Mosses from an Old Manse*. Boston: James R. Osgood and Company, 1876. p. 26.

Chapter 2

HISTORY OF *THE SCARLET LETTER*

In the 1837 short story "Endicott and the Red Cross," Hawthorne visualised his emancipatory 'New Eve' of American literature:

> There was likewise a young woman, with no mean share of beauty, whose doom it was to wear the letter A on the breast of her gown, in the eyes of all the world and her own children. And even her own children knew what that initial signified. Sporting with her infamy, the lost and desperate creature had embroidered the fatal token in scarlet cloth, with golden thread and the nicest art of needlework; so that the capital A might have been thought to mean Admirable, or anything rather than Adulteress.[1]

The Scarlet Letter written between the fall of 1849 and February 1850 has a deep historical background. Hawthorne's long association with his Puritanical ancestral antiquity regarding witchcraft and folklore in New England always haunted his imagination. Hawthorne's reading of books like Snow's *History of Boston* by Dr. Caleb H., or *History of Massachusetts* by Anne Hutchinson perturbed him to discover some dark truths within his mind. His son Julian explained how his father used to read old newspapers, magazines and chronicles to discover the forgotten past and strengthen the verisimilitude of his novels and stories. *The Scarlet Letter* refers to various historical incidents like the death of Governor Winthrop or the Election Day, real life characters like Mrs Hibbins and Reverend John

Wilson regarding whom Hawthorne traversed into the history of Salem. In the book *History of New England* by John Winthrop, James Savage writes in the footnote that governor Bellingham's sister Mrs Hibbins, after the death of her husband, is seen as eerie mysterious 'creature'and is being ultimately given death punishment as she is suspected to be in lieu with the Devil. 'The Salem witch trial' created hysteria not only among the contemporary people but its aftermath can be traced in the fear and trauma of next generations. Hawthorne is scared because the persecuting spirit has been inherited by all his forefathers who have taken active part in Salem Witch Trial as well as genocide of the native Americans. Margaret B. Moore in her essay "The Salem World of Nathaniel Hawthorne" writes that the sense of guilt is "So deep a stain, indeed, that his old dry bones, in the Charter Street burial-ground must still retain it, if they have not crumbled utterly to dust".[2] In the name of chastity and purity, these earliest immigrants in Salem attempted to build theocratic society. His ancestor William Hathorne was famous in the history of America for driving away violently the Quakers, who opposed the Puritanical preaching and the concept of salaried ministry. Hawthorne's ancestors persecuted the Quakers as fanatics, confiscated their properties and hanged them. One such Quaker victim whose blood stained story haunted Hawthorne was Ann Coelman. Like Ann, women who tended to be independent and non-conformist were executed mercilessly. The Salem witchcraft hysteria is repository of Hawthorne's discourse of evil, crime and gloominess. This ghastly historical context always haunted him in his unconscious mind and is therefore reflected in his shame, guilt, betrayal and 'necrophobia'. Whether it is malicious Mistress Hibbins, the dark impenetrable forest of temptation, the macabre mansion of the governor with cabalistic details, shamanistic Chillingworth or the mysterious Black man—all envisage the chronic of Salem horror and Hawthorne's struggle to seek the epistemological truth.

Beside this Salem background, the characters also have historical orientations. By 1841, Hawthorne seems to have focused some of his ideas about the characterization of Dimmesdale and in his *American Notebooks* he explains, "To symbolize moral or spiritual disease by disease of the body—thus, when a person committed any sin, it might cause a sore to appear on the body—this to be wrought out."[3] The naming of Roger Prynne turned to Roger Chillingworth happened to be from the real-life character William Prynne, who has been an anti-Catholic Protestant and is famous for his criticism of King Charles I. Just four years before he drafted *The Scarlet Letter*, Hawthorne writes in his journal, "The life of a woman, who, by old colony laws, was condemned always to wear the letter A, sewed on her garment, in token of her having committed adultery."[4] John Winthrop, in *History of New England* has narrated the story of Mary Latham of Plymouth Colony and James Britton who are condemned and hanged in March 1644 for adultery. Besides, Hawthorne has been aware of Salem's history of Hester Craford, who, in 1688 was "severely whipped" for fornication with John Wedg. Above all, the controversial intellectual woman, Anne Hutchinson on whom Hawthorne has ameliorated and sketched her character, no doubt contributed to Hawthorne's imagination of the character of Hester Prynne. Mrs Hutchinson has been charged for unlawful preaching against Governor John Winthrop's religious words and was finally banished from Massachusetts.

Biographers of Hawthorne always tried to probe into the complex mercurial yet reserved nature of Hawthorne and his reactions to ubiquitous presence of various pervasive women in his personal and professional life. These women not only shaped and influenced Hawthorne's life but also their preponderance can be reflected in his works. It is believed that the character of Hester Prynne is the consequence of Hawthorne's own observation of her widowed mother Elizabeth Manning Hathorne and her struggle to rear children in absence of patriarchal authority. The self-determined and independent rebellious nature of Hester is said to have emanated from Hawthorne's close acquaintanceship with Margaret Fuller. This is asserted most aptly by Thomas R. Mitchell who writes "Through Hester, Hawthorne, on one level at least, continues his now-distant dialogue with Fuller, and attempts to represent, if not actually to solve, the riddle of Fuller and their relationship."[5] Adam Blair by J.G. Lockhart is the undeniable source for Arthur Dimmesdale who, apart from being a Calvinist minister suffered from remorse and guilt for being the lover of a married woman and finally confessed in the rigid theological world and punished himself by resigning from his post and became a soil tiller. Hawthorne's Pearl, the mysterious fiendish child of Hester Prynne originates from his observation of his preternatural daughter Una.

From traditional and ancient practices to contemporary sources, this immortal masterstroke of Hawthorne is multi-layered with innumerable socio-political and interdisciplinary threads. His autobiographical element in the introductory chapter further correlates several personal reflections and professional conflicts which he has expressed through the dexterity of his narrative technique throughout the novel. In a letter to Horatio Bridge dated 4 February 1850, Hawthorne has written:

> There is an introduction to this book—giving a sketch of my Custom-House life, with an imaginative touch here and there—which perhaps may be more widely attractive than the main narrative.[6]

Horatio Bridge played an important role in Hawthorne's life especially in the appointment of Hawthorne to the post of the Surveyor in the Salem Custom House in 1846. Financial crisis had been a perennial problem in Hawthorne's life especially after his marriage to Sophia Peabody and the arrival of the children. Sophia at this time was expecting their second child and Hawthorne has been desperate to secure some permanent job. His experience as the surveyor in the Custom House and the political machinations are effervescent in the Introduction of *The Scarlet Letter*. His attack of the Salem Whig leaders, especially Charles W. Upham who removed him from the post is reflective of his deep seated hatred for this man. The Whigs politically scandalised Nathaniel Hawthorne and as a result his bitterness the lacerating criticism is reflected in the chapter called "The Custom House". This chapter can be considered as the chiasmus of the novel because it entails Hawthorne's ancestry, autobiographical elements, history of his hometown Salem and it also enhanced the thematic development of the novel.

Saturated with history, politics, religion and autobiographical element, *The Scarlet Letter* can be seen as a historical novel. The early American colonial settlements at Massachusetts Bay, Plymouth, and Salem are also historically reflected in the novel. His Puritanical framework which is the backdrop of the novel is primarily forged out of his exploration and research of New England historical records like John Winthrop's *The History of New England* from 1630 to 1649. When Puritanism is seen as the utopian social philosophy, Hawthorne denied such idealism. The Puritanical life is captured in minute details ranging from the description of the harbour, the internal politics and lives of the leaders, buildings and interior household that reflect power and luxury, the dress code of men and women, cultural and social practices, preaching and education for children and the confluence of law and religion. The reference to prison evokes the theme of crime and punishment and also demonstrates how futile the pursuits of the first settlers of the Massachusetts colony were to build an ideal society.

Apart from Hawthorne's brooding imagination that added the romantic essence to the novel, the text is also a commentary on the genesis of nation building. It is not merely a romance or an imaginative escape but it also serves as the essential compendium of contemporaneous America. The most exciting and artistic craftsmanship of Hawthorne lies in his conscious attempt to fuse the seventeenth and nineteenth century America and the consequences of the former in the latter. The cultural settings of the novel reveal the entire gamut of historical, social and literary timelines of America from the day of early colonial period to the Renaissance and Transcendentalism. When Hawthorne started writing the novel, the seed of revolution has already germinated in France, Italy and Austria. The wild spirit of revolution has also touched silently the mind of this isolated author. The nineteenth century European revolutions abroad as well as revolutions at home are all deeply insinuated in his works. In the prefatory essay, "The Custom House," Hawthorne particularly refers to the French Revolution of 1789 when he mentions "Posthumous Papers of a Decapitated Surveyor" hinting at the image of guillotine. The spirit of revolution is also related to the question of slavery, the most controversial aspect of Hawthorne's works which critics have argued again and again.

This quintessential artist of American Literature has contemplated on every socio-political and religious aspects of the United States but his detachment in the matter of slavery is intriguing. His discomforting silence in relation to slavery and racism is deeply rooted in his political background. Being a perpetual Democrat and supporter of Democratic leaders and friends who never felt the weightage and credence for slavery, Hawthorne remained incoherent. President Andrew Jackson who was notoriously famous in driving away the Native Americans was greatly admired by Hawthorne for his boldness and was the epitome of courage. Though 'unfortunate' in its origin, Hawthorne never viewed slavery in the negative light of exploitation and crime. Hawthorne was aware of *The Fugitive Slave Law* of 1850 which affirmed that it is the responsibility of every faithful American citizen to help in the process of capturing fugitive slaves and remain committed to the nation. By portraying Hester Prynne as a dedicated soul in the interest of humanity, Hawthorne perhaps supported *The Fugitive Slave Law*. Exemplifying Hester as the obedient member who accepted the Puritanical punishment, Hawthorne wanted to show how Hester maintained the sanctity and ethics of the society. Critics like Leland S. Person in the famous essay "The Dark Labyrinth of the Mind: Hawthorne, Hester, and the Ironies of Racial Mothering,"[7] has claimed that Hester Prynne is a black slave mother. Person has argued this with Toni Morrison's concept of 'Africanist presence':

> It [Africanist presence] is a dark and abiding presence there for the literary imagination as both a visible and an invisible mediating force. Even and especially, when American texts are not 'about' Africanist presences or characters or narrative or idiom, the shadow hovers in implication, in sign, in line of demarcation.[8]

Morrison, who has claimed herself as America's reformative and revisionary daughter, suggests that even if the white Americans chooses to keep aside the dark African presence, yet the shadow of African presence is undeniable. Though

Hawthorne is extremely fantastic in his play of words and verbal glitter that can beguile or rejuvenate his readers, yet he cannot completely wash his hands off from slavery. Person has identified Hawthornian implicit credo regarding slavery in Hester Prynne's submission but another group of critics believe that since Hester is a white mother, she is spared from death penalty. An anti-Lincoln Copperhead Democrat, on June 15th 1851, Hawthorne has proclaimed in his letter to his friend Zachariah Burchmore:

> I have not, as you suggest, the slightest sympathy for the slaves; or, at least, not half as much as for the laboring whites, who, I believe, are ten times worse off than the Southern negroes.[9]

Such strong racist comment from an American literary exponent is shocking and unbelievable. Such an unambiguous statement from an otherwise ambiguous artist is due to his personal and political orientation. The African-American antipathy is reflective of Hawthorne's democratic ideologies that white Americans are racially superior to make America as the most advanced nation of the world. Such repugnance is reflected always in his works. In *The Scarlet Letter*, the physician Roger Chillingworth after being imprisoned by the Native Americans seems to have undergone metamorphosis inwardly as well as outwardly. Chillingworth's redundant presence is not only disturbing for Hester and Dimmesdale but he is presented as the anomalous in the crowd attired in strange garb and with queer looks. His knowledge in medicine and science has been from the best European institutes but Hawthorne reflected that his knowledge seems to be contaminated by mysterious Native American spirit after his prolong dwelling among them. His evil manoeuvring and knowledge of alternative healing methods are viewed in the light of dark hideous power which he inherited from the natives. Later critics like Jean Fagan Yellin and Jennifer Fleischner researched and justified that Hawthorne purposely refused to stay away from the issue of slavery in his works because for him slavery is neither outrageous nor inhumane.

The Scarlet Letter will always remain an ever demanding and breath taking sensation and exemplar of great literature because of its historical, religious, social, political, psychological and autobiographical density. The various contentions, polemical and political debates, controversies and his artistic allurement of words and ideas are part of his charm as "the American wonder-child with his magical, allegorical insight".[10] His novels and prose never claim conclusiveness but provokes readers to undertake an adventure into the recalcitrant mystery of human mind.

NOTES

1. Hawthorne, Nathaniel. *Selected Tales and Sketches*. Digireads.com Publishing, 2007. p. 98.
2. Moore, Margaret B. *The Salem World of Nathaniel Hawthorne*. U.S.A: University of Missouri Press, 1998. pp. 37-38.
3. *Ordinary Mysteries: The Common Journal of Nathaniel and Sophia Hawthorne*. ed . Lawrence, Nicholas R & Werner, Marta L. American Philosophical Society: Philadelphia, 2005. p. 5.
4. Mitchell, R. Thomas. *Hawthorne's Fuller Mystery*. U.S.A.: Book Crafters, 1998. p. 136.
5. Mitchell, R. Thomas. *Hawthorne's Fuller Mystery*. U.S.A.: Book Crafters, 1998. p. 133.
6. *Selected Letters of Nathaniel Hawthorne*. Ed. Myerson, Joel. U.S.A: Ohio State University. p. xiii.
7. *The Scarlet Letter and Other Writings*, New York: W.W. Norton and Company, 2005: pp. 656-69.
8. Morrison, Toni. *Playing in the Dark: Whiteness and the Literary Imagination*. U.S.A.: Harvard University Press, 1992. p. 46.
9. *Centenary Edition of the Works of Nathaniel Hawthorne*, XVI (Columbus: Ohio University Press, 1962-1997), XVI, 456.
10. D.H. Lawrence described Hawthorne in these words. see Foster, Richard & Sutton, Walter. *Modern Criticism: Theory and Practice*. U.S.A.: The Odyssey Press, 1963. p. 465.

Chapter 3

CHAPTER SYNOPSES WITH CRITICAL INTERPRETATIONS

THE CUSTOM-HOUSE INTRODUCTORY TO 'THE SCARLET LETTER'

Nathaniel Hawthorne initiates the novel with a long introductory essay called "Custom House" which seems apparently incoherent to the main sequential narrative development. This introductory chapter provides not merely the narrative framework but also reflects on the socio-political history of America. When Hawthorne had given his manuscript of *The Scarlet Letter* to his publisher in 1850, the suggestion of the editor was to eliminate the introduction on 'The Custom House' because of the pungent criticism of the Puritanical America. However, in the Preface to the second edition of *The Scarlet Letter* there is an attempt to lighten the satirical rebuff. In the second edition Preface he remarks: "The sketch might, perhaps, have been wholly omitted, without loss to the public, or detriment to the book...."[1] Yet, in his Preface to the second edition, Hawthorne referred to "The Custom-House" as "an introductory sketch." This section also elaborates the source of the novel, the gradual artistic germination of the narrative voice and how the novel has taken shape in the narrator's mind. The narrative discourse in this chapter can be classified into three divisions. The first section is an elaborate description of the Custom-House and simultaneously connects the narrator's forefathers to the history of Salem. It contains the autobiographical element in it. The second section is a satire on the malign politics in the then governmental jobs and the struggle between artistic augmentation and the commercial world. The final section is a way of authenticating the story with historical details and how it is an attempt to re-shape history with new insights.

The narrator introduces himself as the "chief executive officer," or surveyor of the Salem Custom House at Massachusetts, who in order to support his family accepted this appointment in 1846. The very setting of the Custom-House symbolises sterility and dereliction. Situated on a rotting wharf in a half-finished building, the narrator finds life in the custom house to be mundane without any hope of progress. The emblematic American eagle with her wide spread wings at the entrance of the Custom-House is symbolical of ferocity and mischief and the narrator ironically comments that the eagle symbolises American government. To seek shelter and security under its wings is dangerous in reality because one can become an outcast. The eagle with its ferocity and wide spread wings threatens as well as provides shelter. His critical reflection on the stringent Puritanical forefathers is an attempt to unleash the truth about their Herculean task of settlement in the new found land as well as their cruelty and harshness in driving the natives and establishing a new government.

The narrator hints that nepotism is the primary reason of appointment of many of his incompetent co-workers whom he describes as "wearisome old souls". The old General represents some of the heroic qualities as reflected in his compassion and moral strength. Sometimes he presides over the custom house but he seems to be of no importance to the corrupt employee. Since very few ships arrive at Salem, there is hardly any ambience of work except dissonance and corruption. In such dull monotonous existence, the narrator seeks ways and means to amuse himself and stay away from the indolent life of the Custom-House. He recounts one such memorable rainy evening when his curious mind hovered in the vacant part of the building at the second storey. His wandering unravelled a manuscript in a pile of abandoned papers wrapped in a scarlet, gold-embroidered piece of cloth in the shape of the letter "A." He discovered that the piece of writing belongs to a custom surveyor named Jonathan

Prue who lived hundred years back and has documented the local history of mid-seventeenth century Boston in that manuscript.

Commentary

The narrator attempts to unravel American culture and history. The narrator is the reflection of Nathaniel Hawthorne who belonged to Salem and worked as a custom officer. Hawthorne had also lost his job after changes in the political scenario which made him a vociferous critic of Puritanical world. The autobiographical element is evident as the narrator himself cherishes the desire to elucidate 'autobiographical' essay of his three years' experience at Salem Custom-House. Unlike the author's Puritanical ancestors, the narrator deviates as he contemplates on writing as a therapeutic way.

The description of Salem is both nostalgic and a vivid criticism of Hawthorne's frustration in a place of sterility. Salem has been a bustling town in the past and yet he finds his attachment to the place not only disturbing but also uncomfortable. This may be due to his family history and his ancestral root that reminds him of his cruel forefathers who had indulged in bigotry and persecution. Hawthorne explains the dilemma of inevitable acknowledgement of his ancestors and his wilful rejection of the ancestral legacy.

He escapes from the demands of his conventional Puritanical forefathers. He reflects upon the desire of free American spirit and yet he is incapable of completely disentangling from the bonds of family, religion and society. Moreover, his isolation and his sense of forlorn also impart a symbolical meaning to the custom house. His aloofness and his artistic spirit in the midst of incompatible crowd reflect his individualism.

The detailed architectural description of the Custom House is significant. The first storeyed is completely open for all customers and it stands for the public while the secluded second storeyed is closed where abandoned untold history awaits. The entire custom house is also reminiscent of the description of Manse in Hawthorne's *Mosses from an Old Manse*. Manse therefore always reminded Hawthorne of the lingering guilt conscience of his race and their violent act of displacements of the Indians.

This introduction connects with the main narrative plot and with subtlety relates to the characters, themes and the narrator. This narrative discourse consists of Hawthorne's "autobiographical impulse" as well as his technique of withholding "the inmost Me behind its veil." This conflict of disclosure and revelation is another predominant theme that is reflected in the character of Arthur Dimmesdale, the hero of the novel. There is a significant connection between the narrator and the protagonist of the novel, Hester Prynne. Both seem to be alienated from the community of Salem and both are deviant in the Puritanical Society. His anticipated fear of his identity being reduced to a mere custom Stamp, or to a pile of abandoned manuscripts also forms a strong nexus between Hester and the narrator. Hester's identity is symbolically reduced to a mere alphabet and the narrator's fear refers to that. Hawthorn's art of autobiography is mingled with the art of his story telling. In his Preface to the third edition of *Twice-Told Tales*, he states that his sketches "are not the talk of a secluded man with his own mind and heart..., bur his attempts...to open an intercourse with the world."[2]

Hawthorne's art of self-revelation is related to the depiction of the characters in the novel and how one fails to recognize or act upon impulses toward intimacy. Hawthorne's pungent criticism as he is being terminated from the custom house is reflected in his satirical criticism. His seclusion and marginalisation is similar to Hester's ostracisation who has been never afraid to strike a note of individuality. The element of loneliness evoked in this introductory essay is a Romantic trait. More than the sociological aspect, he is interested in the psychological dimension of forlorn and seclusion. Hawthorne like a typical Romantic spirit ponders upon the Imaginative faculty of the artistic self. As he searches for the source of inspiration in the 'moonbeam' or in the 'firelight' for his artistic eruption, he comes across the "rich effusions of deep hearts" among the rubbish. It is interesting to note here that for Henry James, Hawthorne is emblematic of the true American literary spirit especially in terms of American Romanticism. His writing is described as "charming and natural", as having "purity and spontaneity and naturalness of fancy", and as offering "a sort of straightness and naturalness of execution".[3]

Hawthorne's wistful reflection of his ancestors is also a way of unleashing the lurking consciousness of sin. They are described as "dim and dusky", "grave, bearded, sable-cloaked, and steel crowned," who are "bitter persecutors". It is interesting to quote from Hawthorne's *The House of the Seven Gables* where the character Holgrave remarks:

> ...a family should be merged into the great obscure mass of humanity, and forget all about its ancestors. Human blood, in order to keep its freshness, should run in hidden streams.[4]

There is a conscious attempt in Hawthorne to deviate from his ancestors' route. While the Puritans believe that salvation can be achieved through physical ignominy, for Hawthorne repression of natural desire is also a sin. Hawthorne has differentiated sin of the flesh and moral sin of deliberate choice. As a result in the novel we will show how Hester will survive by practising charity while Dimmesdale and Chillingworth die. Hawthorne believed that forgiveness is possible for every sin except where the sinner refuses to repent, as personified by Chillingworth. After Dimmesdale's death, he therefore becomes aimless. If the Puritanical society believes in penitence like socially and religiously imposed punishment on the sinner, then Hawthorne's Protestanism encourages repentance, charity and mercy as a measure of self-purification. Hester Prynne with her free will indulged in adultery and with her free will again, she has chosen charity to humanity and hence Hawthorne shows how the significance of the letter 'A' changes from 'Adultery' to 'Abel'.

In this way, the Introduction is the foundation to generate the curiosity of the readers as well as it builds the fundamental structure of the novel. Like a typical Aristotelian plot, the beginning opens multiple discourses and threads on which the plot is woven. From a postmodernist point of view, *The Scarlet Letter* is the perfect example of a postmodernist text that shows the quest for self-consciousness, endless deferral, multiplicity of meanings and multiple layers of narrative voice.

In this Introduction, we have three shadows of narrative figure, Mr Prue, the narrator and Nathaniel Hawthorne.

This Introduction also ponders on the question of history and its authenticity. The haunting reflection of the past in the present as inescapable truth is also evident in the introductory chapter. The repressed history of many untold things are still scattered which if one wants can observe and narrate. Hawthorne believed that "The past was not dead". It is believed that the story is based on true historical event and there are enough authentic sources. Initially, Hawthorne wanted to include the story of Hester Prynne in a collection to be called as *Old Time Legends: Together with Sketches, Experimental and Ideal.* The element of historicity is reflected in the introductory chapter on the Custom House. The art of restoring and re-writing of previous manuscripts is a novelistic device used earlier by many writers. As a historical novel, *The Scarlet Letter* is essentially important because of the reviewing history of the Puritanical world and his ancestors who have witnessed several Hester Prynne to be persecuted. Hawthorne, from a very early age, had a tendency to conduct a deliberate inquiry into the historical meaning of his local past as reflected in texts like *Seven Tales of My Native Land* and *Provincial Tales.*

CHAPTER ONE: THE PRISON-DOOR

The story begins in a seventeenth-century Boston prison house setting. The focus is on a local congregation of bearded men and some morose women who are mostly draped in grey cloaks and dark hoods. They have all assembled in front of a wooden edifice. The narrator ponders on the requirements of prison and cemetery and he reminds that North America had been one of the penal colonies developed through indentured servitude. Just beside the first burial ground, stands the prison house.

The narrative description is more on the architectural structure of seventeenth-century Boston prison. The door is made of heavy oak wood studded with iron spikes. The juxtaposition of prison and cemetery in the new found land by the Puritans is deliberated by the narrator. The forefathers of Hawthorne have built-up the ideal prison house in order to establish the fact that their new found land should be based on discipline and austerity. The requirement of prison and cemetery in the self-proclaimed 'utopian' dreamland of the settlers is paradoxical. The note of antiquity is reflective in the rusted iron oak-door in this dream land. Sarcastically the narrator says that it seems that this prison edifice has never known youthful era.

The surrounding verdure consists of bushy vegetation, overgrown with burdock, pig-weed and apple-peru. The soil seems to be hostile for anything beautiful and fruitful except for the incongruous wild rose bush with its ethereal blooming beauty and fragrance. This rose bush is perhaps the only effusion of life for the convicts and the source of hope. In the wilderness of sterility and parched prison house, the wild rose bush has strangely survived the harshness of the land but the oak and the pine trees seem to cast a dark glooming shadow on the rose bush. The towns people believe that the wild rose bush at the prison door sprang up the moment Anne Hutchinson,[5] the rebellious woman entered the prison.

Commentary

The necessity of a prison in the colony requires a re-visioning of the historical background. The prison and the cemetery are harsh reality by which Hawthorne meant that how surreal a utopian world is. The Puritanical concept of an ideal society is therefore mocked at by Hawthorne. The ironical utopian world is besotted with darkness and gloom and Hawthorne mocks at the immaterial dreams of the Puritans. Hawthorne's reflection on the prison house is the ironical observation of how the Puritans exercised stringent control over the society. More than safety and security of the settlers, the emphasis is on the concept of crime and punishment. This strategy of punishing the perpetrators relates to Michel Foucault's idea of 'panoptic' and 'surveillance'. Jeremy Bentham's 'Panopticon' is an architectural embodiment where power is exercised in the form of surveillance and yet it should remain unverifiable. Foucault shows the shift in the mode of punishment in the Western world in seventeenth and eighteenth century America. Jeremy Bentham, like many of his contemporaries, had been a utopian who ridiculed the promising

American political philosophy. Instead of a system based on individual merit, Bentham envisioned a utilitarian society where a Central Government would make decisions that would have happy consequences for as many people as possible. Reflecting on Bentham's 'Panopticon', Foucault explains how the prison ensured the exercise of power in order to maintain discipline in the society. According to E. Shaskan Bumas, the author of *Fictions of the Panopticon: Prison, Utopia, and the Out-Penitent in the Works of Nathaniel Hawthorne*, the requirement of a prison in the new world is due to colossal disenchantment. The juxtaposition of cemetery and prison reflect that sin and death are inevitable aspects in life.

The prison at the very opening of the text suggests how punishment and crime has been conspicuous feature right from the beginning of Anglo American history and civilisation. It is intricately woven to the germination of American culture at the dawn of Puritanical society. The readers can anticipate from the juxtaposition of prison and cemetery that the novel deals with sin, crime and protean punishment. The American prison has acquired a range of formal titles ranging from county jail and state penitentiary, federal correctional and detention facility and boot camp and brig. For Foucault, the birth of the prison means the birth of a prison society and hence the Puritanical society represents claustrophobic space of liminality.

The production and function of the colonial space is important. Space is a physical manifestation of political and cultural practices and perpetuation of Puritanical ideologies. The discourse of sin and sexuality are also interrelated to space. Places like prison and cemetery perpetuate Puritanical ideologies of contemporary New England. It is a physical manifestation of cultural and sociological practices. Hawthorne is trying to reflect how the Puritanical America has been a totalitarian society that reflects the incessant tension between power and humanity. The prison door symbolically represents the harsh weather, the severity of life and the hideous cadaverous life in the prison. Interestingly, the novel begins with the prison where the heroine of the novel Hester Prynne resides and ends with the cemetery where the journey of her life ends. The reflection upon the scaffold is significant as it illustrates the exercise of power. It symbolises how human history from its beginning is marked with sin. According to Foucault the prison and the cemetery are heterotopia of deviants. The term heterotopia is first introduced by Foucault in his *The Order of Things* (1966). Hawthorne's reflection on the spatial organisation of puritan Boston focuses on such heterotopia. The heterotopia is a place where the real is challenged, reversed and also reflects disruption against the ordered society. The prison and the cemetery are metaphorical borders between the discipline and punishment.

The rose as the symbol of love and passion anticipates Hester Prynne's story. The rose plant beside the prison door also hints that how human passion and desire are confined and restricted by the society. It stands as the epitome of hope and joy in the midst of dereliction. The rose also creates a resemblance to Hester Prynne's daughter Pearl who is equally wild, passionate and beautiful and mystical. The rose with fragrance and beauty provides not only sympathy to the convicts, but also it reflects the contrast between social and natural. The rose, struggling alone in the land of dereliction unusually, suggests the hope of love and beauty which perhaps Anne Hutchinson hoped for; and Hawthorne exemplified through Pearl.

CHAPTER TWO: THE MARKET-PLACE

The chapter ponders on the question of Puritanical trials and tribulations which range from whipping, scourging or even death penalty in front of the public. Such insightful reflection on the Puritanical punishment followed by public display of the criminal is aimed to teach a moral lesson of the vicious outcome and indignation of crime. The setting is a summer morning in the prison lane where the people of Salem have gathered to behold the severe punishment and shameful exposition of a convict. The excitement is intensified as everybody awaits for the perpetrator to appear from the iron clamped oak door that symbolises restriction and legitimacy.

In this chapter we are introduced to the female protagonist, Hester Prynne, a young woman with her infant emerging from the prison door while the Salem crowd watches this convict to be publicly persecuted. The women's whispering and disparaging comments about Hester indicate that she is involved in a gruesome act. An embroidered ornamented badge on her chest marked as letter "A" in scarlet colour with golden border is the luminary object of discussion in the crowd. The confabulation among women audience in the crowd reveals that implacably they want Hester either to be killed or tortured. Some of them suggested barbarous punishment like putting an iron rod on her forehead. She is described as 'malfactress' and a corrupt soul, who if not punished, will infect the society with immorality and sin. The minuscule physical description of Hester Prynne by the narrator is significant. He explains how she clasps the child tightly as if all her anxiety and fear converge into that little baby while her facial expression is depicted as the mixture of 'haughty smile' and 'burning blush'. Her elegance in her beauty is emulated in her tall stature, bountiful dark shining hair, misty eloquent eyes and her delicate graceful gestures and demeanour. The assembled people are astounded to observe the admirable artistry, calmness and pulchritude in this deplorable woman who is the 'criminal' in the eyes of the Puritans. Besides one cannot overlook the Hester's self-woven scarlet letter which is a reflection of her adroitness and mastery at weaving.

Hester is ordered to move up the scaffold in the marketplace which like the guillotine of the French regime signifies the space of punishment. The scaffold is made of wood and iron and is raised above for public gaze. Hester is displayed blatantly as an epitome of sin and immorality. For the Puritan Salem community she can be an example of debauchery and a licentious woman, but the narrator chooses to focus on the maternal image of Hester Prynne. From the perspective of a Papist she appears to be the archetypal Divine Maternity whose abundant motherhood can be captured in the artist's canvas. The narrator wonders at her indefatigable endurance to wade through the venomous hatred and multitudinous gaze of virulence and acerbity.

The narrative omniscient voice ventures into Hester's mind and is privy to her reminiscence about her home in England and her married life. Hester recalls her simple honest parents at her home in old England and her aged scholarly husband to whom she has been married and finally sent off to the new found land. She is reminded of her penurious house, the white beard face of her father and the tender countenance of her mother. While the reflection on her past life makes her accumulate all the fond memories from the shore of England, the astringent cacophonous Puritanical world anticipates impatiently for the ultimate verdict of Hester's punishment.

Commentary

The description of old Salem as the proposed Utopia where "human virtue and happiness" will reside eternally, is mocked again and again by Hawthorne in many of his writings. In *The Blithedale Romance* he has objected on the utopian imagination as a fantasy while the reality gives an opposite picture. Hawthorne reminds us of Adam Smith's harsh comment on "the man of system" from his *The Theory of Moral Sentiments*. According to Smith, an individual who imagines that a utopia can be established is blind in his limited observation because every individual lives with his or her own ideologies which are "altogether different from that which the legislature might choose to impress upon".[6] This is echoed in Hawthorne's *The American Notebook*: "It is only the one-eyed who love to advice."[7] The irony lies that the supposed Utopia consists of prison and cemetery—crime and death; hence it is already a fallen world. Prison denotes that sin is already known in the colony. The Puritanical doctrine based on original sin is itself a paradox for the utopian dream. Some of the examples of Puritanical punishments suggest how humanity is defiled. The catalogue of characters deserving punishment ranges from rebellious child to be whipped, religious heretic to be beaten and ostracised, or an Indian who dared to take a sip of the whiskey deserves to be lashed back into the forest. The satirical tone highlights racism and sexist prejudices in the name of religion and civilization. Last but not the least, witch hunting and hanging can also be an option. Witches like old Mistress Hibbins, the foul-tempered widow of the local judge, recalls the Salem witchcraft trials where women convicted as witches were hanged. Hanging has been a common form of Puritanical punishment but what is suggestive is Hawthorne's guilt conscience due to his ancestors 'sinful' misrule. The Puritans believed that woman as the weaker vessel becomes easily the diabolical covenant and ready to succumb to the devil. The feminine self is considered to be weak, frail and therefore easily susceptible to sin. Although convictions of witches included both the sexes, yet predominantly the seventeenth-century witches identified were mainly female. Carol Karlsen in the book *Devil in the Shape of a Woman* explains how the Puritanical theology chastised women and never encouraged equality of the sexes.

The Puritanical form of morality in the form of rigorism, ascetism and lack of individuality is not simply criticised by Hawthorne but his purpose is to show the pernicious outcome and destruction of humanity at large. Hawthorne's *Young Goodman Brown* is also another text where his journey into past Salem is an attempt to revision the Half-Way Covenant of 1662, the Puritan Catechism of John Cotton, and the repercussions of The Salem Witch trials. In this chapter Hawthorne describes the power in the ceremonious practice of punishment which aims particularly at the psychological despoliation and the chance of crossing the boundary between sanity and insanity. It is a ritual where sin should be publicly exposed while the sinner becomes the personification of the outcome of sin. Hester's punishment does not cause catharsis rather Hester herself becomes an object of voyeuristic contemplation. The masculine hegemony represented is evident from Hester's silence and the local women's gossip. The women gathering cutting across generations reveals the legitimate narrow construction of femininity. The obsession with sexual disparity is evident in both Puritanical and Elizabethan cultures as we see the same women of Elizabethan lineage blindly supporting Hester's punishment. Strikingly one is reminded of the first American women poet Anne Breadstreet and her struggle as a Puritanical wife. Typically Puritan yet she has raised the voice in her poems for space for women:

> Now say, have women worth? or have they none?
> Or had they some, but with our queen is't gone?
> Nay Masculines, you have thus taxt us long,
> But she, though dead, will vindicate our wrong,
> Let such as say our Sex is void of Reason,
> Know tis a Slander now, but once was Treason.[8]

Hawthorne has not been a feminist nor is completely from chauvinism but he has raised voice about this sexual disparity. Even before he wrote *The Scarlet Letter*, in one of his letters in the *Salem Gazette* he wrote a biographical essay on Anne Hutchinson, the American feminist. In the letter he openly criticises the Puritanical society's marginalisation of Hutchinson as a threat:

> We will not look for a living resemblance of Mrs. Hutchinson though the search might not be altogether fruitless. But there are portentous indications, changes gradually taking place in the habits and feelings of the gentle sex, which seem to threaten our posterity with many of those public-women, whereof one was a burden too grievous for our fathers. The press, however, is now the medium through which feminine ambition chiefly manifests itself....[9]

At the same time Hawthorne never supported equality of sexes. Any deviation from the patriarchal image of submissive woman of purity results in the collapse of the natural order of society:

> Differences between the sexes were total an innate. Women were inherently more religious, modest, passive, submissive and domestic than men, and were happier doing tasks, learning lessons and playing games that harmonized with their nature.[10]

The conversation of the women reveals diverse opinions. Hawthorne calls into question between tradition, morality and the emerging modern America. The wives and the maidens of old English birth who are dressed in coarse fibre are in favour of Hester's death and hanging. They do not hesitate to imagine Hester Prynne being inflicted with hot iron rods which reflects Hawthorne's gender ideologies of women's psychological incapacity to withstand brutality. Moreover no woman is viewed as an individual in the society. The women here seek freedom of judgement by expressing their individual opinions which otherwise seems to be missing in their lives. The momentary thrill of authority among these women reflects their repressed psychology. The women are matriphobic[11] as with great disdain they abuse Hester's illicit sexuality that resulted in the birth of the illegitimate child. The younger generation women seem to be more compassionate as expressed in their comments: "let her cover the mark as she will, the pang of it will be always in her heart."

Hester Prynne's first appearance reflects the Emersonian self-reliance[12] that challenges Puritanical ideology as the American ideal. In this scene, Hester's new self is more confident and ready for ordeal. She seems to be carrying the flag of Hutchinson as an extra-ordinary woman who is cornered by the theocratic Puritans. According to Edward Stone in his essay called *The Antique Gentility of Hester Prynne*—

> ...the edifice of the scaffold in the Boston market place is an important device in the structural symmetry of The Scarlet Letter: not only is it represented as the stage for the initial, central and the final letter revelation scenes, but Hester herself comes in time to feel that is the "whole orb" of her life, "the one point that gave unity".[13]

Hence, Hester's first appearance on the scaffold is significant. Her physical description strikes a note of romantic individualism. She embodies the interplay between sign and emanation. Such rare combination of oppositions in Hester like 'burning blush' and 'haughty smile', 'feminine gentility' and 'desperate recklessness', 'delicate, evanescent and indescribable grace' and 'wild and picturesque peculiarity' reveals that she can be identified with feminine figures like Virgin Mary, Mary Magdalene, Madonna and Eve. Like Coleridge's intermingling of the pleasurable and the sacred in 'Kubla Khan', Hester is the confluence of spiritual purity and eroticism. If she is labelled as the Babylonian whore of the 'Book of Revelation', she is also relegated to as an angel and sainthood at the end of the novel. Though we hardly come across any single word of Hester Prynne yet the insurmountable precipice of her mind is reflected in her facial expressions. Standing alone surrounded by ghastly cruel gazes requires tremendous mental agility. Above all the baby in her arm as a symbol of her adultery and stigma of her sin is psychologically deadening. The way she clasps her baby tightly reveals her motherly self is instinctively protective of her child. Hester is the 'conspicuous object' of Puritanical gaze which is the medium of social strictures and consensus. Hawthorne here reflects on the scopophilia,[14] of the community that relates to the pleasure of looking at the dehumanisation of this fallen woman. Scopophilia is always associated with the sexual innuendo and the libidinous pleasure involved in gazing. This is evident in their imbued sadism as they comment on Hester Prynne: "little will she care what they put upon the bodice of their gown." One of the old women even imagined of stripping Hester's rich gown and drapes her in flannel. Such savage comment reflects the paranoia, superstition, malice and prejudice of the extremist Puritanical community of Salem. Hester is exhibited in the market which is the place of merchandise and thus it reflects commercialisation of human crime.

Hester's dark abundant hair lustrous in the sunlight and deep brow and dark brown eyes captivatingly arrested the narrator's observation. That it cannot escape the gaze of the narrator reflects her abundant sexuality. The alphabet "A" beautifully knotted not only hints at the artistry of Hester but it also suggests revolution. The delicacy and the perfection with which it is ornamented reflects that the exuberant alphabet symbolises her refusal of Puritanical ideals and decree. It stands for her freedom and her rebelliousness.

CHAPTER THREE: THE RECOGNITION

Among several glaring faces, Hester suddenly locates her husband beside a native, who had sent her to America but never fulfilled his promise to follow her. Though dressed in a strange combination of traditional European clothing and Native American attire, she is struck by his countenance and recognizes his slightly deformed shoulders. Through their silent communication, he indicated Hester to remain silent and not to disclose his identity. He clarified from another stranger about Hester's crime and reason for her public punishment. He soon explained that he has been seized by the Indians and remained as convict for prolonged period and was recently released. The stranger informed him about Hester's background as the wife of a learned Englishman who happened to be a physician from Amsterdam but it is believed that he is being drowned. His curiosity to know about the father of the baby soon disclosed that Hester Prynne has kept it secret and the man guilty of adultery also remained silent. The magistrate seems to be very lenient and kind hearted and though the penalty of adultery in Puritanical society is death, yet she is exempted from death and as a punishment she is forced to wear the scarlet alphabet as a symbol of adultery.

While Hester's husband departed with the Native Indian, Reverend John Wilson assigned Hester's trial to Reverend Arthur Dimmesdale for being a better person to understand Hester's situation because of their similarity in age. Dimmesdale, the beloved of the community has been a scholar of one of the great universities of England and in this wilderness he introduced classicism and the spirit of elitism. While the women find him irresistibly charming and pulchritudinous, his eloquent religious enthusiasm, humbleness and innocence have made him charismatic. Dimmesdale commanded Hester to disclose the name of her lover and emphasised that her secrecy is intensifying the sin of her partner. He reminded her about purgation and purification as necessary requirement to enter the heaven. The crowd is amazed at Hester's steadfastness as she answered in a single word "Never". Even after repeated persistency and provocation by tempting that the letter will be removed and the child will be given the identity of the father, Hester makes a bold statement proclaiming that she is endowed with extraordinary strength to bear the suffering and shame of her lover and herself alone. She also confirmed that the child's father is the Heavenly father while her earthly father will be eternally anonymous. As the sun declines, the crowd gradually dispersed and Hester returned back inside the darkness of the prison.

Commentary

This chapter is significant because of the strange introduction of Hester Prynne's husband, Roger Chillingworth whose past life is revealed through nostalgic reflection into history by the narrator. His external appearance is bizarre because the narrator describes that he is dressed in a 'strange disarray of civilized and savage costume.' The admixture of the 'civilised' and the 'savage' is due to his prolong dwelling among the Native Indians but at the same time his scholarly English self cannot be completely erased. However, this ambivalence is the metaphor of Chillingworth's character whose intentions, scholarship and purpose all appeared strange to the people of Salem. His arrival at the crux of Hester Prynne's humiliation makes him stand at the threshold of several possibilities. It is evident that Chillingworth has stepped out of the long wilderness but his accompaniment of the Native Indian with whom he converses so fluently, explains that the man has undergone certain mysterious changes from which is beyond Hester Prynne's perception. Chillingworth's scholarly appearance is unavoidable irrespective of his heterogeneous strange outfit. His physical deformity mixed with super intellectual expression segregates him from the crowd of the Salem community which is the telling symbol of his spiritual deformity and Hawthorne aptly evokes the Biblical reference of knowledge and sin. His scholarship is without humanitarianism and will become the powerful source of his satanic spirit.

Chillingworth's unwillingness to disclose his identity as Hester's husband at that shameful moment when she is epitomised as the exemplary of sin and punishment gives the impression that he is extremely self-centred man for whom his dignity is more important than his relations. His arrival at Salem definitely gives the idea that the man ultimately expects to be united with his wife but the infant in Hester's arms alarms him of some malice of which he is ignorant. Thc abandonment of the hope of re-union juxtaposed by her wife's shameful action causes an immense mutability in the mind of the man which cannot escape his facial cxpression:

> A writhing horror twisted itself across his features, like a snake gliding swiftly over them, and making one little pause, with all its wreathed intervolutions in open sight. (*SL* 92)

The reference of the snake reminds of the Biblical reference of Satan and fallibility of human mind. After such a long gap, when the couple looked at each other, Chillingworth silently hints at Hester that she should be careful in hiding his identity. More than spontaneous love for a long departed wife, the physician is ashamed to be identified as the husband of a sinful convict like Hester Prynne. That he is a man of scrupulous nature is evident in the way he skilfully gathered information about the Hester Prynne's crime pretending himself as an anonymous stranger in New England. With quick recovery from the shameful shock, Roger Chillingworth is supremely playful in his interrogation. The verbal playfulness in his pretentious ignorance like "tell me of Hester Prynne...have I her name rightly?" or his climactic expression "Ah—aha!—I conceive you" are beautifully captured by Hawthorne to reflect how introspective and alert the physician is. His heightened irony is captured when he utters "The learned man…should come himself to look into the mystery" (*SL* 95). Roger in a way asserts his legitimacy in response to the Salem man's misinformation that Master Prynne is dead. At the same time he de-legitimises himself and deconstructs his identity at that very moment when his wife is abused. His determination to identify Hester's partner in the sinful act is reflected as he repeatedly mutters "he will be known". The very act of seeking revenge is the instant pledge that the physician makes at the core of his heart.

We see Hester's feeling of shame and fear as Hester Prynne prefers to stay at distance from her husband enisled by anonymous rebellious Salem community than confronting him face to face alone. It is a chauvinist Puritanical world where men believe that every woman, especially young and beautiful, should always be under man's guidance and vigilance since they are incapable of controlling their temptations and are susceptible to fall. Women represented as weaker vessel unable to stay morally upright without man's intervention is what the Puritanical authority wanted to establish. The root lies in the Garden of Eden myth where Eve is considered as the sole responsive figure in the degradation of mankind. What is significant is the representation of the sinful woman in the public space at a time when rigid sexual boundaries are maintained between public and private. The legitimate feminine space is constricted within domestic space and if there is any allowance for women in public space, it referred to brothels. Hester's retribution in the midst of the market place of Salem is a symbolic representation of how she is seen as a defile woman who personifies sin. However, the public space like market has one more significant connotation. The public space is also an exposure for the woman to the world of experience from ignorance and darkness. This is the beginning of Hester's journey into the harsh outer world. Her education in life is spontaneous and natural. Any form of knowledge to women is considered by the Puritanical world as something like 'forbidden fruit'. This fear of knowledge for women is also reflected in the works of Hawthorne's contemporary writer, Ralph Waldo Emerson especially in his book *From the Memoirs of Margaret Fuller* Ossoli. In this book Emerson admires Fuller's intelligence but at the same time he expresses doubts about her capability to handle the man's domain. Hester Prynne as the deviator can definitely be anticipated as the New Eve with a revolutionary spirit who has gathered knowledge and wisdom after undergoing the Blakian journey from 'innocence to experience'.

The chapter also introduces us to Reverend Arthur Dimmesdale as a study in contrast to Chillingworth. Dimmesdale is introduced through the description of Mr Wilson and he is represented as a man of virtue and of great admiration. Dimmesdale's elevated status quo is reflected in his elitism and education from a great English university. The hero of the novel is introduced with arresting melancholic eyes, 'self-restraint manner' and 'nervous sensibility'. When Mr Wilson suggests Dimmesdale that "the responsibility of this woman's soul lies greatly with you", the irony is that Wilson unwittingly implicated Dimmesdale in the adulterous deed but the literal interpretation is that Dimmesdale is chosen as the community's moral leader and hence he is the best person to judge the woman. When this eldest clergyman of Boston entrusts Dimmesdale to determine the fate of Hester, Dimmesdale's words are paradoxical. Dimmesdale is hinting Hester to disclose his identity but lacks the courage to confess. His words are profoundly manipulative and yet impressive, plaintive but also pleading. Apparently it appears to be sincere but ironically it does not contain any sincerity because he is afraid to confess his partnership with Hester. Dimmesdale's power of eloquence is more emotional than rational, less pragmatic but more semantic.

Thus, Hawthorne prepares his readers for a study of contrast between Dimmesdale and Chillingworth. Hester is the fulcrum in the relationship between the two men and all these three characters—Hester, Dimmesdale and Chillingworth are subject of psychological analysis. Hester's impenetrable silence and Dimmesdale and Chillingworth's duplicitous speeches provoke the readers to explore the reality. The society fails to understand the duplicity of rhetoric and the linguistic art of concealment of thoughts of the two men but ascribes Hester's silence as sin. Hawthorne is also criticising the lack of intellectual nuance of the Puritanical society. In contrast to the manipulative languages of these two men, Hester Prynne with her silence represents the solitary soul antithetical to the Puritanical society. For the Puritanical society, lack of words means stubborn reparative attitude but Hawthorne perhaps suggests that more nuanced, multifarious approach would engender more sympathy and reverence for the human spirit. Both Dimmesdale and Chillingworth have Janus-tongue and at the same time both these men know the power of silence of this woman. Dimmesdale, deep down in his mind, knows that Hester Prynne will never disclose his identity as an adulterer and Chillingworth raising his finger indicating silence to Hester also knows how to dissemble his identity. Dimmesdale uses twinned language to protect himself while Hester's alchemist husband uses artful language to pursue his anonymity in order to reveal the true identity of his adulteress wife's partner.

Lastly this chapter also depicts the public witnessing of crime and shame. Hawthorne's picture of the Puritanical world reveals that the sole decision makers are the all-powerful magistrates. Apart from these magistrates, the colony has not developed any grand juries for criminal justice system; no judge to sentence the offenders neither there is any proper legislative system. The power lies in the hands of a small group of people while the public is only meant as mute spectator. They can mutter and pass comments but must obey the decision without any protest or divergent opinion. The power of a magistrate is the highest power which is hegemonic and autocratic. Hawthorne is critical about these men of highest power whom he describes as rigid, severe and grim. We do not see any proper scene of trial of Hester Prynne in that non-democratic world where she is given the space to defend herself. Without investigating the circumstance and the condition which resulted in the relationship between Hester Prynne and her lover, the autocratic Puritanical world has taken it for granted that adultery is a sin and Hester should be severely punished. In such a circumstance, Hester's silence is revolutionary because it suggests her non-conformity to the society instead of pleading for mercy. Her determination to keep the name of her lover as a secret even at the moment of dire consequence hints that Hester is not the woman of her age.

The most common form of punishment for sex crimes and adultery is whipping in the Puritanical society. The antebellum America is obsessed with this form of punishment since they believe that infliction of physical pain will lead to infliction of guilt. In his later chapters Hawthorne will describe how Dimmesdale as a co-partner of Hester in adultery used to whip himself and then indulges into a sense of repentance and guilt. Hawthorne's choice to spare Hester from physical punishment is to show that the psychological trauma is more atrocious than physical trauma. Moreover, the act of whipping is more prevalent in punishing the slaves as it is reflected in another American bestseller Uncle Tom's Cabin.

CHAPTER FOUR: THE INTERVIEW

In this chapter the narrator visualises Hester inside the prison cell and how the baby struggles after the day's long turmoil. The baby seems to have drunk the anguish and despair of Hester Prynne and almost haunts the prison as she screams and writhes in pain. This illegitimate baby has been wailing incessantly for last ten days and the entire prison seems to be vexed with this furore. The jailer Master Brackett finding the child's cry unbearable informs Hester that one learned physician who is equipped with Christian modes of medical science as well as native knowledge due to his prolong stay with them is being invited for the child's treatment. He believes that Hester should be kept under observation after the psychological turmoil that she has undergone publicly as he is afraid that she may commit suicide and kill the shameful offspring of adultery. This physician is the same man in the crowd whom Hester identified as her husband. Hester is frozen to see him again inside the prison. The physician is introduced as Dr. Chillingworth who requests the jailer to leave him alone for medical examination of the infant in order to pacify the baby. Unceasingly for ten minutes Chillingworth examines minutely the baby looking closely into its eyes, ears, nose and mouth. He examines the heartbeat and pulse and finally commands Hester to give few drops of medicine which he has taken out from his leather bag. In a very sarcastic tone he comments that the child will not respond to his touch since she is not born out of his flesh. Hester is sceptical and doubts that the medicine that he insists to give to the infant may be poisonous. While Chillingworth assures that being a doctor he is committed to rescuing every patient's life, the child magically falls asleep.

Chillingworth has been looking for this private moment to communicate with his long departed wife and clarify regarding the shameful exposition of Hester's adultery and her lover's name. Hester's thudding heart soon confronted Mr Chillingworth's exasperations. He reflects back on his scholarship and his failure to understand Hester. With a tone of sarcasm he blames himself for the conjugal chasm that has gradually increased and his extreme devotion to knowledge and thirst for scholarship which resulted in Hester's detachment from him. He despairs how he has been neglecting his youthful spirit in search of knowledge. He believed that he has deluded himself and is fooled by Hester who is not competent enough to appraise her scholarly husband and is limited within her physical beauty. He has been under the deception that his wife is committed and affectionate towards him. Hester interrupted him clarifying that from the first day of their relationship when he proposed to her, she exonerated with honesty that she has no love, passion except respect and admiration for this man and neither has she pretended of loving him. Chillingworth humbly acknowledges his blunder by betraying her budding youth and then not accompanying her in the New England but he seeks revenge on the man who has indulged in adultery with his wife and therefore he demands the identity to be disclosed to him. Hester inexorably denies disclosure of the identity of her lover but Chillingworth challenges that with his intellectual acumen he will definitely find out the man in the small place like Salem.

When he finds Hester is anxious and awed at his words, he promises that he will never disclose the identity of the fallen man nor kill him for revenge. Revenge means for him psychological turmoil and not relief from sinful existence by murdering the sinner. He believes that the sinner will suffer for his sin and as long as he lives, his suffering will only intensify. Along with Hester's lover's secret, he implores that Hester should not acknowledge or disclose Chillingworth as her husband. He does not want to be recognised by society as a cuckold and the husband of an adulteress. He threatens if Hester ever discloses his identity; he will not hesitate to disclose her lover's identity. The chapter ends with Hester's promise of keeping Chillingworth's identity as a secret while the doctor reminds Hester of the image of the Black Man in him whom the Puritans believed to be ominous evil spirit.

Commentary

We get the glimpse of babies born of incarcerate mothers in Puritanical society. The depiction of Hester and her baby after going through hellish humiliation reflects Hester's indomitable power of withstanding the bitter reality. We see the resilience of Hester's character and her unfaltering motherhood even in the moment of crisis. The relationship between mother and daughter is extremely sensitive and the baby is instinctively responsive to her mother's trouble. Hester's indefatigable power to withstand the child's agitation is the outcome of pure love. The jailer may feel that Hester Prynne could have ended both the lives being unable to bear the ignominy but his mistake lies in thinking Hester as an ordinary woman.

In this chapter, Hawthorne has created intense suspense because of the confrontation between the husband and the wife after a long gap and especially in the aftermath of Hester's public humiliation and exposure of her adultery. It is clear that though Chillingworth has arrived as the physician to give relief to the distressed baby but his intention is to converse in seclusion with his wife. It is expected that Roger Prynne will be taking some severe action against Hester either by divorcing her or taking revenge on the baby born out of the adultery. Hester's fear regarding Roger's medication for the baby as a poison is therefore absolutely relevant. Surprisingly instead of any such outrageous reaction, Roger with calmness lulls the child and converses with his guilty wife with perfect naturalness. When Hester unable to repress her fear, utters her doubt that he can avenge the innocent baby, Roger addresses him as the "foolish woman" who fails to understand that he has no achievement in inflicting torture on the 'misbegotten and miserable' baby. He clarifies that if the child would have been his own, he could do no better for her. But by describing the baby as 'misbegotten' Roger is not merely expressing pity but hints that such unwanted child is the cause of its own existential misery. From his choice of words directed towards Hester Prynne, it is evident that he is extremely scrupulous and shrewd. We get a glimpse of a Machiavellian shadow in Roger's character when he explains that killing as revenge is a shallow act and the real way to avenge is to inflict psychological torture and see the enemy writhe in pain of shame and guilt. Chillingworth has his own book of law and he rejects public law in favour of fanatical service to his personal pursuit of vengeance. Hester's adultery has insulted his masculinity bringing in the question of his potency. To see a child in his wife's arms fathered by another man is the biggest insult and therefore his rage cannot be mitigated by any constitution and law of the Puritanical society. His law is beyond rational and humane and therefore out of violent disdain he pledges to find out the man. He assures Hester that even if the world conspires to hide the man's name, he has the power to locate the guilt in the man's heart. He holds a perverse authority and a palimpsest character extremely difficult to read. It baffles Hester also when she explains "Thy acts are like mercy", "but thy words interpret thee as a terror" (*SL* 114).

The ambivalence of Chillingworth is the strength of his character. He speaks 'half coldly, half soothingly'. Hester's adultery is an insult that depicts him as impotent or asexual but it is time to prove his potency in terms of his revenge. He acknowledges his negligence to his wife and his failure to appreciate a woman of beauty but he also threats politely to Hester that if she discloses his identity as her husband, he will also disclose the identity of the adulterer. Such strategic psychological device explains that his shrewdness and his sense of ownership of Hester Prynne. By assuming the title 'Chillingworth' he has undertaken disguise as his characteristic trait but Hester's title as Prynne suggests that she is still carrying the legacy of her husband's identity. Therefore, Hester and her lover are the sole purpose of his living because they continue his existence and his identity along with them.

In this chapter, Hawthorne gives a view of what the physician has been as well as what he is to become. He has been an ardent scholar, a man devoted to study of human behaviour and psychology, a physician who has gathered knowledge of primitive and modern science of medicine but he discovers that unfortunately his pursuit of scholarship has failed both Hester and himself. He claims that their conjugal relationship has been an 'unnatural relation' between a scholar and an immature girl. His reflection upon his mistakes and his representation of himself as a lonely scholar who has been robbed of his wife initially creates a sense of sympathy but we see the element of his future self-destruction in his grim determination to discover the man who has offended him. In the course of their conversation, we see the strange metamorphosis of a scholar into a vigilant evil spirit.

CHAPTER FIVE: HESTER AT HER NEEDLE

Finally the much awaited day arrives when Hester Prynne's days of imprisonment in the prison are over. This does not ensure exemption from humiliation and freedom. The glowing scarlet alphabet 'A' is the emissary of her sin and a reminder of constant affliction and shame. It has become inseparable from Hester's identity and that she should carry it along with her even on doomsday. Hester has every opportunity to evade the Salem crowd by leaving Salem and by burying all her past she can begin a new life in Europe. She can easily escape among the natives who are not familiar with the rigorous law of the settlers. There are two reasons for which she avoided such step. The narrator comments on the individuality and tenacity of Hester Prynne whose purgation followed by suffering will take place in the same land where she committed her sin. Secondly the two men in her life—her husband for whom still she possess deep respect and her lover whom she passionately loves are all dwelling in the same place. Moreover she cherishes hope that in future her socially tainted relationship can be resolved when her dream of a happy family will be turned into reality through reunion of the father and her child. This little iota of hope in the deepest part of her heart is the source of her strength for existence in that land.

As an ostracised outcast, she selected an abandoned thatched house at the outskirt of the society. The house is located on a rocky ledge above the beach where hardly any cultivation is possible. Detachment from the society does not mean respite for her. She has been always the cynosure of mystery and gossip. Young children peep in to see this mysterious woman and all the superstition surrounding her scarlet letter stitched on her bosom frightened them. If they see her walking with little Pearl, they will run or throw pebbles and make rude gestures. However, Hester's self-dependence is evident in the way she economically has become an independent mother to support her baby and her living. Her adroitness in suturing the scarlet alphabet on her dress is reflective of her artistic skill at needle and thread. In the Puritanical world, the only profession where women are being allowed to venture in, is the artistic domain especially in relation to stitching and needle work; and Hester Prynne has utilised her craftsmanship in order to become financially independent. The Puritan society never encouraged gorgeous dazzling dresses but delicacy is always admired and is a matter of pride when someone has got such artistic delicacy in embroidered gloves, funeral drapes, curtains, baby linen, scarves or towels. As a result Hester Prynne is always busy with her needle and thread fuelled by the increasing demand of her high quality artistic work. Every individual of Salem seems to be wearing some exemplary of her handiwork and soon it became a celebratory tradition to wear crafts of Hester Prynne. This included the magistrate, governor and the entire Salem community who once scorned Hester but now boasted when they wear clothes crafted by Hester's magical touch. Yet Hester's dress remained the most simple of all made of coarse fabric while she always adorned Pearl with fancifully gorgeous attire.

When Hester had earned adequate money for two of them, she always distributed the surplus wealth among the poor and the oppressed. Without any hesitation, she volunteered to distribute food and clothing. She also stitched clothes of the poor instead of investing that time in earning money. Those who insulted Hester are also the receiver of Hester's altruism and compassion. Like a ghost she remained at the outskirt of the society and still very much she is within the society through her action and devotion to humanity. None of them allow her to talk publicly nor are they grateful to her benevolence. Even if she escapes public gossip and goes to the church, she realises that the subject of the sermons is directed towards her.

Incidentally some strange things also started happening at Salem. Hester has discovered the power of scarlet letter by which she has come to know many dark secrets of people but Puritanical austerity in contrast seems hypocritical because it can never emotionally involve the community. Yet the power and beauty of Hester Prynne lies in the way she never disclosed or exposed their weakness to the world.

Commentary

Hester's appearance after her imprisonment is significant. We see Hester Prynne in the light of unique heroism. She is suffering from the fear of emotional excommunication among thousands of men waiting outside to view the adulteress but she is heroic in her individualism. The narrator comments on her 'combative energy' that has the immense power to convert ignominy and shame into 'lurid triumph.' Hester on the scaffold with little Pearl is the defiant prismatic figure in whom the society's repressed tension, fear and anxiety are being reflected. The figure of Hester Prynne reinvokes the rebellious outlaw women of America like Anne Hutchinson or Anne Coleman. This heroism stems from her revolutionary spirit. Her unnatural tension and her pulsating nerves should learn either to sustain the discord or die in shame. The narrator predicts that from this day when her life of imprisonment is over, the real trial will start when every day in her life she has to confront the indignation and shame:

> The days of the far-off future would toil onward, still with the same burden for her to take up, and bear along with her, but never to fling down; for the accumulating days and added years would pile up their misery upon the heap of shame. (*SL* 118)

But Hester Prynne's silence is her revolution. She is like the goddess of liberty reminding us of revolutionary images of 1848-49, the first Bastille Day.

This chapter marks the passage of time when Hester's life of imprisonment is over. The first question that the narrator ponders is why Hester Prynne chooses to stay in the same land where her future is abominable especially when she could have easily escaped into some parts of the world. The narrator offers several explanations and is left for the reader's choice to decide. Interestingly many of Hawthorne's characters with artistic propensity are seen to be motivated out of repressed love and emotions because of their inability to express in social and political circumstances. Hawthorne's artists repress their desires because of social circumstances or the lack of courage and their emotions find outlet through artistry. If Arthur Dimmesdale excels as an artist of oration, then Hester excels in sewing and in embroidery. In the restrictive Puritanical society, the only mode of communication and expression of love for each individual person is the medium of art. Even in his *The Marble Faun*, the character Kenyon is seen to be an excellent sculptor whose untold love for Hilda is expressed in his artistic masterpiece. Similarly Hilda, in order to protect her chastity as the guardian of the shrine of the virgin is unable to express her feelings which find expression in her paintings. In the Blithedale Romance Miles Coverdale and Zenobia express their love through artistic creation. In his short story "The Artist of the Beautiful," Owen Warland creates great art because he falls in love with Annie and lacks the courage to express that to her before she marries another man. Hester's extraordinary embroidery is a testimony of her unfathomable passion and deep emotions. Her artistry whether in the form of curtain, scarf or her own scarlet alphabet is a self-expression and the signature of her identity as a woman of fineness and flair. Hawthorne thus explains the intensity of her passion:

> She had in her nature a rich, voluptuous, Oriental characteristic,—a taste for the gorgeously beautiful, which, save in the exquisite productions of her needle, found nothing else, in all the possibilities of her life, to exercise itself upon. Women derive a pleasure, incomprehensible to the other sex, from the delicate toil of the needle. To Hester Prynne it might have been a mode of expressing, and therefore soothing, the passion of her life. (*SL* 125)

The 'voluptuous' and 'Oriental' elements are therefore contradictory to the Puritanical world. This element of display of passion in the Puritanical society thus marks Hester as the transgressive figure.

The narrator makes an ironical observation when he explains how Hester's needle work is a work of great admiration and yet the people of Salem believe that by allowing Hester Prynne to work for them, it is a kind of charity they are performing towards this poor woman. This contemptuous attitude is best exemplified in their refusal to allow Hester sew garments for wedding which they think will be contaminating and violating the sacredness of marriage. Whether it is the governor, military men, ministers or the common men and women of Salem, all of them are seen to wear Hester's needle work in various forms. In the patriarchal Puritanical society, Hester Prynne is seen to be engaged in traditional 'feminine' art which patriarchy has reserved as feminine 'craft'. However, her thread, needlework and weaving are reminiscent of the ancient mythology of three Fates called Moirae (lot/destiny) in Greek who gave humanity at birth the power of good and evil. The first Moriae, Clotho spins the thread of life, Lachesis gives and determines the length of string while Atropos cuts and brings an end to life. Similarly Hester Prynne embroiders the scarlet letter with golden scarlet thread and determines her own fate, she allots to the entire

Boston community through her artistry a new life and a new dimension of charity, and finally at the end of her life when she has crafted her own destiny, the thread of her life is cut and she is buried near the burial of Dimmesdale, the man whom she loves. Her ornate needlework embroidered in gold thread is anti-Puritanical because of excess of ornamentation which is strongly discouraged by the Puritans. But her embroidery is the epitome of Hester's artistic fertility, the gorgeous fantastic innovation of the mind much like her creator Hawthorne with whom she shares so much of resemblance. Apart from sharing the same initial alphabet 'H' of their names, both Hester and her creator have attempted to revise the Puritanical world. Thus, Hester Prynne in her artistry has given a new definition and meaning to the scarlet alphabet. She has thus re-written the meaning of 'A' from 'adulteress' to 'Abel' and finally to 'Angel'. In the process, she has constructed her own identity. The only extravagance in Hester's life of abstinence is Pearl's outfit and attire. Her bright tunic with abundant embroidery reflects how Pearl represents the passion and emotions of her mother. Pearl is the ultimate source of joy and she evolves all the hues in her mother's life. Through Pearl's grandiloquent decoration Hester reflects the fecundity of her passion and creative frenzy.

Hester Prynne is therefore a cultural paradox in whom we see a single working mother in the Puritanical world, a skilled domestic woman, an artist, a whore and a saint. She is frightening for her daring nature and yet delightful because of her creative spark. She is sensuous, fantastic, grotesque, monstrous and divinely. In Hester Prynne, Hawthorne reflects American historical consciousness, the American Puritanical unconscious and the cultural index of American subjectivity. We see Hester's life at the outskirt of civilisation as a symbolic representation of penitence, expiation and transgression. As an outcast and a stranger to human companionship, Hester is the fugitive figure in the Puritanical world. This exiledom is a curse and a penance. Like the wilderness, Hester is untamed by the Puritans and she absolves the sin she has committed through a process of peregrination. In this way Hester reminds us of the history of literary characters like Shakespeare's Timon of Athens,

Eustacia Vye from *Return of the Native* or *King Lear* in the middle of wild forest. Hester Prynne is the rebellious symbol of immorality, frailty and sin. However, in this Puritanical politics of marginality and Hester Prynne's oddness as circumstantial luminosity, there is an adamant rebellious self of Hester against the viciousness of Puritanical world. The harshness of the land, the threatening frontier of the Indians and the unyielding soil are symbolical setting for Hester's confrontation with her sin and guilt. The sterility of the land where Hester's has found her cottage is dislocated from the Puritanical society of Salem. The mystery and gloominess associated with the cottage evokes the gothic element of an abode of witch where humanity can hardly dare to venture in.

The theme of public and private disclosure that so greatly marked Dimmesdale's speech in Chapter three, is again reiterated in this chapter, but this time the scarlet A on Hester's clothing is associated with the theme. Though the alphabet symbolises sin and evilness of Hester Prynne, yet it endows Hester with the extraordinary power to recognise the sin of the society. The last section of this chapter concentrates on Hester's psychosis of fear because of the children and the entire society who treat her like a ghost, an abhorrent pariah who is inside the society and yet outside it. Nathaniel Hawthorne strikes her indefatigable egoism in her seclusion. She stood the test of time and never succumbed to self-destruction like Dimmesdale.

CHAPTER SIX—PEARL

While Hester Prynne is learning the art of living in desolation and loneliness, her little girl Pearl is growing up into a brilliant beautiful baby. She is enthralling and sprightful and possesses umpteen charms that draw any body's attention. The narrator comments on the connotations of her name in relation to her significance in Hester's life. She is Hester's sole treasure achieved after much struggle and pain. She is as precious as pearl in her life and her appraisal as Hester's richest treasure of the world is increased day by day as the narrator reflects how intensively the mother and the daughter become dependent on each other. Hester's greatest anxiety and awe surrounding the child has been that since Pearl is an illegitimate child not born out of sacred wedlock, the sin may be manifested in some way or the other.

Pearl's physiognomy never manifested any such deformation. She is endowed with boundless energy, always rollicking, jumping and gathering flowers in the woods or cavorting along the beach compelling Hester to walk down the memory lane of her childhood in England. She is exceptionally mature given her age and is such a blithe animated spirit that one can hardly see her crying or frazzled. Nevertheless, she disregards rules and can never remain confined within regulations and restrictions. No authority can restrain her whether it is her mother, church or the town people. Even after several attempts of Hester to interrupt her impulsive behaviour, Pearl is at her own disposition and renounces with laughter. When Hester Prynne helplessly cries for her inability to instil discipline in her child, Pearl laughs more loudly or scowl with anger. Hester soon realises that the child exists outside human limitations.

Pearl's individualism is so severe that she abandons Hester's dream of seeing her child intermingling with other children. Pearl is least concerned about the distance the rest of the children maintain as they want to avoid her thinking that she is some supernatural spirit. On the contrary she cherishes her own self-invented games and if by chance any child approaches her, she would throw stones and pebbles at him or her. It seems that Pearl being aloof all through is more comfortable in her solitude than among the children who think of her as other worldly creature. If they show any interest in her it is less out of befriending her than out of curiosity to mistreat her. Nature seems to be Pearl's greatest friend and she is most jovial among the trees, rivers, sky and the sea. Spontaneously, she exchanges her words with the pine trees, the wild flowers or waves who seem to be responding by whirling, whispering, tossing and dancing along with her. Hester has also witnessed her anger for those natural elements which she cannot withstand. She will uproot unwanted plants like Ragweed, flinging them into air, stamping insects into dust or scatter piles of rocks. As Hester Prynne is scared to witness such attitude of Pearl, she questions the Almighty regarding such anomalous behaviour of Pearl.

The Scarlet alphabet, which Pearl has been witnessing unconsciously from the day she is born, has become Pearl's obsession. She will either grab it or throw wildflowers at it with immeasurable laughter and joy. When her mother interrogates her asking her identity, she is intelligent enough to explain that she is her mother's little Pearl and will reject such Heavenly father whom Hester would like to introduce to her. Pearl's dauntless rejection of the heavenly father intensifies Hester's fear and reminds her of the Salem rumours that Pearl is the monstrous demonic offspring borne out of Hester's sin with some devilish purpose.

Commentary

This chapter focuses on the fruit that Hester Prynne has conceived out of her passion and love. Hawthorne here develops the mysterious character of Hester's daughter Pearl, who seems to be exclusively individual with abundant vitality. Pearl's bounteous beauty is like a wild immortal flower that becomes more adorable as she grows every day in the midst of natural surroundings. The narrator focuses on the significance of her name that reflects the invaluable presence of this child in Hester Prynne's life. She has no resemblance with serenity and tranquil lustre of pearl but the name signifies the richness and rarest possession of it in Hester's life. To explain how precious Pearl is in her mother's life, Hawthorne defines her as "her mother's only treasure". There is also a significant Biblical allusion to the name Pearl. Jesus Christ described heaven as 'a pearl of great price'. Hawthorne is extremely satirical when he explains that what humanity has stigmatised as sinful outcome of Hester Prynne's adultery is in God's yardstick reproved by the birth of this adorable child. Pearl may symbolise sin, adultery, unlawful passion and illegitimacy but Hawthorne explains that Pearl "was worthy to have been brought forth in Eden; worthy to have been left there, to be the plaything of angels after the world's first parents were driven out" (*SL* 134). Pearl also represents Hester's salvation and pride. Though Pearl is the living scarlet letter and the tormenting reminder of Hester's sin, yet she promises a new dimension to womanhood of future and will be the cataclysmic revelation to guide Dimmesdale to moral ending. In the 1980s, T. Walter Herbert, Jr. published "Nathaniel Hawthorne, Una Hawthorne, and *The Scarlet Letter*: Interactive Selfhoods and the Cultural Construction of Gender" in which he explored the connection between Hawthorne's daughter, Una, and Hawthorne's literary creation, Pearl. He discussed some of the troublesome qualities of Una as reflected by Hawthorne in Pearl.

Child Pearl with her 'native grace' is adorned by her mother's artistic spirit and imagination. She is seen as the only source of radiance in the dark gloomy cottage of Hester Prynne. Pearl reflects her mother's deviant nature as she rejects all patriarchal rules. Thus, Pearl is the metaphor of wild unrestrained beauty, freedom and variety of life. She is vigorous, wild, passionate, impulsive and capricious. Pearl's childish lawlessness is a reflection of dormant spirit of her mother Hester Prynne. Hawthorne emphasises the organic element in Pearl since like nature, she is unpredictable. Sometimes she is like morning radiance and sometimes she is like whirlwind or tempestuous storm. In the Puritanical society children cannot be left at their whims. They need strict guidance, regulations and restrains but Pearl is against all such precedents. John Robinson, the Puritanical minister proclaimed:

> There is in all children, though not alike, a stubbornness and stoutness of mind arising from natural pride.... It is a natural corruption and root of actual rebellion against God.[15]

The Puritanical doctrine suggests that natural corruption and rebelliousness are natural things in children since their foreparents are Adam and Eve. Hence Parents are advised to restrain and repress such stubbornness and willfullness of children. Otherwise the evil spirit will develop in the child. However, though Pearl is born in the Puritanical era, yet she cannot be caged within such exclusiveness and bigotry. Though Hester Prynne has been afraid of her guilt and feared that as Pearl grows up some anomalies must be reflected in the child's body which little Pearl did not show, yet she failed to control Pearl's wilderness or to reinforce endorsement of Puritanical authority. Hester's fear is not strange as it reflects the religious preaching of the ministerial figures. John Winthrop in his *The Journal of John Winthrop* describes grotesque malformed body of children whose parents have committed sin. One such Winthrop's descriptions of a child who appears to be a hybrid of human and demon explains how the child "had a face, but no head...over the eyes four horns, hard and sharp...all over the breast and back full of sharp pricks and scales like a thornback."[16] Being the nightmarish child of parents who have been followers of Anne Hutchinson, the child is supposed to represent the disease dormant in the Puritanical society. The narrator explains Puritanical family disciplinary methods like harshness, rebuke and the use of the rod are remote to Hester's ways of rearing her child. Yet the child's obstinate nature, sudden yelling or whims make Hester doubt whether Pearl is influenced by some evil spirit. Histories reflect that children of Salem in the Puritanical world have been the subject of political and religious reforms. In the New Found England where safety and healthy sustenance are considered as the primary mode of settlement, like crops and plantation, unwanted orphaned or illegitimate children are not only discarded but considered dangerous to the development of the society. In "Description of New England", John Smith solicits "fatherless children" of least value in the American social system. The history of Puritanical children as the future generation of America entails such stories of Pocahontas, the native Indian girl who saved John Smith from execution from her father's hand, conformed to the Puritanical order by converting to Christianity and marrying a tobacco planter, John Rolfe. The Puritans took pride in proclaiming this as John Smith explains to Queen Anne how Pocahontas "rejected her barbarous condition" to become the "first Christian of the Nation, the first Virginian that ever spake English, or had a child in marriage by an Englishman."[17] The barbarous capturing of Pocahontas in her childhood is justified as the symbolic potentiality of taming of American wilderness and barbarity into 'civilisation'. In contrast to the Indian child Pocahontas' successful 'negotiation' and 'cultivation', who addressed Smith as "Father", rearing of Hester's child is a dangerous violation to Puritanical order. Hester rejected the Puritanical paternal surrogation and preached little Pearl that her father is Heavenly Father. Pearl's existence is Hester's emotional centrifuge and therefore she cannot tame and chide her through drastic action and violence. Such resonating passionate bondage between the mother and child is depicted by the narrator when he explains how Hester seeing Pearl in her weird behaviour, used to grab her near her bosom and kiss her with tears in her eyes fearing that the child can be drawn towards the evil spirit.

In the absence of a father figure who is equated to a ruler in the colonial Puritanical world, Hawthorne describes Pearl as "a born outcast of the infantile world. An imp of evil, emblem and product of sin, she has no right among christened infants" (*SL* 139). This process of 'othering' Pearl from the rest of the children is to avoid 'contamination' of the evil spirit since the Puritans believed that a child's body and mind is the fertile ground with the potentiality of getting influences, as John Locke's theory of 'tabula rasa' or the 'empty mind' suggests. Pearl's savagery is considered as detrimental influence on the rest of the children. Pearl's bizarre behaviour of throwing stones at meddling children is a natural reaction if we see it as the psychology of a child secluded from the society but Hester fears this behaviour as "witch's anthemas in some unknown tongue." Pearl's unruly passion symbolises the mystery of her mother. So instead of implementation of Puritanical strict disciplines on the child, Pearl serves as the expression of the ardent discipline on Hester reminding of her guilt every time.

CHAPTER SEVEN—THE GOVERNOR'S HALL

This chapter focuses on Hester Prynne's visit to the mansion of Governor Bellingham since she has to deliver a pair of gloves which she has fringed and embroidered at his disposition. She is also keen to meet him because of the gossip that Pearl will be segregated from her mother since it is believed that Pearl being the child of the Demon, will never allow her mother's redemption. Governor Bellingham is the sole contriver of this idea and he believes that if Pearl would have been a human child, then salvation would have been possible for Hester and it need not be necessary to send Pearl to the Puritanical church.

The narrator focuses on the architectural construction of the mansion of Bellingham. The house is embellished with deep red front door and latticed windows made of heavy cast iron nails which symbolise affluence and wealth. The iron nails are meant to display wealth and the governor's house as the most prestigious building is expected to have maximum of these nails.

The day Hester visits Bellingham's mansion, Pearl also accompanied her, dressed in crimson velvet outfit and embroidered with golden thread. The wooden mansion seems to be one of those fairy tale houses and a misfit in the Puritanical New England. Little Pearl's pristine soul is attracted by the glistening sunlight that has fallen on the shimmering window and door. When she asks her mother to gather the sunlight for her, she refuses advising her to find her own sunlight and since she is devoid of any light in her life. After several knockings on the door, the servant appears who has been in bondage for seven years in exchange for his travel expense to New England from England. The servant as a newly arrived person is unaware of Hester's story and therefore when he observes Hester's beautifully crafted scarlet letter and her angelic daughter, he allows Hester Prynne inside thinking that she must be a gracious lady.

Inside, it is modelled after the great baronial home of Renaissance and medieval England. The large windows have illuminated the dark rooms and in a series, the portraits of Bellingham's stern forefathers robed in armour and waistcoats are hanging on the wall bespeaking his noble lineage. The centre of the hall consisted of a complete coat of armour which governor Bellingham has worn during Pequod War. While Pearl is excited to see such armour, Hester is afraid to see how her image is distorted in the glass. The only bright visible thing is the scarlet letter and the rest of herself seems to have disappeared or insignificantly visible. For a moment she felt that some imp in disguise must have taken Pearl's form and waiting to torment her with some hidden power. Averting the armour immediately, she directed Pearl into the garden which seems to be a reduction of ornamental England gardens. It is overgrown with weeds and scantily few cabbages and pumpkins are hanging. The little child Pearl is again captivated by the red roses in the garden and when she has become uncontrollable in her nagging demand for the rose and screaming loudly, the governor appears along with his other companions.

Commentary

This chapter is a continuation on Pearl's conflicting existence in the Puritanical world. Hester's visit to the Governor Bellingham's house with a pair of gloves that she has embroidered for him is primarily to protect her child from being snatched away by the Puritanical governing body. The fear of deprivation and abandonment of the child has caused turmoil and furore in her mind so that her frantic motherly self is desperate to preserve Pearl. Governor Bellingham and the rest of the elected Puritanical polemic authority have decided for a restrictive life of Pearl which they think immoral Hester Prynne is incapable of giving to her child. This is especially due to condemnation of illegitimacy in the Puritanical society. During the Interregnum (1649-60), and the passing of the Adultery Act of 1650, the Puritanical ministers strictly maintained records in the parish registers. The anxiety of Hester Prynne is not extremity because history of Salem reflects that illegitimate children by the Massachusetts Code in 1648 are condoned. Single motherhood is not at all encouraged especially to those who have dissuaded from Puritanical ideals and are not morally worthy to carry forward the next generation. Hester Prynne is considered as licentious cancer staining Winthrop's 'City Upon the Hill American Politics'.[18] The Puritans believed that allowing single mother to raise their children is dangerous because the child will be polluted by the mother's vicious nature. Hence Pearl as a child born out of fornication is entitled to become custody of the Puritanical ministerial authority.

Accompanied by Pearl who is always the cynosure of attention with her mesmerising bright eyes and instinctive actions, Hester does not hesitate to dress her daughter in the fiery passionate hue of life that Hawthorne describes as "brightest little jet of flame that ever danced upon the earth" (*SL* 152). This extremity of colour in the child's dress seems like another scarlet letter that drew attention of the children who wanted to throw mud at Hester and Pearl. The colour reflects Hester's taste for the gorgeous luxuriant elusiveness. But Pearl seems to be self-sufficient waging war against the entire world to defend her mother and herself.

The description of Governor Bellingham's palace is like a fantasy world. Hawthorne with bitter satirical tone comments on the luxury of Bellingham who is the predominant leader to propagate the Puritanical propositions of a life of restriction and restrain. The gorgeous abode is the sign of luxury and extravagance. The opulence is revealed in the walls adorned with fragments of intermixed broken glasses that glister like diamond in the sunlight, the cabalistic pictures drawn in the stucco and the large giant wooden door represent a world outside Puritan ideals. The exotic furniture like 'ponderous chair' designed with 'oaken flowers', the pewter tankard in the middle of the hall and the series of ancestral portraits of Bellingham's forefathers reflect the high aristocratic class consciousness and the desire for finesse in the art of living. These Puritans like Bellingham who propagated that Puritanism embodies true Christian belief in self-denial and exemption of individual desires. Bellingham's unrestrained individual luxury is not an interrogative discourse but Hester's adornment of Pearl's dress is objectionable. Hawthorne's prolong description of the mansion is not unnecessary poetic explication but there is a strong undercurrent of irony and criticism in it. Above all the bright panoply especially "manufactured by the skilful armourer in London" that consists of gorget, graves, pair of gauntlets and swords reflects how the governor cherishes to be worshiped not merely as a governor but also a great warrior, ruler and statesman. All these reflect the desire to meet the exigencies of comfort, ornamentation and a life of profligacy.

Besides the governor's garden where implantation of European crops and vegetables are cultivated in the soil of New England implies some ironical suggestions. Hawthorne clearly explains that this is the "effort to perpetuate on this side of the Atlantic, in a hard soil, and amid the close struggle for subsistence the native English taste for ornamental gardening" (*SL* 159). This domestic space is a frontier of colonial enterprise. It is a kind of a desired replica of Europe with a purpose to contextualise the picture of 'civilisation' in the New Found Land. Bellingham's mansion and garden are therefore medium where the dreams of the settlers are stored centripetally while in its centrifugal aspect, it dissipates the message to replenish the native space with a new taste.

The governor's white servant who is a slave for seven years is "as much a commodity of bargain and sale as an ox, or a joint stool". This brings in another interesting aspect of Puritanical religious world. Massachusetts has been the first slave-holding colony in New England and primarily the slaves consisted of the Indians. The Puritanical ministers and governors thought of themselves as God's elect. The Calvinist doctrine of predestination supported the Puritans in a superior position to surrogate the natives and dominate them by imposing the justification that they are condemned and cursed by God. But Hawthorne describes him as a "freeborn Englishman" which means he has been in debt and is sold to other people by the court. Depending on the amount of their debt, they are brought for specific time period in the New England. This group of people in the emerging capitalistic society is also called 'indentured servants' who do not suffer from racial inferiority unlike the black slaves. Bellingham's white slave therefore exemplifies the minister's superior status quo and politics of racial selectiveness.

CHAPTER EIGHT—THE ELF-CHILD AND THE MINISTER

As the men gradually approached towards Hester, Governor Bellingham is seen in a robe that most powerful men used to wear in the Puritanical society. With grey hair and alert eyes he stepped in lightly followed by Reverend Wilson who is trying to convince the governor about the possibility of growing crops like peaches, pears and grapes. Two other men also entered and they are Reverend Arthur Dimmesdale and Dr Roger Chillingworth, Hester's husband who is trying to explain Dimmesdale about the concept of overwork and exhaustion. It is heard that Dimmesdale has been suffering lately from lassitude and fatigue. While Governor Bellingham scorned disdainfully when he has come across the mother and the child, Reverend Wilson with sarcasm asks Pearl about her orientation and why her mother dared to dress her so outlandishly. With enough intelligence,

Pearl replies that she is her mother's child but Wilson leaves no room to remind that their present discourse has been about the child of adulteress Hester Prynne and how a gallant and unfaithful woman can allow her daughter to dress so gaudily and walk the streets.

Soon Bellingham discloses that recently the most controversial contention in Salem is Pearl's upbringing and the authority of rearing the child in relation to her unchaste mother Hester Prynne. They are surprised to find her audacity to enter inside the mansion but in a way they think it is necessary to confront the ostracised woman to disclose the truth to her. He acknowledges that being in power they will decide about the immoral soul of Pearl and they cannot allow her to stay with a fallen woman whose soul already resides in the pitfalls and the dungeon of the world. According to him, the child should be preached under the rigorous strictures of Puritanical church and must be disciplined properly which Hester Prynne is incapable and not worthy of. He orders Hester to speak on the matter. Hester, with humbleness and in most civil manner, answers that the scarlet letter is a big lesson for her and it still indoctrinates her with knowledge about life and enables her to explain the ethical and unethical aspects to her child.

When the governor instructs Wilson to examine the child, he repeats the same question about her creators. Hester Prynne has not been Puritanical but she knows the lessons of Bible which her parents have taught her in England. She has imparted the same knowledge to Pearl who could have easily answered from her lessons of Westminster Catechism in a better way than any child of Salem but unfortunately after much delay she replies that she is being plucked from the wild rose bush outside the prison door. Bellingham exclaims that the child is awful and signifies her dismal future and her sinful soul. At this Hester becomes irresistible and frantically explains that God has given her this beautiful gift at the cost of all that is bereft of her. Pearl is her only hope, her happiness and her punishment for her survival in the barren desolated life and if any one tries to disunite the mother-daughter relationship, both of them will end their lives. She appeals to Dimmesdale to stand by her, claiming that he has known her heart better than anyone in Salem and he is the best person to realise the significance of the child in Hester's life where everything has been drained away. Though stunned at sudden transgression of Hester, he favours her.

Dimmesdale seems to have undergone complete metamorphosis from the day when Hester Prynne appeared on the scaffold with her baby on the bosom. He looks much older than his age, sick and battered with pain. He has developed the habit of keeping his hand on his chest when he speaks on difficult matters. In that painful gesture, he explains beautifully from the Bible on the relationship between mother and child. Dimmesdale explains that only a mother with her special senses can connect with the child which no one else can ever perform, no matter how well intentioned that person may be. Though the child is the product of her father's guilt and her mother's shame, yet when god has decided upon this life, it is meant with some purpose. For him the child is sent as a form of blessing which humanity finds it difficult to discern. Raising a child is the most difficult thing and it is another way of retribution for Hester Prynne. It is another way of salvation and the child's dress reflects the nitty-gritty about her pure affection and care, her intense attention to nurture Pearl most eloquently. He thinks that the child and the mother are intrinsically related and they teach each other how to seek and gain salvation. He therefore implores the authority to let them stay together since the Almighty has decided in that way.

After this oracular speech of Dimmesdale which he is eternally gifted with, Wilson and Bellingham are convinced and they acknowledge their incapacity to think the way Dimmesdale has thought. Chillingworth is sceptical about Dimmesdale's excess of earnestness but the governor decides that as long as there is no more scandal and defamation regarding Hester Prynne, he is convinced to allow the mother and the child to stay together. Little Pearl seems to be amazingly attracted by Dimmesdale and all of a sudden she takes his hand in her own and laid her cheek softly against it. When Reverend Dimmesdale attempts to kiss her, she quickly springs and vanishes from the room. This charm of the child cannot even escape Wilson's observation, but Chillingworth addresses her as an 'elf' and attempts to determine the father of the child by observing her nature and countenance. Wilson finds it a vain attempt since it depends on God to disclose the identity of the biological father.

When Hester and Pearl depart from the mansion, the narrator takes a glimpse of the sister of the governor Bellingham, Mistress Hibbins who will be hanged few years later as a witch. Mistress Hibbins beckons Hester and invites her to come into the forest tonight and join the revelry with The Man in Black. To this Hester denies and explains that Pearl requires her attention and if the Salem authority would have snatched Pearl away from her, then she would merrily go and sign the bond of The Man in Black with her own blood. As she closes the window, Mistress Hibbins is yet hopeful that Hester will join the community gradually.

Commentary

This is a significant chapter in the novel because it allows the novel to reach its climactic point. First of all we come across the interaction of Pearl, the illegitimate child of Hester Prynne and the Puritanical ministers who tease and test the child in the presence of her mother and her biological father, Dimmesdale. We also find a natural inclination and fondness of Pearl towards Dimmesdale whose true filial bond with Pearl is unknown to the world. Moreover, in this scene of anxiety where Hester helplessly clamours to prevent separation of the mother and child, Dimmesdale's support in her favour germinates the doubt in Chillingworth's mind who happens to be an introspective shrewd reader of human mind. This chapter brings together all the important characters of the novel that we encounter at the beginning.

Hawthorne's portrayal of these ministerial figures is an attempt to deconstruct the stern rigidity and the shallow disciplinary life of the Puritans. This has been a repeated subject in Hawthorne's writings. In his short story "Young Goodman Brown" he attacks the Puritanical characters like Goody Cloyse, Deacon Gookin, Minister, Faith, and Goodman Brown. Behind the curtain of the mansion, Hawthorne reflects that the real devotional life of luxury and comfort which they enjoy in full gusto. Their 'legitimate taste for all good and comfortable things' "suggested that pears and peaches might yet be naturalised in the New England climate, and that purple grapes might possibly be compelled to flourish against the sunny garden-wall" (*SL* 162). Pears, peaches and purple grapes are symbolical representation reflecting the impetus of these Puritans to embrace the seducing life of material comfort. Far removed from a life of simplicity, they lead a life of luxury and enjoyment. The way Mr Wilson and Bellingham taunt little Pearl reflects that the Puritanical world preferred harshness and cruelty instead of love and affection for rearing of the children as well as in the process of selection and rectification of them. These aged men without any tenderness and affection but with a sadistic bent once more reiterate that acerbity and brutality are the characteristics of the Puritanical mind. The anti-climactic catalogue of names that Mr Wilson jeer at in relation to Pearl's identity ranging from pearl, ruby, coral, red rose and elf signifies that they are not merely impolite but also the ethics of austerity and discipline are deceptive. As they regard Pearl's soul to be immoral, they alleged Hester Prynne of being incapable to educate Pearl with discipline and instruction. They can see insatiability in Hester's Prynne's 'badge of shame' but the narrator observes that it is for her a way to salvation.

Pearl's defiance and rebellion against Puritanical order is explicit over here. She portrays her mother's rebellious nature, as her muteness is a protest in answering questions related to catechism. Pearl's answer regarding her origin is extremely incisive of patriarchal authority. She denies naming any paternal figure and instead claims that her mother has plucked her from the wild rose bush that grew near the prison door. Just like her mother chooses to be a single mother and obstinately never mentioned the name of her father, similarly Pearl, like her mother, remains tight lipped about her father and chooses to ignore the paternal contribution. Women in the Puritanical society are always seen as the "weaker vessel" on whose soul the devil can easily take possession. Such pessimistic ecclesiastical perspective is the principal reason behind the harsh treatment of Pearl. Hawthorne rationally explores child psychology and Pearl's refusal to answer regarding her origin appears, therefore, as the natural propensity of children to hesitate in front of strangers.

We also witness tremendous strength in Hester Prynne to wage a battle alone in the patriarchal world. The desperate frantic effusion of eloquent words from Hester's mouth to avert the segregation of the mother and the child is a spontaneous overflow of anguish and emotion which otherwise remains pent up in this woman's secluded life. Her coherent argument is extremely compelling because she speaks out of her suffering and shame which she undergoes every moment. After the scaffold scene, once more we come across the powerful rebellious spirit of Hester Prynne who can abandon all Puritanical theocracy to protect the only source of her survival in this world. It is this extraordinary spirit of the woman among the most powerful patriarchal figures of the society that makes her perennially fascinating. She invokes the fledging spirit of feminist revolt of Anne Hutchinson, as Hawthorne explains:

> Alone in the world, cast off by it, and with this sole treasure to keep her heart alive, she felt that she possessed indefeasible rights against the world, and was ready to defend them to the death. (*SL* 168)

When she exclaims that Pearl is the oxymoronic source of happiness and torture, an incessant reminder to her sin and punishment, Hawthorne deconstructs the human vision of sin and goodness, heaven and hell echoing the Miltonic Satanic discourse that it is the individual mind that decides suffering and joy, heaven and hell. However, her sudden outburst at Dimmesdale as she exasperates: "Speak thou for me" followed by "Thou wast my pastor, and hadst charge of my soul, and knowest me better than these men can" reflects that Hester Prynne in her moment of frantic effort may have reached the edge where she can no more keep the secret about the child's father. The latent rebellious spirit may apparently appear 'unwomanly,' but it is this dissident spirit that appears threatening to Dimmesdale who woke up from his slumber at Hester Prynne's provocation. This tempestuous spirit of Hester Prynne also unleashes a gamut of unexplained darkness in the lives of Puritanical women. One can recognise the feminist voice in her that explains the tragedy of aimless existence of outcast women and their frustration.

In contrast to Hester Prynne's crescendo of rebellious spirit, Arthur Dimmesdale appears 'careworn' and 'emaciated'. Empowered with gift of the gab, every time he utters his precious addictive words, he retreats within. Under compulsion when he justifies Hester's demand as awful sacred relationship between mother and child, Arthur denies to confront his own crime. By proclaiming Pearl as the outcome of her 'father's guilt and mother's shame', he steeps himself into self-deception and evasion of filial responsibility. His words do not contain anything new apart from what Hester Prynne has ushered but they are garbed in ornament and their shimmering beauty pleased the Puritanical authority. Simultaneously, the narrator also portrays the metamorphosis of Chillingworth as if the evil spirit is invoked within him. Arthur Dimmesdale's earnestness for the child and the mother leaves enough evidence for him to persecute Dimmesdale psychologically. Though others cannot identify the nullity of this man yet the old physician is quick enough to catch his abhorrent falsehood as a game of abstract ideas and surcharged oration. Dimmesdale's attempt to defend Hester and Pearl is motivated predominantly by self-centredness and rescuing himself from confronting the shame. If Hester Prynne is the epitome of revolt, she also suggests that revolution is life while Dimmesdale's evasiveness is death. At the end, Hawthorne explains that when—

> The young minister, on ceasing to speak had withdrawn a few steps from the group, and stood with his face partially concealed in the heavy folds of the window curtain; while the shadow of his figure, which the sunlight cast upon the floor, was tremulous with the vehemence of his appeal. (*SL* 172)

One can understand the symbolical significance of this description. Dimmesdale confessed without confessing, he is awaiting for his exit. His attempt to hide behind the folds of the curtain is the instinctive nature of the character that the narrator has captured. His shadow anticipates his future existence which is present-absent.

The satisfactory end of the tribunal is further enhanced by the next emotional scene of father-daughter relation. Pearl with her tender lips caressed her father's hand while Dimmesdale spontaneously kissed her forehead. This obscure acknowledgment of fatherhood by Dimmesdale cannot escape the physician's observant mind. It is a step towards progression of the climactic disclosure of the father-daughter relationship. It symbolises gradual intimacy reminding simultaneously the first scaffold scene when Pearl gazed silently at Dimmesdale. Pearl therefore represents a better destiny for humanity than that contrived by the Puritanical theology and interpretations. Pearl as 'elf-child' as the title of the chapter suggests is the Puritanical interpretation while in reality she represents mankind as "an infant immortality, being capable of eternal joy or sorrow."

The introduction of Mistress Hibbins as the figure of darkness and the reference of Black Man gives another picture of superstition and witchcraft in the Puritanical world. It is juxtaposed when Mr Wilson accused Pearl to be under some evil power. Hester's brief interview with Mistress Hibbins is purposely devised by Hawthorne in order to reflect on her mental condition and she explains she would have readily sold her soul to the devil if Pearl would not have been with her. This re-invokes the Salem history of witch hunting where Puritan women outside social convention are seen as threatening. Those who are accused of witchcraft are generally widows without children. Between 1692 and 1693, the Salem witch trials occurred in colonial Massachusetts. The belief was that the devil attacks and recruits bodies which are weaker and under his power, the witch can cause harm to any extent like murder, shipwreck, illness and death. Hibbins is the fictional characterisation of the historical Salem witch Ann Hibbins who was executed. She was trialled and convicted in the year 1655. The history of witch-hunting has led to the historical name of Salem as 'witch-city'. Hawthorne's inclusion of the historical character of mistress Hibbins is to hint what Hester Prynne could have easily become if Pearl would not have been there. Moreover, Hester's refusal to accept Hibbin's friendship reflects that she still believes in Christianity. It can be that in the character of Hibbins, Hawthorne is trying to reflect the 'other' Hester Prynne.

CHAPTER NINE—THE LEECH

This chapter primarily focuses on Roger Chillingworth and his identity. By excavating the past, the narrator reminds that after his release from the Native Americans in the wilderness, he discovers that his wife is the emblem of sin and instead of being a faithful wife awaiting for her husband's homecoming, she has indulged in adultery. He is ashamed to acknowledge her identity and out of fear of dishonour of being the husband of an unfaithful woman, his disguise and his new name becomes a great medium of his revenge. As everyone believed that Hester Prynne's husband died in a shipwreck, so also he has buried his original identity deep inside the sea and has introduced himself only as a physician with a new name called Roger Chillingworth. A physician is as rare as the arrival of God in New England and the people chiefly depended on quacks. Hence Chillingworth's presence is precious especially when he has been an outstanding doctor in the cities of England.

He is not an orthodox Puritan by heart and his religion is mainly medicine and human body. There is no doubt that he is extremely knowledgeable in his field because of his awareness of the recent scientific advancement in the Western world and at the same time he is also equipped with ancient knowledge because of his prolong stay among the natives. His knowledge on the vast array of medicinal herbs, roots, leaves and the various heathen ways of ailing diseases has equipped him with profound expertise and he has been honest in acknowledging his faith in both European and heathen science of the natives. He lives up to the Puritanical ideals—working hard, attending church services if not for religious rituals but for political purpose and lives a modest life without any crash exorbitance in his dress or dwelling.

When Dr Chillingworth happens to become the personal physician of Salem's beloved minister Arthur Dimmesdale, he has been cordially accepted in the heart of each Salem inhabitants. They are happy especially because of Dimmesdale's deteriorating physical condition. He seems to have lost all his vivacious energy and has become extremely pale and thin. They assume this to be the outcome of his excess of work, starvation and fasting, and the superabundant attention he pays to his parishioners. It seems that this spiritual man through his extreme devotion to humanity is searching for redemption of the sins of entire world. There is also a fear that he may die prematurely because he is too holy to live in this sinful world. To this Dimmesdale has an alternate individual explanation which is that he is too weak and ineffectual to serve the Almighty. When Chillingworth appeared in this land, the Puritanical society found it God's grace to send such a learned scholar in this land of harshness because he has sacrificed his wealth, honour and fame. Moreover Chillingworth's intense interest in Dimmesdale is taken as an obvious indication that this man is like a saviour sent by God to save the pious spirit of Dimmesdale. Like a parishioner he is attached to Dimmesdale and after winning his heart by meandering a strong friendship and intimacy in the lonely world of the minister, he pretends earnestly to restore his health and vigour. Dimmesdale often tries to avoid the medicine but it seems every Sunday after he has delivered his sermons from pulpit, he becomes thinner and paler. It has now grown into a habit of putting his hand over his heart. Reverend Wilson finally convinced him that if he does not accept the help of this man in ailing himself, then it will be a sin to reject the providential messenger. Arthur on the contrary clearly states to Chillingworth that to ease the concern of the mass, he is accepting his service but he would prefer him to serve the community.

But more than the disease, this doctor is interested to explore the character of this young clergyman and hence he started spending more time with him. They often go for strolling along the beach or deep inside the forest. While the doctor gathers herbs and medicine, he suggested to Dimmesdale that he should refresh himself in the midst of nature, breathing fresh air and stay away from his stressful life. Their conversation ranged from philosophy and science to religion and history and the Reverend is impressed by Chillingworth's thirst for knowledge. His philosophy of treating his patient is to know his soul in order to cure his body and therefore he attempts to venture deep inside the psychology of this man, exciting him, clarifying his taste and his discourses. For Chillingworth is an incredible reader of human mind, he knows the secret ways to reach one's heart. He can read silences, twisting and avoidance of subtle questions, disappear all of a sudden or listen to things which the speaker in his monologue often utters to himself. Dimmesdale at some point also detests his company because irrespective of the doctor's versatile knowledge, the minister is more comfortable with religious aspects. For the benefit of the treatment of his patient and in order to keep a close vigil on his patient, he came up with the proposition that both of them should live together and henceforth keeps close watch on his life, his movement and his living. When they together rented rooms from a widow in the same house, Dimmesdale and Chillingworth live separately but can easily pass into each other's room. While his paleness has disappeared yet he is often seen in daydreaming and hallucinating.

On the other hand, some shrewd members of the Salem community have started observing certain ugly spirit in Chillingworth and some suspicious evilness in his eyes unlike his first arrival when he looked calm and scholarly. The local women started gossiping that sometimes Dimmesdale appears to be haunted and it seems that some Satan with his evil force is trying to disturb him and they are suspicious that the doctor must be the diabolical source of evilness.

Commentary

The Leech, as the physician Mr Chillingworth is referred to, reflects the allegorical figure of Lucifer. He is the symbolic old serpent. Hawthorne's metaphorical choice refers to Chillingworth's power of infiltration in the lives and psyche of Hester and Dimmesdale. As the leech draws the blood away from a man's body hence Chillingworth too consumes the life force of Dimmesdale. His relentless search to gradually insinuate into the heart of Hester's lover is a way of dispensing poison in their mind and body.

Hawthorne explains that the physician's decision to percolate in the life of Salem is not to support his fallen wife's misery and ignominious life but rather to avenge the man who has insulted his existence. This chapter builds the foundation of the relation between the protagonist and the antagonist. Chillingworth's dark psychology is reflected in his mysterious existence in Salem as people wondered why such a talented man chose to stay in this land. His past is mysterious as he presents the story of being in captive of the Native Indians while in reality he seems to be in good terms with them. His friendship with the Native Americans reveals how manipulative this man is who can adapt to any situation for his personal benefit. The consort and comradeship is noted from the beginning when the character of Chillingworth is introduced. His conversation and nexus with the natives appear as if Satan with the other fallen angels are cast off into another land where the knowledge of good and evil is not restrictive to Puritanical ideologies.

His calculative steps in life reflect in his name "chill" which suggests that he is a man of psychological insights. Utilitarian by nature, he presented himself with his skill in medicine like a gift from heaven for the Salem community. But in reality he will dispense poison in the life of Dimmesdale and Hester Prynne. His decision to choose Dimmesdale as his neighbour and companion is deliberate because his revengeful enterprise is to find Pearl's biological father. Aiming to elicit the truth about Dimmesdale's weakness and physical illness, Master Pryne disguised as Chillingworth uses all the psychiatric reconnaissance. He becomes his confidante, constant attendant and intimate friend. His presence in the form of a saviour and physician is like a catalyst triggering the patient's psychodynamic effect. Chillingworth is sharp and shrewd enough to aim the arrow of doubt on the right person. During Hawthorne's days, the branch of psychiatry has hardly developed which Michel Foucault much later rigorously pondered how the branch of psychiatry as the essential clinical study is being neglected for centuries.[19] In Chillingworth, Hawthorne anticipates the outline of a modern psychiatrist for his techniques are scientific and rational. His cold scrutiny of Dimmesdale's mind and body involved attuning his mind to that of his patient. Whether it is at the cost of betrayal of friendship or exploiting the privilege of the profession of a doctor, he aimed to trespass the precinct of the mindscape of Arthur Dimmesdale. He is therefore the parasite of Dimmesdale whose existence is completely dependent on the existence of the host.

Arthur Dimmesdale on the other hand is a bundle of contradiction. As his name suggests, 'Arthur' associates him with romance and chivalry of the legendary king Arthurian world. However, his last name 'dim' is a contradictory to the first. His dimness and faint perspective lies in his incapability to confess his sin and proclaim his love for Hester Prynne. The etymology of 'dale' refers to some bent or hollowness or the gap between two hills. Hence Dimmesdale's love for Hester is hollow since he can never dare to stand publicly beside Hester Prynne. Even in his religious world, he is hollow for though he proclaims acute impressionable dictions yet he hardly follows them in his life. Dimmesdale's escapism cannot evade Chillingworth for he comments sarcastically:

> Youthful men, not having taken a deep root, give up their hold of life so easily! And saintly men, who walk with God on earth, would fain be away, to walk with him on the golden pavements of New Jerusalem. (*SL* 183)

We see brilliant manoeuvring of Dimmesdale by Chillingworth. It seems like a grave digger Chillingworth is excited to dig the ground of Arthur's mind and the deeper he ponders, the uglier he becomes. The people of Boston have noticed how the learned man's face has undergone transformation as if the fire of hell is burning in his face. Though he appears evil in his purpose yet there is bitter truth in his doubt and apprehension. Further his wondrous mechanism of treatment and detection involved the interaction of mind and body. The doctor reads the face to venture the minister's egoistic self-defensive silence. Chillingworth exacerbates his depth of guilt as a perpetrator that weighs him down.

In this chapter Hawthorne also reflects Chillingworth's extraordinary talent to win the heart of a man polar opposite to his nature, character, profession and age. To explain such bizarre company of people, the narrator explains such friendship and intellectual discourses appeared like—

> a window were thrown open, admitting a freer atmosphere into the close and stifled study,... But the air was too fresh and chill to be long breathed with comfort. (*SL* 184)

Thus, Hawthorne is hinting that Chillingworth's treatment through connection of body and mind is anachronistically modern.

CHAPTER TEN—THE LEECH AND HIS PATIENT

The narrator comments on the metamorphosis of Roger Chillingworth who at the beginning may not be affectionate towards anyone in this world but remained composed, ethical and honest. His search to solve the mystery of his adulterous wife, and her lover now appears as the primary pursuit in his life. Unlike his scientific knowledge that only employs human intelligence, he realises that human emotion is uncontrollable and unpredictable. He soon develops strong fascination to know the dark mystery of Arthur Dimmesdale's heart and is obsessed to unleash the innermost secret. His dark passion to venture into the recalcitrant darkness is so strong that he is compared to a grave digger or a determined miner searching for gold. At some point, some of the abstract clues encourage and assure him that he may succeed in achieving what he aims for. He soon started feeling that Dimmesdale is not as pure and spiritual as everyone thinks and that his intense passion for religion is a hint that he must be passionate for other things in life. He often beckons and captivates Dimmesdale in his trap in order to succeed in his vent for truth but he finds that he is concerned with congregation, salvation and love for the Heavenly father. If Dimmesdale would have been in good health, he would have easily realised the aim of this man but his poor health is the greatest predicament for the physician to discover the truth.

One day when Dimmesdale clarifies the source of the mysterious coloured leaves and weeds which the physician has gathered to prepare some drugs, the physician ensures that they are plucked from the trees born out of the human carcasses in the graveyard. The trees are mysteriously dark because they reflect the dark secret of the dead bodies which the world never came to know. The physician hints that confession is the best healing medicine for humanity and nature also supports that. To this Dimmesdale asserts that besides God, no one possesses the power to help in revelation of human souls. It is kept in store for the Judgement Day finally when the soul will be set free. As they started pondering over the power of confession, Dimmesdale is reminded by the physician that some sinful souls still prefer silence. To this Dimmesdale replies it is just like some people still love to serve God knowing that they are impure and carrying the burden of guilt. For the physician, the greatest sin of humanity is to confess the truth and hence the best way to serve God is that the sinners should perform purgation through confessions. To intensify Dimmesdale's suffering at that juncture, he gives the example of Pearl as an outcast who with her mother has been walking down the street at that point. When Pearl hears the physician's voice, she is desperate enough to throw flowers at him and warns her mother that she must stay away from this Black Man who has already captured the soul of the minister Dimmesdale. When he further exemplifies Hester with her scarlet letter, Dimmesdale appreciates Hester's immense strength since her life is an open book while others' who lack the power to confess, suffer from both concealment and sin.

The doctor soon ponders on Dimmesdale's life and he doubts that his patient has not exposed his mind to him for proper treatment of his body and still holds back certain secrets. He doubts his physical suffering is due to psychological turmoil. He claims that a doctor is specialised in suffering whether it is of mind or of body. When he insists the Reverend to confide in him his deep buried secrets but Dimmesdale is agitated as he slams the door and leaves the room claiming that confession is a transaction between God and the sinner, and the physician has no right to stand in between the sufferer and God. Late afternoon, the minister has fallen asleep in his room after such censorious debate when he almost became hysteric because of excessive unexplained emotional furore. The physician leaves no stone unturned to utilise this vulnerable moment of the minister and therefore as if pretending to medicate his patient's stimulated nerves, he enters in his room. His utmost curiosity forces him to unbutton Dimmesdale's shirt while the minister in deep slumber remained ignorant of this terrible violation of human ethics. Master Prynne seems to be over powered with demonic force as he discovers the greatest treasure in his life. In his satanic rejoice he appears to be victorious as if he has succeeded in corrupting another favourite soul of God who is to be banished from Eden.

Commentary

This chapter focuses how for one year, with intense devotion Chillingworth has succeeded in his unethical clinical study of Dimmesdale's mind and body. Consolidating his position as the minister's intimate friend, his heightened alertness and vigilance are unique and unearthly. His selective discussions with Dimmesdale related to most volatile topics like hidden sin which shows his implicit method of exposing the sufferer's guilt conscience. The crux of his sadistic treatment of Dimmesdale is amaranthine in nature. He explains to Dimmesdale that the ugly weed that he has plucked from nearby graveyard contains the secret guilt of the corpses. He knows the art of pricking the conscience of a guilty mind and therefore the weed he refers to is Dimmesdale's adultery which will haunt even after his death. One can feel an incessant silent battle is going on between Dimmesdale and Chillingworth.

The burning eyes of the physician refer to fire of hell suggesting his trepidation and his dynamism when he senses victory over the perturbed mind of the minister. Hawthorne's comparison of this old man to a judge, a miner or a mathematician is intriguing and impeccable. He explains:

> He had begun an investigation, as he imagined, with the severe and equal integrity of a judge, desirous only of a truth, even as if the question involved no more than the air-drawn lines and figures of a geometrical problem, instead of human passions, and wrong inflicted on himself. (*SL* 193)

Few lines later he compares Chillingworth to a miner:

> He now dug into poor clergy man's heart, like a miner searching for gold; or, rather, like a sexton delving into a grave, possibly in quest of a jewel that had been buried on the dead man's bosom, but likely to find nothing save mortality and corruption. (*SL* 193)

A judge and a mathematician are persons who work rationally devoid of any emotion. They work rationally on the basis of evidence and reason. The ultimate motto of the judge is to affirm truth and confirm crime and punishment while the aim of the mathematician is to solve the problem. In Chillingworth, we see the loveless and passionless heart toiling day and night for framing an equation and impinging punishment by self-made law for a crime where there is hardly any proof. But we cannot say that Chillingworth is free from intuition. Both Chillingworth and Dimmesdale work on the basis of intuition and nurture reciprocal suspicion without definitive confirmation. The comparison to a miner reflects the aspect of selfish greed and avarice. Here, this physician is least bothered about the psychological turmoil and erosion of the mind and the body of Arthur but his greed is to confirm his suspicion and find the truth. Chillingworth has sensed the dual personality of Dimmesdale and therefore he thinks that beside the aesthetic aspect, there is 'animal nature' inherited by the minister. Chillingworth is not a true Puritan since he does not believe in the fervent Christian belief of salvation and repentance. Hawthorne describes his patience and indomitable determination are the sole purpose of his living. Just like a miner, after immutable struggle when he comes across rubbishes like love, sentiment, pity inside Dimmesdale's heart, he diverts his direction but never abandons his effort. The greater the limbo, the greater is his cruelty. It is a search for pathogenic secret repressed deep down. Thus, Chillingworth appears as a crafty man nefariously aiming to precipitate eternal torture in Dimmesdale's mind.

Chillingworth is also Hawthorne's foil to disclose Arthur Dimmesdale's heart to the readers. By introducing this character Hawthorne foreshadows discovery and introspection of human mind. Chillingworth's strength is his adroitness and patience while Dimmesdale's weakness is his self-doubt. Both the men cohabit suffering but their form of sufferings is different. Chillingworth suffers insult and blistering wound because of Dimmesdale's sexual fulfilment which he cannot perform. His dissatisfaction has given way to interpret Dimmesdale's sexual gratification as 'animal nature'. This causes impotent rage and hence his aim is to unman Dimmesdale in the service of the oedipal father's need to punish the disobedient son. This aim to avenge is a pure narcissistic gratification in a homophobic culture of disruptive eroticism.

Chillingworth's demonism reaches its apex when Pearl's floating laughter from outside interrupts their contemplation on human sin and secret guilt. The benign motive finds the source for investigative procedure and utilising the opportunity, Chillingworth raises question about little Pearl's evil origin and Hester's sin. Chillingworth has stricken the raw nerves of the minister since it relates to his repressed guilt and his own offspring. For a moment it seems both the men confronted the ugly spirit of each other under the veil. In the game of power, Hawthorne's leech seems to be most powerful because he is igniting the fire in Dimmesdale's purgation and at the same time compelled Hester to be tongue tied by extorting and threatening. Significantly, Pearl appears to be the guiding star to the conscience of these two men. When she flung the prickly burrs at Dimmesdale out of her strange whims, it is as if she is rebuking her father for his denial. When Pearl utters:

> Come away, mother! Come away, or yonder old black man will catch you! He had got hold of the minister already. Come away, mother or he will catch you! But he cannot catch little Pearl! (*SL* 201-02)

It seems that Pearl is her mother's guardian angel but she denies help to protect her father because of his repressed guilt. While the two main protagonists and the antagonist silently confront each other, Chillingworth appears victorious in the dynamics of power. Dimmesdale's self-incrimination is worst at this juncture. Pearl's allusion to 'blackness' in describing the physician is obviously a reference to Mistress Hibbins' Black Man in the forest who is malevolent and epitome of some unearthly fiendish power. Being a captive of the native Indians and acquiring knowledge about their world, it seems Chillingworth is the emissary of the Devil. It is as if the devil has enticed the minister into a bond, torturing him excruciatingly till the end. Hester has also entered into a misaligned contract with this black man to keep his original identity as a secret. However, through Pearl's comment, Hawthorne is trying to suggest that all the three characters are involved in an allegorical silence which is the greatest hamartia in this tragedy.

The final section of this chapter is on the dialectical tension of body and mind and their co-relation. This has been an age old disquisition in philosophy, theology, religion and literature. When Chillingworth explains to the minister that—

> A bodily disease, which we look upon as whole and entire within itself, may, after all, be but a symptom of some ailment in the spiritual part.

He then further emphasises that Dimmesdale's disease is of the spirit than of the body:

> a sickness, a sore place, if we may so call it, in your spirit hath immediately its appropriate manifestation in your bodily frame (*SL* 204-05)

Body is always seen as the temporal reflection and necessary garb to define the soul's dimension. The 17th century philosopher René Descartes in his work called De Homine (On Man) explains mankind as automation possessing a divine soul. Descartes believes that body and soul/mind are different 'substances' and the unity of the two is termed by him as Cartesian dualism. For Descartes, the body affects the mind since it receives signals from the body and the mind also affects the body since it responses to its plans. The nineteenth century American writer Henry David Thoreau has often reflected on the discord of body and soul but concludes that empathy exists between the two. The interdependence of body and soul is recognised by Thoreau as "mysterious interplay between matter and spirit" so that—

> certain labours of the body may invigorate the spirit; certain spiritual contemplations may elevate the body. And it is the truly successful man...who learns to support his body and his spirit 'by one and the same means.'[20]

Chillingworth's words in this context therefore open the great debate of the dualism of body and soul. His formulation regarding Dimmesdale's psychosomatic disorder is rooted in modern medical science. Chillingworth's ardent interest in both Dimmesdale's body and mind is to dissect and see the precipitated throbbing illicit desire and sin in recalcitrant darkness of psychic and bodily sphere. Thus, Chillingworth represents Hawthorne's brand of characters like Ethan Brand, Aylmer, Rappaccini, whose job is to remove the surface illusion of social contract and purge the soul for the purpose of extracting the truth. Through this subtle unuttered conflicting bond between Dimmesdale and Chillingworth, Hawthorne is anticipating the deferred future of America. The cumulative psychic pressure that the physician is creating is like a tangible lash on the conscience of the suffering soul and this is seen in the instant reaction of the minister who, with furious rage denies unleashing his heart to an 'earthly physician'.

After this minor confrontation when Dimmesdale falls asleep, the greatest treasure of the miner is discovered. Trespassing all forms of morality, he sees the naked chest of the minister and witnesses the replica of Hester's scarlet letter. Rejoicing in the discovery of the greatest treasure of this earth, the physician is saturated with the damnation of his own soul as well. This is the turning point that anticipates Arthur Dimmesdale's spiritual death and affirmation of Roger Chillingworth's final fall. Through this microcosmic discovery of Chillingworth, Hawthorne is also interrogating the greed and unlawful intrusion and exploration of native America by his forefathers.

CHAPTER ELEVEN—THE INTERIOR OF A HEART

Initially the aim and purpose of Chillingworth's life at Salem has been to search for the sinner who has conjoined with his wife in the shameful act. Now the motive has changed with a latent malice. While pretending to be the closest friend and confidant of the minister, he is inwardly pitiless and tortuous, making Dimmesdale suffer endlessly without any respite. Dimmesdale also feels some evil presence around him but he is unable to identify the emanation of that spirit. He feels the old man's gnarled and terrible attitude intolerable but cannot see any reason behind it. He therefore concludes that it is the external manifestation of his own guilt and shame which he tries to locate in others. His distrust is nothing but due to his hidden sin and dark history.

The more intense is his suffering, the more powerful has become his delivering of lectures. His wound seems to be pouring out in his sermons which easily pierce the heart of common men unlike those older sober scholars whose high dictions and rhetoric hardly seem convincing for the mass. Perhaps Dimmesdale would have preferred to remain as one of the elevated theological preachers, but his guilt conscience and the burden of his secret have pulled him down to the level of common men. Every Wednesday and every Sunday, he decides not to decline from the pulpit until he confesses the actual sin but he plays with words and he remains in disguise. There remains a gap between his intention and utterance. The more Dimmesdale proclaims himself as the sinner who requires God's mercy, the Salem audience believe it to be his extreme humbleness to make others confess their guilt and sin easily. No one can ever think about this play with words and hence Dimmesdale's suffering intensifies day by day because of his complete awareness of his inability. His lack of boldness to confess the truth publicly gradually turned him into a sadist so that every night, when he undresses himself before going to bed, he uses the scourge to lash himself several times, feeling the razor edges metal stars shredding his flesh and thereby rejoice in the pain inflicted on himself. Further, his endless deprivation included incessant fast so that the body may become pale and frail. He spends sleepless nights, pondering over his countenance in the mirror or praying on his knees. Dimmesdale has also started having hallucination seeing some apparitions like his parents turning away from him or Hester Prynne accusing him pointing her finger at the scarlet letter. During one such night when sleep has departed him completely, and he is suffering from intense back pain because of self-scourging, he decides to dress in his best, as if preparing to preach in front of his congregation and moves towards the marketplace where Hester Prynne has been publicly persecuted.

Commentary

In this chapter, Chillingworth's revenge after his confirmation is elaborated. Hawthorne now clearly shows the split between the interior and the exterior of the physician. It also reflects shadow between the sacred adorable public image of Dimmesdale and the guilty soul that Chillingworth has come to know. The poisonous morbid spot marked as the scarlet alphabet on his chest is the secret way into the cavern of the heart of the minister. The title of the chapter refers to the secret transit of Dimmesdale's heart that unlocks all the morbid repressed guilt and crime. This chapter is reminiscent of Khalil Gibran's poem "On Crime and Punishment":

> Oftentimes have I heard you speak of one who commits a wrong as though he were not one of you, but a stranger unto you and an intruder upon your world.

But I say that even as the holy and the righteous cannot rise beyond the highest which is in each one of you,

> So the wicked and the weak cannot fall lower than the lowest which is in you also.
>
> And as a single leaf turns not yellow but with the silent knowledge of the whole tree,
>
> So the wrong-doer cannot do wrong without the hidden will of you all.[21]

Gibran is claiming that crime is the part of the same body and soul which we love and admire. The shy, sensitive and humble minister's darker side of the character therefore can be found within each of us. The minister's conflicting self has the urge to confess yet at the same time the fear of the curative effect of confession makes him retreat. Confession is a way of recognition of one's sin and is supposed to be the beginning of repentance. On the other hand, Hawthorne explains that—

> After the incident last described, the intercourse between the clergyman and the physician, though externally the same, was really of another character than it had previously been. (*SL* 209)

Now it seems that after seeing the Reverend's secret, Chillingworth has emasculated Dimmesdale, repaying the anguish and insult which he has undergone one year back. This vengeful punitive physician has obsessively penetrated into the conscience of the minister and hence Hawthorne explains the sheer wild pleasure of Master Prynne:

> the very inmost soul of the latter, seemed to be brought out before his eyes, so that he could see and comprehend its very moment, He became, thenceforth, not a spectator only, but a chief actor in the poor minister's interior world. He could play upon him as he chose. (*SL* 210)

The word 'play' denotes how he relishes in extracting the pleasure out of the barbaric psychological torture of Dimmesdale. Like a mutated Faustian sufferer of Christopher Marlowe, Dimmesdale is the victim of the game and illusion of another Mephistopheles that is Chillingworth. The abject sinner is now intensified in self-loathing. But the irony that Hawthorne mocks at is that Dimmesdale being a sinner becomes a greater minister. For Dimmesdale is merciful, benevolent, generous and humanitarian in contrast to moralist John Wilson. Through the character of Dimmesdale, Hawthorne is trying to reflect on the double aspect of the Puritan reformers. The endorsement of so-called 'morality' through the so-called 'immoral' experience in personal life is Hawthorne's area of speculation. Such ironic predicament is revealed when Arthur Dimmesdale in his deliverance of the sermons subjects himself as a sinner and "an abomination" while the congregation is impressed with his modesty. Hawthorne also reflects how the strong bond of sin and suffering are inextricably interrelated that personify humanity.

This chapter focuses on the psychological realism of human beings which relates to the interplay of psychology, sociology and literature. Though Hawthorne's *The Scarlet Letter* is a pre-Freudian text yet we can anticipate Freud's discourse in the character of Dimmesdale. In Dimmesdale we see a conflict of Freudian 'id' and 'superego'. In the previous chapter when the physician refers to the 'animal self' of the minister which he has inherited from his forefathers, it is the 'id' that he is reflecting upon. This 'id' to which he has succumbed to is in conflict with his 'superego' that wants Hester to confess his name as a co-sinner. We will witness soon how at one point his ruling superego will usurp the 'id' when he will plan to elope with Hester from New England. Dimmesdale's mindscape is the perfect graph to study the intricate relationship of 'id', 'ego' and 'superego'. E. Michael Jones in the essay "The Dimmesdale

Syndrome: Why Confession is a Necessity" from Culture Wars has coined the term 'Dimmesdale syndrome' after Nathaniel Hawthorne's fictional character to explain the outcome of self-deception, repression and suffering. The most tormenting element in Dimmesdale's life of secrecy and guilt is anxiety which is a significant component of Freudian discourse. We can see Freudian 'defence mechanism' into action as Dimmesdale cannot take the initiative to deconstruct his social image.

Dimmesdale's character opens another controversial area of Puritanical world which is Ministerial sexuality. In the book *The Feminization of American Culture*, Ann Douglas explores the most sensitive issue of the relationship between women, ministers and cultural values. Most of these ministers found women as the "second sex", isolated from the public world and as the listeners of their religious sermons; they are the blind believers who have no rational interrogation in their mind. The ministers with their religious and institutional power can convince women and indulge them in ministerial concupiscence. Such lusty desires give way to ministerial anxiety and Arthur Dimmesdale's character highlights this hidden truth. Unlike American fictional characters of divine lechery like Elmer Gantry or Thomas Marshfield, Arthur Dimmesdale represents loft adorable exquisite refinement in his words and physique.

Through the parallel reflection of Dimmesdale and Chillingworth's characters, Hawthorne is also problematizing the question of American masculinity. Hawthorne's biographical details explain that after the demise of his father, Hawthorne is reared in his maternal family. His life had been full of struggle, hardship and economic crisis till towards the end of his life he managed to build a house of his own. The struggle of this man through tremendous self-doubt, frustration and failures has bagged loads of praises from his friends in whose eyes he has been the epitome off true manliness reflected in his consistent struggle and toil to achieve success and triumph at the end of his life. Yet the same man writes:

> I grew up without a root, yet continually longing for one-longing to be connected with somebody—and never feeling myself so. (XII 27)

In colonial America, the concept of masculinity is essentially important. The young man's struggle to establish a successful life of prosperity in the turbulent new found land is the most crucial aspect of manhood. His firmness and self-command are seen to be essential factors in determining his civilised race and his masculinity. Dimmesdale's indecisiveness is contrary to American masculinity especially in an age when Ralph Waldo Emerson is propounding the concept of masculinity in New England by asserting self-reliance of manhood. Both Dimmesdale and Chillingworth feel that their manhood are impaired in individual ways. We find that Dimmesdale's world of anxious solitude is not self-sufficient, no matter what morals and virtuous words he utters in front of the audience. His agony to wrestle against his guilt conscience and yet incapable to find a solution for retribution is the biggest dilemma in this man's life. The paradox of understanding an evil presence in Chillingworth's company and yet incapable of preventing him venturing into his life is the tragic dilemma in his life. That gender is a social construction has been unknown during Hawthorne's time and it is taken for granted that it is naturally oriented. True American masculinity is therefore complemented by pure womanhood that relates to concept of 'home' and a happy peaceful domestic life. Chillingworth therefore fails to assert the quality of American masculinity because he has failed to control his wife Hester Prynne within the domestic sphere. Hester rears a child not born of the wedlock not with Chillingworth but with Dimmesdale. This triggers not only ignominy but self-doubt in the physician. She has therefore failed to assert the selfless devotion to husband which is perceived as the essence of womanhood. She is not the domestic angel but almost repulsive whore for the Puritanical society. To avenge Hester's lover is therefore to restore his masculinity and to see Arthur suffering is a kind of discharge of libidinal energy that he has repressed for a long time.

To preserve the purity of woman is also a part of American masculinity and it is a matter of shame and disgrace for one's manhood whose wife is impure and corrupt. Just before Hawthorne's marriage with Sofia, he described his wife like a pond lily which is transcendently pure. He explains—

> How the pond-lily derives its loveliness and perfume.....I possess such a human and heavenly lily...and wear it in my bosom.[22]

The word 'possess' reflects that manhood referred to proprietorship and assertion of power over woman in which Mr Chillingworth failed. Being in this way, Chillingworth's obsessive self-containment is ironical because it resulted in self-denial of libidinal energy and ignorance of Hester. In contrast to these two men, Hester Prynne depicts certain Puritanical 'masculine' qualities by being the master of her house and becoming the maker of her fortune. Hester Prynne has constructed in New England what these two men cannot—a frontier selfhood and a self-reliant personality. American Revolution may have excluded women directly from political frontier but Hester Prynne's character ushers in a new economic and social place for women.

Dimmesdale's weakness is reflected in his lack of courage to equivocate the truth. Worse than that, he misrepresents the truth about his secret in his sermons. His masochistic way of scourging himself with a whip is a morbid form of penance. Such perverse delight by self-abnegation, fasting and scourging are all bodily inflictions which cannot be equated to public confession and acknowledgement of Pearl as his child. This is an easier way to punish than demean his position and tarnish his elevated image. Dimmesdale is afraid to acknowledge his libidinal wishes because it appears sinful to him. Therefore to punish his fleshly pleasure, he indulges in fleshly pain. Excess of narcissism withholds him from confessing and public acknowledgement. Masochism is subdivided into three categories namely erotogenic, moral and feminine. Dimmesdale's masochistic form is erotogenic masochism that involves deriving sensual gratification from physical pain. Moral masochism concerns torturing of the ego incessantly by superego and whose desire for punishment becomes so irresistible that he is constantly tempted to commit those deviant acts that will result in self-castigation. Dimmesdale however seems to be very protective of his ego. Feminine masochism refers to men who desire to assume the 'feminine position' and women who dare to transcend the social parameter. For Dimmesdale, we do not see such type of masochism. The Puritanical society believed in regicide as the necessary step for punishment which Dimmesdale avoids. The condemned body needs to be punished publicly before being executed in order to teach the community the punishment of such transgressive act. In this way the focal point of punishment is more psychological than physical.

In the colonial America, judiciary system is intrinsically related to religious systems. Religion and law are identical in Puritanical world. Lawrence Friedman explains:

> it would be hard to overemphasise the influence of religion…in shaping the criminal codes, in framing modes of enforcement, and, generally, in creating a distinctive legal culture. The criminal justice system was in many ways another arm of religious orthodoxy.[23]

The Almighty Father in the Puritanical eschatology is cruelly disciplinary and for him severe punishment is the only way to control mankind. Dimmesdale being one of the religious figures is aware of justice that only seeks infinite punishment. Being one of those chosen and elected members, he deserves more punishment than anybody else according to Puritanical doctrine. If Dimmesdale's secret is revealed, social stability will be disturbed because being one of the ecclesiastical figures, his indulgence with Hester Prynne is a reflection of libidinal excess. It is said that Puritanical society in New England practised erotic-endo colonisation where any sort of deviant pleasure like rape, masturbation or adultery is considered sin.

Against Dimmesdale's masochism, Chillingworth is a perfect occult sadist. Chillingworth's sadism seems to be congregation of the sadistic excess of the Puritanical society. Dimmesdale's scarlet alphabet "A" on his chest can ironically signify androgyny in terms of Puritanical masculinity that supported robustness of men. However, Chillingworth's avenging pleasure at the personal level can be seen as not merely sadistic but sadomasochistic since it relates to erotic rivalry between husband and lover of Hester Prynne. Though pretending to be a scholar and a physician, Chillingworth is a warden in the 'moral hospital'[24] till the patient is cured. Chillingworth's subterfuge asserts Foucault's discourse that knowledge and power coalesce within modern disciplinary technology. In this course of private space of masochism and sadism, we see both the men undergo tremendous physical and mental metamorphosis. This can be best explained in the words of Charles Dickens who has elaborated such private way of punishment which appears invisible to eye and yet erodes the soul inside:

> I hold this slow and daily tampering with the mysteries of the brain, to be measurably worse than any torture of the body, and because its ghastly signs and tokens are not so palpable to the eye and sense of touch as scars upon the flesh; because its wounds are not upon the surface, and it exhorts few cries that human ears can hear; therefore I the more denounce it, as a secret punishment which slumbering humanity is not roused up to stay.[25]

CHAPTER TWELVE—THE MINISTER'S VIGIL

As if in a trance, Dimmesdale reached the market place in a moonlit night. He started watching the scaffold where several years back Hester Prynne has undergone public humiliation. As if some mysterious force has beckoned Dimmesdale and he climbed the steps of the scaffold. The sky seems to be a canvas of canopy of black clouds and the narrator comments that if the throng of people present during Hester's trials would have been present today, it is impossible to visualise the face on the scaffold through this impenetrable darkness. The precinct of Salem is lost in slumber and the minister alone on the scaffold is horrified to think of his sinful past and how it is continuing in the present. Out of repulsion and disgust he screamed with full gusto echoing off the roofs of the village houses. It is expected that all of them by now will rush to see the letter on his chest which will spontaneously answer his crime that remained in oblivion for several years. No one is stirred except the old physician in a nightgown and a cap, with a lamp is seen to be standing at the window of Governor Bellingham's house. From another window light emanates and this time Mistress Hibbibs, the sister of the governor of Salem appears startled by the scream. It seems as if she is longing to join some unholy spirit in the darkness but she quickly disappears extinguishing the lamp when she found light in her brother's window.

While the chill breeze is blowing and Dimmesdale is still standing on the scaffold, in the distance he observes a tiny light moving towards him. Illuminating bushes, fences and doors as the light appears nearer, he finds Reverend Wilson who is returning from Governor Winthrop's house. Governor Winthrop has passed away in the midnight and Wilson has been present to witness the final departure of the holy soul from his earthly abode. Though Dimmesdale hoveringly tries to utter a word, he fails while Wilson passes the scaffold without even noticing him in the darkness. Suddenly the laughter of a child strikes his ears and he soon visualises Pearl and her mother Hester Prynne. Hester discloses that they are returning from the deathbed of Governor Winthrop and she should go home and prepare a robe for his funeral. All of a sudden he requests Pearl and Hester to come and stand along with him on the scaffold which he should have done when seven years back Hester with her child appeared for the first time. When the three in silence stand in that dark night, for Dimmesdale it seems that his mind and body are relieved from agony and torture. At this point Pearl enquires whether in the day light the minister will stand along with them. The minister replies to Pearl's query that on the Final Judgement Day, they will unite again. To this Pearl roars into laughter while in the sky several meteors strike across the sky and three meteors form the red incandescent shape of the alphabet "A" illuminating the sky. The entire Salem is enlightened and Dimmesdale notices Roger Chillingworth at the edge of the sidewalk.

Dimmesdale probes Hester if she knows anything about the physician's background since that man is tortuous and fearsome for him. While Pearl all of a sudden claims that the physician is the Black Man, Hester remains silent as she remembers the promise made to Chillingworth. Chillingworth beckons him to come along with him and both the men then move towards their destined house. Next morning which happens to be a Sunday, Dimmesdale seems to be immensely compelling and impressive in his sermons and it is believed that his eloquent delivery of sermon touched miraculously several souls of Salem. The sexton hands over a pair of black gloves to the minister. He believes that these gloves of the Reverend found on the scaffold of the convicts are being stolen by some evil power who wants to dishonour the minister but the spirit's attempt fails because Dimmesdale is untainted and holy. Sexton further informs that last night when the pious soul of John Winthrop has demised, the entire firmament was illuminated with the alphabet 'A' which symbolises that Governor Winthrop was transformed to an Angel.

Commentary

This chapter reflects Dimmesdale's midnight excursion towards the scaffold in the market which is the apotheosis of Hester Prynne's sin. Dimmesdale's midnight ordeal seems to be like his nightmare and one is reminded of Garden of Gethsemane where Jesus Christ as the divine among mortals is full of sorrow to see human sin, suffering and pain. There appear apparently three observers who witnessed Arthur Dimmesdale's secret attempt to confess his sin. Governor Bellingham is one of them as a representative of the civil government appeared near his window after hearing Dimmesdale's shriek. Dimmesdale has the opportunity to confess to him but he fails. Mistress Hibbins, who is the witch of the town, also appeared in the course of her midnight adventure but Dimmesdale is not bothered. Reverend Mr Wilson also passed by after witnessing the departure of the soul of Governor Winthrop but Dimmesdale chose not to interrupt him. The three realms of power in Puritanical world are represented—civil, demonic and divine but Dimmesdale failed to ally with any one of them. In this process of fallacious nocturnal vindication, it appears that Dimmesdale has lost his sanity but his narcissism and self-aggrandisement are still lingering in him and hence he purposely chose to remain obscure in the darkness of guilt and fear.

Hawthorne like a modern symbolist writer has brilliantly described the surrounding atmosphere of that dark night. The 'unwearies pall of cloud [that] muffled the whole expanse of sky from zenith to horizon' (*SL* 221) is a symbolic representation of the confused mind of Dimmesdale. The reverberating sound of his shriek is a metaphorical representation of the novel's attempt to represent human passion and emotions. His shriek reflects the basic interpretative role of Hawthorne throughout the novel. This shriek like Pearl's sudden outburst is full of mystery. It reflects the intensity of emotional chaos and the repression he has been accumulating inside. The narrator comments that in the obscure night of early May if the same crowd that has witnessed Hester's ignominy would have been present, they would not been able to see the minister's bodily existence. Such absent present in the chiaroscuro of the night reflects the ambiguity of the mind that lacks the courage to confess publicly. This shriek is the metaphorical exclamation of individual anxiety verses Puritanical social norms. His defensive self is well aware that he is safe from discovery. With a tone of intense mockery Hawthorne writes:

> Crime is for the iron-nerved, who have their choice either to endure it, or, if it press too hard, to exert their fierce and savage strength for a good purpose, and fling it off at once! This feeble and most sensitive of spirits could do neither, yet continually did one thing or another, which intertwined, in the same inextricable knot, the agony of heaven-defying guilt and vain repentance. (*SL* 222)

Hawthorne is not critical about Dimmesdale's crime but his comment hints at the excess of self-delusion in the man. His half-attempt to confess the truth in the middle of the night is 'the mockery of penitence' (*SL* 222) which caused the 'angels blushed and wept'. This reminds us of Milton's Paradise Lost (Bk 6, II 824-52) or Blake's Songs of Experience: "When the stars threw down their spears,/ And water'd heaven with their tears."[26] The fallen disobedient angels who along with Lucifer rebelled against God regretted their betrayal and are now full of shame. What Hawthorne wants to suggest here is that Dimmesdale's hypocrisy lies in self-deception and is comparable to Lucifer's fall.

Dimmesdale is suffering from hallucination at this point on the scaffold. Hallucination is a sensory experience that does not happen or exist in reality but is the result of figment of imagination of a guilty mind. Such hallucinations give rise to anxiety, depression and shame. Dimmesdale's illusion reflects his wish to confess the truth. This chapter focuses on Dimmesdale's prolong hallucinations which Hawthorne termed as 'lurid playfullness' (*SL* 227). Such conversation between Dimmesdale and Reverend Mr Wilson does not take place in reality but it is the external manifestation of his internal desire to confess to Mr Wilson. Such deep psychological prognosis by Nathaniel Hawthorne is an extremely modernistic approach. It is interesting to note that when Hawthorne was attending Bowdoin College, one of the faculty members Thomas C, Upham, who was a philosopher psychologist and was known as a professor of Mental Philosophy made tremendous impact in Hawthorne's life. It is said that Upham had greatly influenced Hawthorne with his various theories like 'trifaculty psychology' that explains how human mind is schematised into intellect, sensibilities and will which if studied carefully can reflect various motives, hidden scruples and guilt conscience. Thomas Upham's famous book *The Interior Life* is interesting in this context where he has commented on the conflict with evil force and the conflict is intensified the more perfect the soul of the man is:

> Thou hast contended with Satan, and hast been successful. Thou hast fought with him, and he has fled from thee. But, O, remember his artifices. Do not indulge the belief that his nature is changed. True, indeed, now he is very complacent and is, perhaps, singing thee some siren song; but he was never more a devil than he is now.[27]

Upham explains that conflict with evil will continue but if love sustains he will be able to win over evil. In case of Arthur Dimmesdale the question is what the priority in his life is—Hester and Pearl or his bloated ego and the much worshipped self-image. Upham believed that love can dismantle selfish pride but we hardly see till the end of the novel that Dimmesdale has been able to sacrifice his hollow reputation.

The arrival of Hester Prynne with Pearl on the scaffold is the second of the three scaffold scenes in the novel. Interestingly in the first scaffold scene where Hester was condemned of adultery, Reverend Arthur Dimmesdale remained detached from Hester's ignominy and suffering. In this second scaffold scene in the dark pitch night when he has arrived for self-condemnation followed by self-consolation, Hester Prynne chose to stand by his side. Dimmesdale's summoning of Hester and Pearl: "Ye have both been here before, but I was not with you. Come up hither once again, and we will stand all three together", (*SL* 229) is a selfish act that reflects his own cowardice nerves that search for a partner to share the suffering of his guilt. Like the fallen angel Lucifer, Dimmesdale searches for his partner to fill the empty void of loneliness and sin. This is evident in Arthur Dimmesdale's reply to Pearl's question whether he is willing to stand on the scaffold with the mother and the daughter next morning in front of the entire community. Dimmesdale's denial reflects that he is still not ready to abandon his bloated ego and afraid to confess the truth. Nathaniel Hawthorne has been well versed in Biblical studies and in Yesterday With Authors, James T Fields comments:

> Hawthorne was a diligent reader of the Bible, and when sometimes, in my ignorant way, I would question, in a proof-sheet, his use of a word, he would almost always refer me to the Bible as his authority.[28]

Hawthorne must have the intertextual reference of Denial of Peter in his mind when after repeated persuasion of Pearl; Dimmesdale's failed to answer the exact day when he would be ready to bear the burden of his yolk along with Hester and Pearl. In the Gospels of the *New Testament*, it is explained how in the Last Supper, Jesus with his disciples predicted that Peter would disown him twice when time comes before the rooster crowed. Next morning when Jesus was arrested, Peter denied acknowledging Jesus but when the rooster crowed, he broke down which is known as Repentance of Peter. Dimmesdale has not reached that stage yet and hence his denial stems from the fear of ignominy.

The mysterious meteors in the sky as if witnessing the secret congregation conspired to warn Dimmesdale about his perdition and Hawthorne writes with gothic flair how in the horizon the alphabet 'A' is designed. However, we have to remember that the mysterious 'A' might be the result of Dimmesdale's hallucination and therefore it is ambiguous. This hieroglyphic reflection appeared to the others as angelic because they believed that the demise of the divine soul of Governor Winthrop just before the incident is related to the mysterious alphabet in the sky. Last but not least, the mysterious impenitent figure of Chillingworth is seen in his persistent pursuit of revenge. With the appearance of this 'fiend' in the scene we finally see all the four major characters of the novel are present who in some way or the other are entangled in sin.

CHAPTER THIRTEEN—ANOTHER VIEW OF HESTER

Pearl is now seven years old. The narrator comments that time is the greatest healer and even hatred can be transmogrified into love if it is not lacerated again. Even Hester with her glittering golden alphabet holds nothing new for the Salem community to be awed or terrified. She has accepted the world as it is without any complaint. Hester never contests the insults and harshness inflicted upon her. On the contrary, Hester has become more compassionate day by day. There is not another Salem inhabitant who has been so kind to the poor as Hester is. As a result people have become sympathetic towards Hester. Moreover she lives a life of abstinence far detached from the worldly privileges and works for minimum requirements in order to survive with her daughter. Now, the adulteress Hester is the spring of effusion of human tenderness and has ordained herself as Sister of Mercy. Her burning shame on top of her bosom now becomes the solacing place for the sufferer and the poor. As a result the symbolic interpretation of "A" is no more adulterous but Able. Hester's help and service is unconditional and she is the first person to be seen where agony and suffering turn humanity lonely and desolate. But Hester is never seen in any mirthful jovial gathering because she knows that to share the joy and happiness, there will be enough mortals in this world. Even the rulers and the authorial class now share some compassion for Hester although Hester never expects anything in return. They now see the scarlet letter as the cross on the nun's bosom which can win her any danger in this world.

There have been stupendous changes in her physiognomy. Hester's beauty is astrayed in the process of her secluded magnanimous service to greater humanity. Her dazzling brilliant hair always covered under the cap has never known sunlight. Her gracefulness is lost into oblivion and the colours of life are all burnt under the effect of scarlet letter. She has become a skeleton of a tress bereft of leaves and flowers. Her plain dress, elegant feminine body, reserved manner and lifeless gaze arouse passion no more. Lonely, sequestered from the rest of the society, Hester now lives a life of contemplation and reflections. She has not conformed to the Puritanical society and within Hester lies the germ of revolution but her freedom is in her thought, in her imagination and in her buried hopes. Moreover, Pearl's eccentricity and irregular freakishness often perturb Hester as she contemplates on the future of the child. But this child like a saviour also prevented Hester to become another Anne Hutchinson. Some of her reflections are extremely emancipatory and enlightening. Hester's experience in life has enabled her to deconstruct the normal confinements for women in the Puritanical New England. She therefore strongly thinks that the society should be reconstructed where the power dynamics between the sexes should be equal.

At times when darkness surrounds her mind, she becomes extremely pessimistic thinking heaven is the best place for Pearl and abandoning her own life can bring relief to this constant struggle for survival. At this point her recent interaction with Dimmesdale petrified her. For seven years Hester has buried the secret of her relationship with Chillingworth and never disclosed to Dimmesdale and to the whole world. She realises immediately after the meeting with the minister at midnight on the scaffold, that the physician is acting as the harmful catalyst to erode the minister internally. She is amazed to observe that the minister has lost all his moral strength and sometimes behaves like a child completely frivolous. Understanding that the Reverend is standing at the edge of madness, she blames herself for hiding the truth about Chillingworth. During all those years of isolations, she has evolved internally as a more cultivated woman and she feels that she has every right to help the minister from destruction. Her encounter with her husband in the prison, her blemishes and public insolence that she has encountered every day and her single motherhood has bolstered her to take firm decisions. Hester thinks that their dual crime or sin in the act of this undefined relationship has linked them together for ever and hence it is her responsibility to look after him. She is also aware that Chillingworth in seeking revenge has undergone a sharp moral decline and therefore she is determined to meet the physician in order to rescue her lover. Within few days, in the peninsula where Hester is strolling with Pearl, she came across the physician who with a basket of herbs is seen sauntering for roots and leaves in the midst of nature.

Commentary

Through Hester's metamorphosed impersonation, we get a glimpse of a budding feminine prophetess among ordinary women. The title of the chapter "Another View" is suggestive of Hawthorne's attempt to reflect another dimension of Hester's personality. We see a great transformation from the vibrant passionate lustrous beauty to a cold, desolate woman who is only surviving as if for the sake of repentance through her philanthropic activities. The flow of love and passion has all evaporated and her charity and benevolence have become the routine of her life. Being a absent-present figure who is ostracised and rejected by humanity, she remained as the untouchable, unwanted ghostly figure at the fringe of a sanctimonious civilisation.

Apart from her general concern for poor and the sufferer of Salem, Hester's ember of love for Dimmesdale is revealed when she is worried about the minister's health and tottering self. Hester could have easily remained detached from Dimmesdale after consistent blows and shuddering pain. Being physically apart from the minister, yet her strong sensibilities make her aware that Dimmesdale is gradually moving towards the edge of lunacy. She blames herself for not preventing Chillingworth in his vicious method of annihilating Dimmesdale. By not revealing to the minister about the true identity of the physician, she thinks she has committed another blunder. She therefore determines to rescue the minister. Till the end of the novel, she desperately tries to save the decaying spirit who on the contrary wants to escape from shame. She is so courageous and firm in her love that she now decides to venture and confront her husband at any cost in order to save the minister. Though her love for Dimmesdale is unwavering, yet we do not see any male characters in the novel worthy to become a partner of Hester Prynne's remarkable personality.

Unlike Dimmesdale or Chillingworth who are so much preoccupied in their individual suffering, Hester Prynne has been able to feel the melancholic world and the gradual deterioration of the minister. Keeping aside her own sorrowful world, she feels the pain of others. Dimmesdale can be a remorseful hypocrite, Chillingworth can be a sadomasochist but Hester's love reminds us of Thomas Aquinas who despite being a stringent moralist has explained that whether love is sinful or a virtuous act, it "includes an inordinate turning to a mutable good".[29] This betrothed woman still has the dying embers of love within her and therefore she thinks of rescuing Dimmesdale. Hester's endurance and patience are extraordinary and the readers develop admiration for this woman because of her immense strength to forbear the entire trauma that life has in store for her. She has not interfered between Dimmesdale and Chillingworth for the sake of the minister's safety. Afraid of Chillingworth's threat of exposing Dimmesdale's name, she has remained silent for all these years but now she has recognised the 'terrible machinery' at work which is corroding Dimmesdale's mind and body.

Hawthorne explains how the entire community has now altered their opinion when they witness Hester Prynne being reduced to a mere lifeless creature who has chosen philanthropy willingly. Hester's life is a loveless chasm where living is for the sake of survival but her affection for Dimmesdale has not yet withered away. Hawthorne writes:

> there lay a responsibility upon her in reference to the clergyman, which she owned to no other, nor to the whole world besides. (*SL* 240)

Her only source of survival and remnant of affection that reminds her of Dimmesdale's lingering presence is little Pearl who has now reached seventh year in her life. On the other hand the social satisfaction revealed in the sympathy of the society for Hester Prynne suggests how empowerment of women or liberty to express their desire is scandalised as social disruption. They prefer this new evolved Hester Prynne, abiding selfless maternal figure than the relentless passionate woman with untamed desires. Hester Prynne now as "Sister of Mercy" invokes an interrogation in the mind of the readers: has Hester's incomprehensible patience to bear Puritanical hatred and hostility caused this transformation or is Hawthorne's mimetic view in the course of the novel is indicative of a better world of compassion and love? However, we can say that this beautiful woman who once defied customs of her times is transmogrified into a woman without any voice. Hawthorne questions on this long struggle between individual and collective identities of the self of Hester.

The narrator tries to get a grasp of the psychopathology of Hester Prynne. In the past, Hester's body has been the symbolic representation of patriarchal anxiety, fantasy and disillusion and now it is the site of social control and Puritanical hegemony. Throughout the novel Hawthorne has shown the oscillation of the figure of Hester Prynne between 'good' and 'bad', purity and impurity in the eye of the society. 'Another view' is now the representation of Hester Prynne who seems to have yielded to the patriarchal cultural codes. Perhaps Hester's acceptance of the conventions is because her creator is a male author. If her creator would have been a female author she could have become another Anne Hutchinson, Sojourner Truth, Margaret Fuller, Elizabeth Peabody, Adrienne Rich or Charlotte Perkins Gilman. But in this chapter Hawthorne has hinted that if there are characters like Delilah, Helen or Eve who caused the destruction, then women also have the potential power to change and influence the society. Hester's radical individualism is stronger than Dimmesdale or Chillingworth who have only caused either impairment or silent violence in the society. Yet she is grounded in her 'Otherness' and therefore even after unending benevolence, the Salem community does not allow Hester to be present in any sacred or auspicious occasions. Cultural feminists have seen Hester Prynne's femininity is the strength of her character and her weaker counterpart is Dimmesdale. Previously Hester's independence is marked in passionate and sexual transcendence, after seven years with the maturity of her age and under the burden of shame and suffering now, her individuality is noted in her independent thinking. She has the intellectual revolutionary spirit and is much ahead of her time. Hawthorne explains the immense transformation of this woman who has nothing to lose, no desire for worldly privileges nor any attempt to preserve her hard earned money for Pearl.

Besides her physical beauty, this chapter describes the inner beauty of the soul of Hester Prynne. Her virtuous convictions and selfless devotion to society is so pure that the narrator comments how she is the first person to arrive during the pestilence and—

> Her breast, with its badge of shame, was but the softer pillow for the head that needed one. She was self-ordained a Sister of Mercy, or, we may rather say, the world's heavy hand so ordained her, when neither the world nor she looked forward to this result. (*SL* 243)

Hawthorne, from this chapter onwards, is trying to emulate the tragic element in Hester Prynne. She transforms her love directed for one into devotion for many. Her self-abnegation is a lesson to Dimmesdale and Chillingworth who cannot overcome their narrow personal self-interest. The narrator's retrospective sigh is noted in the line when he explains "her rich and luxuriant hair had either been cut off, or was so completely hidden by a cap, that not a shining lock of it ever once gushed into the sunshine" (*SL* 245). This picture of Hester Prynne stands in opposition to dark-haired Hester like virtual Madonna with her baby outside the prison gate. Hawthorne emphasises that the public tableaux is so important that Hester is now transformed and seen in the light of saintly penance.

The analogy of Hester Prynne and heretic Anne Hutchinson is intriguing and invokes historical intertextuality. At the beginning of his career, Hawthorne has sketched Anne Hutchinson titled as "Mrs Hutchinson" and also referred to her character in his book *Grandfather's Chair*. Just like Mrs Hutchinson never accepted the Puritanical idea of predestination, similarly Hawthorne suggests that if Pearl would not have arrived in Hester's life, she would have become another Anne. Both the women are susceptible to threat and suffering because of their violations of theocratic patriarchal society. Both are exemplary in the Puritanical society because of their concern for humanity. Such interpolation of fictional and real characters reflects that Hawthorne perhaps hinted at the feminist alliance of the two. This is revealed as the omniscient narrative voice carefully construes the unanswered questions within Hester's mind:

> Indeed the same dark question often rose into her mind with reference to the whole race of womanhood. Was existence worth accepting even to the happiest among them? As concerned her own individual existence, she had long ago decided in the negative, and dismissed the point as settled.... As a first step, the whole system of society is to be torn down and built up anew. Then the very nature of the opposite sex, or its long hereditary habit, which has become like nature, is to be essentially modified before woman can be allowed to assume what seems a fair and suitable position. (*SL* 248-49)

Such desire in Hester's mind to destabilise the patriarchal norms is drastically radical. Hester Prynne is therefore the figure that embodies feminist potential. She is the foremother of a radically unique visionary woman who is not only farsighted to see the future of women but also imparts the lesson of how to seek a better world.

CHAPTER FOURTEEN—HESTER AND THE PHYSICIAN

In order to converse directly to the old doctor, Hester Prynne purposely wants to keep away Pearl from the bitter exchanges between the mismatched husband and wife. She instructs Pearl to play in the midst of nature so that she remains engaged in her childish prattle. Like a falcon without any destination, Pearl is lost in her world of abysmal freedom. After seeing her reflection in the water of a pool she invites the other face to become her playmate. She is beckoned by the charming little girl from inside the pool and Pearl discovers her white bare feet when she daringly steps in the pool.

Old Roger Chillingworth is sarcastic in his tone and when Hester approaches to him, he mocks at her recently developed fame and goodness. He derides that if Hester is so determined to wear the scarlet letter even when the ecclesiastical authority is thinking of removing it after witnessing her generosity and kindness; she should continue wearing the artistically embroidered stigma on her bosom. Hester is shocked at the degradation of the man's moral character as reflected in his face. He does not epitomise intellectuality and cerebral qualities for which she admired him at one point in life. She detects the inquisitive mind and a burning desire mingled with scepticism on his face. It appears that the broiling fire of revenge is always conflagrant within him and his long devilish intention has turned this man of brilliance into a devil.

When Hester Prynne appeared, his favourite topic is definitely Hester's lover since he relishes sadistically as Hester in afflictive shame wiggle and suffer. Hester boldly confronts him by proclaiming that to protect Dimmesdale's honour, she has hidden Chillingworth's true identity and on the contrary the physician has taken advantage of it. While Dimmesdale is unaware of this vilifier with whom he is dwelling under the same roof, Chillingworth tortures him every moment; avenging him scrupulously and making him feel the pangs of death. Chillingworth defends him by reminding that both of them should be obliged to him because if he would have disclosed the truth, Dimmesdale would have faced the catastrophic abatement from a life of honour and respect to shameful death in the prison. Hester exclaims that perhaps it would have been a respite for him than suffering in the tortuous hell of Chillingworth. The doctor confesses that it is most satisfying to see his patient in this ordeal. He knows that Dimmesdale's excess sensitivity makes him aware of some vigilant eye upon him and yet the poor minister thinks that it is his fallen state that makes him feel the world as evil. The physician knows that Dimmesdale is incapable to wear the scarlet publicly and hence his sting of remorse cannot let the man free his heart ever. The doctor confesses that while relishing and satisfying his vengeful heart, he has metamorphosed from a scholar to a devil. With nostalgia, this man recalls how he has been a humanitarian, a scholar and a man of high acumen but now reduced simply to a demon. Hester out of her disgust interrogates why she is being spared from the same torture that he is inflicting on Dimmesdale because both of them have been responsible for this transformation of the physician. The physician believes that the scarlet letter has avenged enough and his respite lies in that.

Hester's dauntless spirit does not hesitate to say that she has been poisoning the minister's life by burying the secret about

Chillingworth and she should not delay anymore to disclose the truth since the physician will never stop avenging. She knows that this can provoke the physician to declare publicly the truth about Dimmesdale but she is not going to beg for mercy any more. It is of no use to live a deadly life of awful emptiness. Her extreme frustration is revealed when she explains that the future is desolating and nebulous for not only herself, for the physician or for the minister but also for Pearl. Chillingworth expresses his pity for Hester because if she could have chosen a better soul than marrying him, all her virtues would not have been wasted. In return, Hester expresses pity explaining that the physician should leave tormenting the minister for the Judgement Day and try to invoke the scholarly self within him. Their conversation ends in futility as Roger explains that he is bereft of any power to pardon and mercy the sinner. Hester has planted the seed of evil and now everything is left in the unknown hands of faith.

Commentary

This chapter focuses on the transformation of Chillingworth's character within the span of seven years. Hawthorne writes:

> But the former aspect of an intellectual and studious man, calm and quiet, which was what she best remembered in him, had altogether vanished, and been succeeded by a eager, searching, almost fierce, yet carefully guarded look... there came a glare of red light out of his eyes, as if the old man's soul were on fire and kept on smouldering duskily within the breast, until by some casual puff of passion it was blown into a momentary flame. (*SL* 254)

His obsession with revenge has been so intensed that Hester is shocked to see the man of respect transformed into a person of hatred and disgust. After their first private encounter inside the prison, this is the second interaction but Hester discovers how the physician has morally degraded. This internal transformation is reflected in his external feature. The old man acknowledges that he has become a 'fiend' and he is aware of it. He reminds us of all the ancestors from the past—Milton's Satan or Mary Shelley's monster. He represents the digression in nature, and like Satan, the fallen angel, he has become the revengeful adversary and a castaway. So, Hester Prynne is a publicly known castaway but Chillingworth along with Dimmesdale are alienated figures in their own world of desolation. Their conversation reflects that Chillingworth is still defensive of his act and he blames Dimmesdale primarily more than Hester for the ruin. Hester blames Chillingworth for Dimmesdale's gradual destruction and ebbing away of his life force. There is hardly any chance for this old scholar to retreat into his past life of glory. He confesses that the reason for his survival is to see the minister being excruciatingly tortured.

Strangely as we understand through Hester's view point how Chillingworth has degraded from a man of honour and respect to a fiendish antagonist, we also feel pity because all his scholarship and knowledge that he boasted off throughout his life has been in vain. He had been at a point, a man of beauty because of his wisdom and knowledge but that is now metamorphosed into hideousness. His rawness in seeking revenge has almost erased the last vestige of humanity within him. Sometimes he is horrified to imagine such metamorphosis within him and intuitively he senses the consequence of this transformation. In this chapter, Hawthorne penetrates into the intricate mind of this scholar who otherwise is difficult to assess. In his confession he actually indulges into an introspective analysis of the self and is terrified. His fear is not merely because of his transformation but also due to his foreshadowing that he will finally lose in the battle. The tragic element is heightened as Chillingworth in his moment of discovery realises his sharp fall. Like Satan, Master Prynne's revengeful act does not anticipate victory but defeat. Like the archetypal sinner, his act leads to shame, pain and death. On the contrary, Hester Prynne regains and recovers glory through patience and suffering.

Interestingly when the physician greeted Hester, he hardly uttered the word 'Prynne': "Aha! And is it Mistress Hester that has a word for old Roger Chillingworth?" (*SL* 253). His purposeful rejection of his original surname is a way of denial of his previous identity as well as denouncing Hester from the matrimonial bondage. There is enough sarcasm in using the epithet 'old' before his name especially in front of Hester Prynne because implicitly he wants to prick Hester's conscience by reminding that one of the primary reasons of Hester's adultery is their gulf of age difference. Roger cannot forget the truth that it is deficiency of love which resulted in Hester Prynne's inevitable rejection of him. Hawthorne with a modernistic approach is raising the age old debate about the incompatibility in marriage and the search for true happiness. Hawthorne wants to deconstruct the age old concept of an older man as an appropriate husband to dominate his wife. This reminds one of Walt Whitman's poem "A Woman Waits For Me" from *Leaves of Grass*. Whitman was always ahead of his time and it is reflected in this excerpt:

> Sex contains all, bodies, souls,
> Meanings, proofs, purities, delicacies, results, promulgations,
> Songs, commands, health, pride, the maternal mystery, the seminal milk,
> All hopes, benefactions, bestowals, all the passions, loves, beauties, delights of the earth,
> All the governments, judges, gods, follow'd persons of the earth,
> These are contained in sex as parts of itself and justifications of itself.[30]

Whitman has given a beautiful dimension of sex in deconstructing all the moralities of society. Hawthorne similarly wants to denounce the Puritanical morality as reflected in this interaction between Hester and Roger. He wants to focus on the catastrophe in their conjugal life which is the outcome of the patriarchal ideology that a husband is a protector and proprietor of his wife. Like Hester, women with their eternal love have always stood the test of time but their lovers have failed so. Roger Chillingworth proclaims that Hester has committed mistake twice—first by marrying Roger and second by loving Dimmesdale, both of them do not deserve and are not worthy to have Hester Prynne in their lives. No one knows better about this than Roger Chillingworth and hence he says:

> Thou hadst great elements. Peradventure, hadst thou met earlier with a better love than mine, this evil had not been. I pity thee, for the good that has been wasted in thy nature. (*SL* 260)

At the end of the novel we find that Dimmesdale and Roger both annihilate in their respective hubris and Hester Prynne not only survives but evolves with new wisdom out of her suffering and pain. It is interesting to note what Virginia Woolf in her novel *Mrs Dalloway* has written:

> Through all ages—when the pavement was grass, when it was swamp, through the age of tusk and mammoth, through the age of silent sunrise, the battered woman—for she wore a skirt—with her right hand exposed, her left clutching at her side, stood singing of love—love which has lasted a million years, she sang, love which prevails, and millions of years ago, her lover, who had been dead these centuries, had walked, she crooned, with her in May; but in the course of ages, long as summer days, and flaming, she remembered, with nothing but red asters, he had gone; death's enormous sickle had swept those tremendous hills, and when at last she laid her hoary and immensely aged head on the earth, now become a mere cinder of ice, she implored the Gods to lay by her side a bunch of purple-heather, there on her high burial place which the last rays of the last sun caressed; for then the pageant of the universe would be over.[31]

Before meeting her husband, Hester believed that her love for Dimmesdale makes her feel her responsibilities towards him but she has nothing for Chillingworth. But in the course of this conversation when Hester is baffled by the awful change in her husband, her guilt conscience and introspective speculation made her realise that she is also responsible for Chillingworth's ruination. The subterraneous message that Hawthorne wants to focus on through the discourse between Hester and Chillingworth is the inherent self-defensive nature of human beings where the victim victimises the perpetrator. Hawthorne uses the analogy of mirror where through each other's face as the reflecting glass, the couple recognises each other. When Hester Prynne begs that he should give respite to the minister from infernal torture, Chillingworth cannot restrain his admiration for Hester's 'majestic' despair. Though he does not blame Hester as much as he blames Dimmesdale, yet he is sadistic enough to taunt her benevolence towards humanity and her scarlet letter. One has to be very careful with Chillingworth's double edged words. He is a man of lesser words but whenever he speaks, his carefully chosen dictions are lethal enough to hurt and act like poison. He relishes the opportunity of invoking repeatedly Hester's past. Hester is also aware about the danger of speaking and of remaining silent. We do not expect simple reply from Hester and that triggers more pleasure in Chillingworth. If Chillingworth's weapon is his noxious words, Hester's power lies in her honest words. Her strength and endeavour to rescue Dimmesdale is so intense that she reminds Chillingworth that forgiveness is also a way to restore his moral and intellectual positions. Hester is much ahead of her time and she is ingenious enough to catch Chillingworth's scientific inveterate ways of torturing the minister. When the physician defends himself justifying that if he wished, he could have killed his enemy; Hester tacitly explains that death is a respite to the minister than "to die daily a living death" which Chillingworth is imposing on him. In the name of retributive justice, this man has indulged in relentless study of Dimmesdale's tortuous heart for seven years persistently. Thus with her intellectual clarity she has astounded her husband that Hester Prynne is no more the immature woman whom she married long time back. If Chillingworth has undergone transformation, there is also a huge disparity between Hester Prynne of England and Hester Prynne of New England.

As these both characters depart, Hester's hatred for Chillingworth grows deep. She realises how his sympathetic healing power for his patient has transformed into destructive monstrous power. Hester being transformed as Sister of Mercy hoped that mercy might claim all the demands of justice. Hester Prynne inwardly despises her former husband and regrets for her past respect and adoration for the same man. As she pledges Chillingworth, she is also aware that all the four characters—Arthur Dimmesdale, Hester Prynne, Roger Chillingworth and

Pearl are all leading towards the destructive end without any hope of respite:

> There is no good for him, no good for me, no good for thee. There is no good for little Pearl. There is no path to guide us out of this dismal maze. (*SL* 260)

Such fearful anticipation of Hester reveals that she is the only character who has grown above possessive individualism while the rest of the two men in the love triangle are immersed in their intrusive personal worlds incapable of seeing anything beyond that. At the end of this chapter however, we see that this interaction between Hester Prynne and Roger Prynne contrarily allowed Hester's tide of affection flow automatically which was so long being restrained because of guilt conscience. She has no hesitation to proclaim in front of her husband that through all these years of contrition when she has repressed the truth about Chillingworth's identity, she has committed a blunder and now she will try her best to rescue the minister from his silent tyranny.

Chillingworth remains committed and bounded by his need for revenge. He is determined to blossom the tragic "black flower" of May and his end speech addressed to Hester in this chapter reflects that Fate has nurtured the black flower planted by him. This black flower is contrasted to the wild rose that little Pearl has always been attracted to. Perhaps Hawthorne wants to indicate that "Providence" has decreed to blossom a beautiful flower in the shape of little Pearl out of this blackness of human soul.

CHAPTER FIFTEEN—HESTER AND PEARL

When the physician departs after such bitter exchange of words, Hester wonders what herbs and roots the man must be collecting. The Earth sensing his evilness should offer only what is deadly and destructive. His malicious nature can corrupt the antidote into detrimental substance. When the man is gradually disappearing into distance, Hester wishes that why not the earth swallow him before this evil spirit spreads his wings into the sky and disappears. She clearly utters that whether it is a sin or not, but intense hatred is the only thing that she has for her physician husband. Hester reminiscences her redolent conjugal life in England when this scholarly man in the evening emerges from his deep insightful study and bask in the warm smile of his wife. He then asserted that Hester's smile is a rescue from the dark loneliness of his world of scholarship. At one point she considered those evenings as the happiest junctures of her life but now witnessing the evilness of the same man, she wonders how she can even imagine happiness in the company of this man. For Hester, the greatest sin in her life is to marry a man like Chillingworth and she repents for allowing that man to hold her hand, to look into her eyes and to kiss her. With her passing of age and maturity in life, she realises that Chillingworth's crime is worse than hers since that man has taken advantage of her youth and innocence and took it for granted that once she reaches maturity, she would realise happiness in their marital bond. She feels herself betrayed by this man and her betrayal is the outcome of Chillingworth's deception. The narrator elucidates that when a man decides to hold the hands of a woman, he must make sure of winning her passion for him as well or else the result will be like Roger Chillingworth's fate whose wife's heart is robbed by another man. More than repentance, she finds justification in her indulgence with Arthur Dimmesdale. This realisation would not ever happen if she would not have encountered this man in his present state.

After Chillingworth departed, Hester beckons Pearl who is gambolling among horseshoe crabs, star fish, jellyfish and sea foam scattered in the breeze. In her amusing world she has draped with gathered seaweeds like a miniature mermaid and from her collected pebbles in her apron, she is pelting stones at the flock of sea gulls. Discovering some eel-grass, she fashioned the alphabet "A" on her breast like her mother, but this time it is green in colour. Hester Prynne observing the letter on little Pearl's breast queried the meaning of it. Pearl answers that just like the minister keeps his hand near his chest, similarly she wants to make something significant on her chest. Pearl does not know anything more than this but she perceives with her strange childish senses that the old physician with whom her mother has been talking, may know the connection between the minister's hand on his breast and Hester's scarlet alphabet.

Though Hester finds it as a mere childish observation yet suddenly she realised that Pearl's maturity and gradual development has set some buoyant breeze of hope in her mind that her daughter can become her best friend. She never expected anything in return of her love for Pearl but suddenly in an epiphanic moment, she is excited to think that Pearl can be her best friend in this world in future days when she will confide everything to her daughter. Pearl's intrusiveness about the letter has always appeared for Hester as the source of her punishment and justice but a fresh reflection arrives into her mind. She started thinking that there can be a divine purpose of mercy and kindness at work. While Hester's mind is overwhelmed in analysing her relationship with Pearl, the little child's ceaseless inquiry about the significance of the letter is insistent. Hester realises that she cannot pay such a heavy price of telling the meaning of the alphabet for the hope of Pearl's friendship in her world of desolation. She rebukes Pearl for her willingness to know about things that are prohibited to children and for the first time she has lied to Pearl that she does not know the reason behind minister's hand on his chest. The scarlet letter has always been her moral guidance, the guardian spirit but to control little Pearl, Hester Prynne has to lie. The chapter ends with a glimpse of Hester's motherly stringency. Pearl's obstinate nature continued in her interrogative expedition regarding the meaning of the scarlet letter and Hester soon warns her that she will lock little Pearl inside dark room if she continues annoying her mother.

Commentary

Just after Chillingworth's departure in the previous chapter, this chapter reflects on Hester's nostalgia about her days with Chillingworth. Hawthorne has juxtaposed the two relationships that Hester shared with the two men. Hawthorne never concludes about human relationships in terms of morally 'right' and 'wrong' unlike his Puritanical forefathers. Like a critic he leaves it for readers' interpretations. The permissive public view of adultery is presented by the author but at the same time he ponders deep down to reflect on the complexity that led to adultery. Nathaniel Hawthorne in his writings always reflected that marriage and family is one of the means for pursuit of happiness. But through

Hester's reflection upon her past, he clarifies how an incongruous marriage can become a predicament and cause of tragedy. And then infidelity or adultery becomes the key to unlock the prison gate of constriction and thereby escape hoping for happiness. After several years of her married life with Chillingworth when Hester walks down the memory lane, she evolves with a new awareness that Chillingworth has consciously betrayed her, taking the advantage of her youthful ignorance. For the first time she realises that Chillingworth has done more injustice towards her than she has done towards him. Dismissing all social, theological and legal norms of the society and gathering her juridical conscience, Hester Prynne becomes her own judge and recounting her disjoined memories of a short conjugal life, Hester now realises that Chillingworth is unworthy of all her sense of guilt that she suffered all these years. The central question in the novel is 'adultery' and how religion and society see it as a sinful act. Chillingworth's revenge is the outcome of such inherent social concept that adultery is a social sin and a violation of religion, law and custom. For him Hester Prynne is his personal possession and whether he has been neglectful of his duties as a husband, denied affection and love are not of priority, more than that what has left a deep bruise is that Dimmesdale has dispossessed him from his right. Even when he arrives in New England, he dominates his wife by successfully blackmailing her, threatening her of public exposure in order to pursue a vengeance more damaging than death. He has failed to think of Hester as an independent soul and thinks it a rightful claim to seek vengeance even after knowing that Hester Prynne has never given her heart to him.

The discourse regarding the punishment of an adulteress by the patriarchal society has already been deconstructed several years before by one of Chaucer's budding feminist characters Alison, or the Wife of Bath in *The Canterbury Tales*. This is also a subject of reflection of John 8: I-II. That passage explains how Jesus Christ saved an adulteress from death who was inflicted with pelting stones. Jesus Christ forgives her raising a question about such patriarchal violence and its destruction. Hawthorne perhaps critiques such Protestant Christian culture that perpetuates violence. It is the same culture that has encouraged men like Chillingworth to seek revenge although he has failed to be a true husband. Hawthorne brings in the central question of love which is completely lacking in the relationship of Hester and Chillingworth and therefore in some way or the other, their relationship is subjected to lack of faith, lack of understanding and is destined to shatter. No one recognised how a loveless marriage of compulsion is a crime. No one questions how Chillingworth has violated the sanctity of a human heart by fooling Hester Prynne into a marriage. How come Hester Prynne has abrogated the holy institution of marriage when Chillingworth has violated it at the beginning by deceiving her? To see a man of his dignity suffering the dishonour of cuckoldry is unpardonable, but it is also true that a man of knowledge and science like Chillingworth in pursuit of beauty and self-satisfaction has cunningly duped young immature Hester Prynne for his own selfish ends.

Loneliness has personified Hester's life. Her recollection about her conjugal life reflects that Chillingworth remained secluded in his world of study while Hester silently nourished her husband with her beautiful fresh smile. Such refreshing smile which "He needed to bask himself...in order that the chill of so many lonely hours among his book might be taken off the scholar's heart" (*SL* 263) reflects that Hester's requirement in Master Prynne's life has not been more than a 'seducer' and a 'servant'. In her essay entitled "The Economics of Sex", J. Scutt views marriage as the legalised way of selling women's sexuality in order to achieve security in the society. Who can bring justice to such selfishness and disregard from Chillingworth? Hence Hawthorne suggests:

> Let men tremble to win the hand of woman, unless they win along with it the utmost passion of her heart. Else it may be their miserable fortune, as it was Roger Chillingworth's, when some mightier touch than their own may have awakened all her sensibilities, to be reproached even for the calm content, the marble image of happiness, which they will have imposed upon her as the warm reality. (*SL* 264)

So, whether one blames Dimmesdale or Hester, this tempest was long due especially for a woman of unbounded passion like Hester Prynne. Hester's ennobling recognition in this chapter is a message from Hawthorne about chauvinist self-petrification in egoistical intellectual triumph and obsession with self-glorification at the cost of abstention from what is natural. What is tragic in Chillingworth is his intellectual clarity to understand his fall. But being a man who believes in science than predestination, he now applies scientific means to study human mind which he has done with natural phenomena in the past. Perhaps within this realisation, Hester finds Chillingworth's figure in the distance as "crooked' and "deformed" (*SL* 262, 264).

Juxtaposing Hester's emancipatory understanding and confidently becoming her own judge, the narrator describes the same budding spirit in Pearl who fascinated by her own image in the water tries to assert a place for herself in nature. This is symbolical where the woman must recognise her worth in the otherwise patriarchal world that tries to neglect her. Pearl appears to be self-sufficient among 'impalpable earth and unattainable sky', snails, jelly-fish, tide, breeze, snow-flakes, birds and the sea. Unlike Chillingworth who attempted to tamper the natural world, Pearl is in accord with it. Hester's lost opulent beauty can be restored in Pearl in the midst of nature. Pearl's image in the pool of water is Hester's Pagan self. Hester and Pearl are like goddesses of nature who cannot be tamed and controlled by mere empirical knowledge. What is shameful for Hester is a matter of pride for little Pearl and hence she imitated her mother's 'scarlet' alphabet on her bosom with 'green' eel grass. For Pearl it means life, vitality and untamed spirit.

Finally Hester's loneliness is the subject of speculation in this chapter and the narrator reflects how her intense depression propelled her at one point to confide in little Pearl her repressed agony. She wanted to escape from this unending entrapment through her selfless nobility but she is entangled more and more. Both Pearl and her mother stood in the same circle of seclusion and exclusion. Hawthorne is anticipating the power of female friendship in the form of various relationships. The mother-daughter relationship is so pure that Hester at one point is compelled to confide in her little child than the two men in her life. The question of female integrity and faith is perhaps most untainted in this relationship than any other. One cannot forget the friendship history of Hawthorne and Margaret Fuller in the literary world. While both these writers have been trying to establish their literary career almost at the same time, Hawthorne's sole purpose was to establish a stable career in order to marry his idealised woman Sophia but Fuller wanted to support her family and herself. Fuller wanted to deny marriage and motherhood for the sake of intellectual desire. Though Fuller fell in love with men like Sam Ward or Emerson who called her "the queen of a parliament of love", yet she has never been satisfied in these relations. It is evident in her words:

> Once I was all intellect; now I am almost all feeling, Nature vindicates her rights, and I feel all Italy glowing beneath the Saxon crust. This cannot last long; I shall burn to ashes if all this smoulders here much longer.[32]

Fuller's magnetic power remained incompatible with any men of her time. Hawthorne has acknowledged Fuller's profound power to influence any individual soul. Hester Prynne like Fuller remained unparalleled in the contemporary world of Puritanism and one can say exactly about Hester Prynne what Sarah Freeman Clarke has commented about Fuller:

> She broke her lance upon your shield. Encountering her glance, something like an electric shock was felt. Her eyes pierced through your disguises.... Though she spoke rudely searching words, and told you startling truths, though she broke down your little shams and defences, you felt exhilarated by the compliment of being found out.[33]

CHAPTER SIXTEEN—A FOREST WALK

Hester is extremely impatient to convey to Reverend Dimmesdale about the risk of being in touch with the physician. She wants to avoid visiting Dimmesdale's house to prevent any further controversy. The physician's vigil and surveillance is also in Hester's knowledge and therefore to rescue Dimmesdale she is determined not to meet him at any such place which Master Prynne can easily sought out. Hester is aware that Dimmesdale often indulges in long stroll deep inside the wood and therefore she aims to see him in the midst of the solitary jungle. One morning when Hester comes to know that Dimmesdale has gone to some Indian native village to spend the night and to visit Apostle Eliot among the Indian converts, she is determined to meet him in the forest on his way back. The dark forest appears to her like moral wilderness and this is further intensified by the grey clouds that have gathered in the sky and have created a sombre atmosphere. The chiaroscuro of shadow and light is beautiful as if playing hide and seek in the forest. The mother and the daughter have their most intimate conversation where Pearl believes that the sunlight is purposely avoiding Hester because of her shining scarlet letter but she can catch it because she does not wear a letter like her mother. It seems that Pearl has absorbed the sunlight within her and her wild energy is just like Hester's paramount strength with which she has been able to survive when sorrow and humiliation are the only things left in her life. Pearl with her childish prattle cherishes to know the story she heard from Mistress Hibbins about the Black Man who offers his iron pen to people in the wood to sign their names with their blood. She has also come to know that Hester's Scarlet Letter is the signature of the Black Man who meets her mother in the woods at midnight. Her mother acknowledges that she has met once the mysterious Black Man who has marked her with this bright dazzling Scarlet Letter. Pearl seems to be a part of this forest, like the brook emanating from some mysterious source and dazzling and flowing in its own rhythm. Pearl remains busy in her play with flowers and trees and Hester anticipates the minister's arrival when with heightened consciousness she listens to the rustling sound from the distance. Hester soon attempts to intercept in order to draw attention of the minister.

Commentary

The forest has always been symbolical for its wilderness. If the Puritanical world tries to establish a utopia in New England, then the forest with its untamed wilderness is the 'heterotopia', a deviant place as Michel Foucault has elucidated. It is deviant because it is a place where the deviants of the Puritanical society saunter in and is not considered as part of the society. Against the Puritanical attempt to begin with a radical newness, Hester Prynne, Arthur Dimmesdale, Pearl and Mistress Hibbins are the deviants who are found venturing in the space of heterotopia of deviation. It is the antique fugitive world without the social boundaries of moral and immoral. It is the boundless jungle of incredible freedom and the space for naïve moments and secrets to be disclosed. This natural forest perhaps mocks the artificial superimposed laws and regulations of the Puritanical world. This primitive forest is as mysterious as those characters who venture in. It is also the discursive manifestation of the repressed desires, wishes and emotions of these characters. Pearl indulges in the narcissistic quest of her spirit, Hester and Dimmesdale find it as the perfect refuge to resonate into each other's warm affection and finally Mistress Hibbins finds this wild exuberant forest as the place of Eros and Thanatos. The Puritans may find Hester's untamed virulent sexuality similar to the wild sagacity of the forest but for Dimmesdale this wild forest is the therapeutic sensation to the bruised soul and shameful spirit. Hester Prynne therefore chose the forest as the perfect abode for the kinesis of their spirits in contrast to Dimmesdale's restrained domestic space of vigilance. In the *Bible*, the wilderness of the forest is seen to be a place of alienation and purgation for the suffering soul, overgrown with thorns that pricked the disobedient soul of Adam and Eve. This wilderness is the place condemned by God for suffering and resurrection and thus the Puritanical world justifies their civilized new found world in New England as an attempt to tame and discipline the world.

Hester desires to meet Dimmesdale under the open sky and Hawthorne has chosen this forest as the private place for the final secret interaction of the couple before the story ends. The description of the 'primeval forest' begins with narrow dense footpath that symbolises the constrictions in Hester's life. The chill and sombre weather reflects the tension and uncertainties in the mind of Hester. The unending war between social expediency and moral righteousness is represented by the sunlight and the dark cloud. Hawthorne is almost preparing his readers for a psychodynamic study of the secret lovers of his romance. The cornucopia of green colonial America is explored by Hawthorne.

The image of the deep wood with "luxuriant heap of moss", "a gigantic pine with its roots and trunk in the darksome shade", the impending branches of the trees and the "brown sparkling sand" beside the brook all surround the mother and daughter and it seems that nature has provided them a cordial shelter when humanity ostracised them. From the restrained Puritanical cage, the forest is therefore the symbol of freedom and liberty. Hester's tangible desire to meet Dimmesdale with full freedom is the most anxious moment for the readers. Such anxiousness is intensified when Pearl interrogates her mother about the Black Man.

The story of the Black Man and his signature though seems to be the popular superstition of the time but Hawthorne uses it with greater significance. The Puritans often associated blackness with some evil force and is converged with the devil. The stemming of such belief is due to the association of the natives or the Indians with the evil power. It is a way of racist reduction of imagining the 'other'. Pearl's curiosity about the Black Man who has signed the scarlet letter on her mother's bosom is a reminder of the popular myth of the witches and their nexus with the devil. Hawthorne is perhaps trying to evoke what Freud will be terming as the 'uncanny'. The feeling of uncanny is more psychological that reflects the repressed fear of the society. To explain the source of the uncanny, Freud writes:

> An uncanny experience occurs either when infantile complexes which have been repressed are once more revived by some impression, or when primitive beliefs which have been surmounted seem once more to be confirmed.[34]

In the New England, the forest with its wilderness is the unfamiliar zone and the Black Man is the figment of imagination. In reality, this Black Man is personified as Roger Chillingworth. In the earlier chapters, Hester and Pearl have already addressed him by this name. The recurrent image of the Black Man throughout the novel has intensified the ambiguous setting of the forest scene. His malignity lies in corrupting the human soul, compelling them to sign the bond and mark them with his signature. The haunting imaginative story of the Black Man in the backdrop is not simply to heighten tension but reflect the evil spirits of humanity. Hawthorne in his short stories "Young Goodman Brown" and "Rappaccini's Daughter" represents the forest as the active player with its malignant force in the novel. The Black Man is also introduced in the second story that represents the Devil's power of temptation. Hawthorne's representation of American natural world always carries some gothic element in it. Pearl in the midst of mysterious conspiring nature becomes more enigmatic with her free flow of imagination and wilderness.

Pearl's association with the nature is indicative that she is the child of nature. The murmuring brook that continuously flows is like little Pearl, gushing out the life force spontaneously in its own rhythm. The sunshine is also associated with Pearl because she is the source of warmth and happiness, the reason for her survival. Like Wordsworth's Lucy, Pearl has an intimacy with nature. Hawthorne's creation of a wild illegitimate child in the novel holds in balance the contradictory tendencies of imperial rhetoric: authority in balance with nurture, domination with enlightenment, debasement with idealization, negation with affirmation, exploitation with education, filiations with affiliation. Pearl's story is coterminous with that of imperialism where the cross fertilization between childhood and primitivism becomes important since both need growth and maturation. In John Locke's theory of childhood, the concept of tabula rasa, blank mind or absence is significant in the imperial enterprise where the negation of colonial space is a necessary preparation for the great civilizing mission. Pearl therefore represents the untamed wild spirit that needs to be controlled as Governor Bellingham and other Puritanical authoritative figures already proposed seven years back. One is reminded of Montaigne's essay "On Cannibals" where it is suggested that cannibals live in an Edenic state of purity and simplicity while Rousseau compared the child's mind to a wild plant that symbolises the uncontaminated nature. When Pearl wanders away in the bush after Hester's instruction, it seems that hardly any boundary exists which Pearl recognises. When she sang along with the murmuring of the brook while gathering violets, it seems she represents a timeless world and appears to be a partner of primitivism. It is reminiscent of the Wordsworthian lines where Nature says:

This Child I to myself will take;
She shall be mine, and I will make
A Lady of my own.[35]

Pearl with her innate burgeoning tendencies, the sportive animal spirit and mysterious language to communicate with Nature seems to be gaining a natural grace that corresponds to her physical beauty. In Pearl, Hawthorne will manifest a talismanic force which is anti-Puritanical. She symbolises the pre-lapsarian stage and therefore she has already answered to Mr Wilson that her mother has plucked her from the wild rose plant outside the prison door. Against the Calvinist backdrop, this 'elf-child' learns the art of living from Nature itself.

CHAPTER SEVENTEEN—THE PASTOR AND HIS PARISHONER

When she encounters Dimmesdale face to face, she observes how the minister with his hand upon his chest has lost all the life force and looks weary and exhausted. Each of them appears like a ghost to one another, as if meeting some supernatural creature. When Hester asks whether his mind has achieved peace and solace, Dimmesdale touches Hester's cold hand with his chill and dearth hand in order to convey with umpteen feelings. They go into the shaded part of the wood and for a time being they have been speechless only to realise internally that after a long time, they are together. They started their conversation with the fear of the approaching storm in their lives. Dimmesdale confides that instead of peace, intense sadness and afflictions have seized him. When Hester consoles him elucidating the abundant love that Salem pours on him, he explains that the deep faith of the people of Salem has epitomised Dimmesdale as the divine effusion of celestial light of heaven without knowing that the evil resides within him. He feels that he has succumbed to temptation because he has certain flaws. A ruined soul like him is incapable to save others and he deserves only hatred and abomination in reality. He considers Hester to be fortunate to wear the scarlet letter openly while he is damned to wear secretly inside. He desperately wishes for a friend or an enemy to whom he can confess and shed off his burden and guilt. At this juncture, Hester gathers all strength to disclose the truth. She reveals that for long time

Dimmesdale has been living under the same roof with his enemy. She declares Roger Chillingworth is her husband and explains her compulsions which restrained her from confiding to the minister.

Dimmesdale is shocked, full of anguish and then he repents why he had failed to realise the man when his heart has given him the inkling. Dimmesdale claims that Hester is unforgivable because of this reprehensible act of hers but Hester drowned in emotions, embraces Dimmesdale and begs for exoneration since she never expected that the outcome of her silence will be so detrimental. Dimmesdale affirms that he has forgiven Hester and they are not the worst sinners in this world because for him Roger Chillingworth is worst in his covetousness than them. When Dimmesdale is apprehensive about the physician's undertaking of disclosing his identity as Hester's lover, Hester Prynne encourages the minister to migrate to England and begin a new life. She bolsters Dimmesdale that he should regain his mental and physical strength, must alter his name and should not end his life in despair. When Dimmesdale exclaims that he is devoid of strength to revitalise his life alone, Hester hints that she has planned to escape from this tormenting New England along with Pearl and Dimmesdale, and that is the only way one can wipe out the past and stop ruining the future.

Commentary

This scene in the novel is one of those passionate rare moments of emotional climax. The readers anticipate extreme emotional tension since for the first time they are going to witness the private moments between the heroine of the novel and her lover. The excitement of such long awaited meeting is given full eloquence when Hawthorne writes:

> So strangely did they meet in the dim wood that it was like the first encounter in the world beyond the grave of two spirits who had been intimately connected in their former life, but now stood coldly shuddering in mutual dread, as not yet familiar with their state, nor wanted to the companionship of disembodied beings. Each a ghost, and awe-stricken at the other ghost. (*SL* 285)

Such diffidence and disbelieve to trust the presence of each other in seclusion is almost like a dream. The forest is the crossroad of sin and joy, libidinal excess and freedom of expression. The first touch of the two cold hands in the middle of this wood shows a spontaneous uninhibited reaction. Their quasi physicality in the midst of darkness of the forest is evidence of their mental stress. Their immediate touch of each other brings an exquisite solace and confidence in the desolate hinterland of their souls. Thus, Hawthorne has already evoked an evanescent essence of romanticism even in the middle of crisis and tension. Nathaniel Hawthorne embraces American Dark Romanticism[36] and this forest scene is a bold depiction of the writer's essentialism and individualism of his own romantic spirit. The readers witness the peace and purity of happiness in the lovers who are stigmatised as sinners by the society. What can be simpler, pure, and natural than when in the sublime strangeness of the forest, these two lovers discover the plurality of the self?

Whether this scene arouses sympathy or condemnation of the lovers, Hawthorne leaves it in the form of an interrogation. At this point, it is significant to note the distinction made between natural and civil liberty made by John Winthrop, one of the Puritanical leaders. Natural liberty is common in man and beasts and man being superior, has the power to exercise this liberty for evil or good purpose. In contrast, civil liberty is related to covenant between man and God and this should be the ultimate purpose of all authoritative force. The Puritans believe that civil liberty is always aimed for good and benefit of mankind. They find civil liberty in marriage and ministerial authority. Marriage is seen as God's will and sanction and therefore Hester Prynne's adultery is sinful. Hester's disobedience is seen once more at this point where she not only suggests that they should elope from this land of sterility but also that their love is self-sufficient and does not require any accreditation. Their love is outside the code of civil liberty and falls into the category of natural liberty.

Gradually Hester ventures into the existential dilemma of Arthur Dimmesdale before she discloses the truth about her former husband. Hester's nursing potential is revealed when she comforts the minister to release the latent anxiety within him. With her wisdom born out of suffering, she becomes the gargling fountain of humanity in the purgatorial unyielding world of the Puritans. She is the oasis in the deserted heart of Dimmesdale when the stray, unforgettable silhouetted moments of past connects them in the present. In their respective desert the presence of the other is like the much awaited coming of the crusading night bringing life back to the parched land. But it is Hester only who tries to unlock the pent up flood of feelings residing in Arthur's. Whether Hawthorne supports natural liberty completely is not transparent since Hester Prynne and Arthur Dimmesdale are not successful in their plan. What is intriguing is that the patriarchal hierarchy in civil liberty is deconstructed here. The Puritans believed that the relation between the husband and the wife should be the microscopic reflection of the rulers and the ruled of the Puritanical society. This is primarily based on the principle of absolute loyalty. Unlike this principle, Hester and Dimmesdale's relationship is outside the institute of marriage, and we see Hester Prynne is taking the leading role of devising some ways and means to escape. The dilemma of justice and sympathy for these two characters against the repressive Puritanical world is unresolved. The couple's love and strong attraction for each other perhaps shows the imperfection of the Puritanical society that has failed to judge Hester Prynne's 'youthful mistake'. There are alternate options to correct Hester's mistake like sanctioning divorce. If Hester has committed mistake by performing adultery, then she also committed mistake by marrying Roger Chillingworth. Moreover, we cannot forget that Hester Prynne's attraction for Dimmesdale developed when Hester and Dimmesdale are under the misconception that Roger Chillingworth is dead. This leads to further argument whether repressions of certain passions are necessary at all for the civil society or will it lead to hidden 'sins' like that of Hester Prynne and Dimmesdale. The question leads to re-evaluation of sexual reforms in the society. Is Hester Prynne at all guilty of anything? Did Hester and Arthur Dimmesdale desire in their unconscious mind Chillingworth's death in order to facilitate their mutual attractions for each other? But a pure untainted emotion like love should be unconditional and cannot be restrained by any law of this universe. Marriage is an institution based on patriarchal power dynamics and gender politics. This is problematized when Hawthorne introduces his philosophy of punishment and forgiveness against the conflict between Puritanical law and natural law.

When Hester discloses the truth about the physician, Dimmesdale's self-disgust and anguish for Hester's silence is heightened. Hester Prynne momentarily has stricken Dimmesdale's injured ego. He is left with internal struggle because he feels betrayed by Hester as well as by himself. He has always sensed that the physician appeared intolerable but failed to grasp the evil within him. Physically his abrupt actions demonstrate that he is distraught. Hester's grandiose self finds it hard to resist the physical intimacy in order to pacify Dimmesdale's tempestuous madness and hence Hawthorne, with heightened passionate flair, writes:

> With sudden and desperate tenderness she threw her arms around him, and pressed his head against her bosom, little caring though his cheek rested on the scarlet letter. He would have released himself, but strove in vain to do so. Hester would not set him free, lest he should look her sternly in the face. (*SL* 292)

One can sense the power in Hester's words and emotion. Dimmesdale cannot neglect the abundance of love in Hester's heart irrespective of her silence for all these years. He is absorbed in her gushing passion and love.

This chapter also gives space to Dimmesdale's clarification about his real identity that has been oscillating between appearance and reality, his public image and his personal secrets.

We come across another new dimension in Hester Prynne's character. Her dormant love for Dimmesdale is as steady and unalterable as before and hence she tries to convince her lover that he has repented enough and self-punished enormously. She leaves no stone unturned when for Dimmesdale's sake she decides to elope from New England. We see a strange contrast between Hester and Dimmesdale. Hester is confident to overthrow all Puritanical rules and regulations while Dimmesdale finds it impossible. He is reluctant to leave because he believes God has chosen his ministerial position for him. It is this dilemma and lack of confidence in Dimmesdale that mismatches him with Hester Prynne. Arthur is in his nadir of despair and Hester is trying to pull him with all her vitality and encouragement. Such revolutionary spirit in Hester during this colloquy inside the forest can be seen from the patriarchal point of view as the subversive temptress Eve chooses to establish a self-proclaimed law. This is heightened by Hawthorne as Hester's sex, youth and beauty all of a sudden seem to be vivacious under the effect of the piercing sunlight. But if she takes the initiative to plan for umpteen freedoms, it is primarily for Dimmesdale. There is a role reversal as Hester tries to reassure Dimmesdale pragmatically. Hawthorne has explained at the beginning of the novel that Hester Prynne could have escaped from this land but it is only the power of her love that has compelled her to undergo the retributions and yet be together with her man in the same land. Even after seven long years of almost without mutual reciprocation of love and emotions, it seems the intensity has not been reduced as evident in her addressing of the minister as "Arthur."

The minister has always been a guiding light in the life of the people but in this secret rendezvous, he seems to be like a child who seeks solace and guidance from Hester: "Think for me, Hester! Thou art strong. Resolve for me! Advise me what to do" (*SL* 295). Hester with her unbounded faith in her love and confident in her lover's intellectual acumen takes the initiative of guiding Dimmesdale. Though Dimmesdale fails to comprehend Chillingworth's psychology, Hester is much ahead in the race of psychological battle. She hits the nail when she explains to Arthur that the physician has got "a strange secrecy in his nature" but she is confident that Chillingworth will not waste his venomous poison for revenge by publicly declaring the truth about Dimmesdale. Hester now projects and imposes her energy in Dimmesdale by promising her guiding presence in his life. Dimmesdale's childlike dependence reflects Hester's emancipatory power. He desperately requires Hester's resolution, support and love without which he is weak and fragmented. Though their plan did not succeed in the end, but Hawthorne leaves a question mark that if a spiritual man like Dimmesdale is incapable to resurrect and survive, could Hester Prynne with her feminine 'magnetic power' of love elevate and recover this man if he would have remained under her care and supervision? Undoubtedly she has stupendous strength in her words:

> Hast thou exhausted possibility in the failure of this one trial? Not so! The future is yet full of trial and success. There is happiness to be enjoyed! There is good to be done! Exchange this false life of thine for a true one. Be, if thy spirit summon thee to such a mission, the teacher and apostle of the red men. Or, as is more thy nature, be a scholar and a sage among the wisest and the most renowned of the cultivated world. Preach! Write! Act! Do anything, save to lie down and die! Give up this name of Arthur Dimmesdale, and make thyself another, and a high one, such as thou canst wear without fear or shame. Why shouldst thou tarry so much as one other day in the torments that have so gnawed into thy life? that have made thee feeble to will and to do? that will leave thee powerless even to repent? Up, and away! (*SL* 298)

Hester has assumed the role of a guiding force in the dyad, but what shall we call this? Is it an artful persuasion, play of words to control one's mind or an attempt to recapitulate the lost vigour through a psychodynamic usage of words? Her frantic exasperation for reunion acts like an electrifying force. Towards the end of the novel, we will see how Hester will propagate that speaking as an art of expression must have the freedom, reminding us of the historical figures like Anne Hutchinson and Margaret Fuller. Like a doting mother, Hester insinuates new spirit in the minister with her rhetorical brilliance. She dreamt of a picture of a true happy family which failed with the physician before. The irony is that Arthur Dimmeadale who has been playing with his words and malleability of language failed to understand the same weapon that Hester Prynne has used.

CHAPTER EIGHTEEN—A FLOOD OF SUNSHINE

Arthur Dimmesdale is taken aback at such dauntless decision of Hester. Hester's freedom of thought is the natural outcome of her ostracised life. She has been the rebel, the deviator with her note of individuality but for the minister who is one of the central authoritative figures of Puritanical world, this appears abstract and beyond his wildest dreams. She belongs to that wilderness where everything is chaotic. Her world has been the wild untamed world of the forest observing human institutions from distance. She is more like the Native Indians who are beyond Puritanical social order, who cannot be tamed in the name of civilisation and whose presences are threat of violations because of their non-conformist attitude. Hester Prynne has been carrying the passport of violation, the daring identity of scarlet letter has given her the audacity to venture into such prohibited places which other women dare not. The minister has never dared to choose the precarious and audacious paths. His sin is the sin of passion and his incapability to confess it or to shield it is impossible for the minister. The difference between Hester and Dimmesdale is clearly evident. While the former seems to have been preparing for this second deviation, the latter is caught in the dilemma of 'to be or not to be'. Dimmesdale's difficulty is making a choice because to escape from this land without confessing appears to him like a criminal and to stay back and remain silent is also hypocritical. Everyone is afraid of death and shame and Dimmesdale's incapability to confess is a natural human principle of self-defence. The narrator compares Dimmesdale to a defeated castle which can never regain its lost glory but can only be prevented from further attack from enemies.

Dimmesdale realises that he cannot survive without Hester's power and tenderness which are the source of his sustenance. He fails to take a decision but Hester's determination and insistence affords some distant hope of happiness. Hester as his good angel is the harbinger of new hope to the captive spirit of the minister who seems to be caught in a dungeon. To erase the past and to welcome a better future, Hester takes a bold step. She expels the scarlet letter and throws it away. It seems as if her spirit is set free and she is assuaged from shame and disgrace. Further, she removes her cap that has hidden her long cascade of shining hair. It seems that the milk of tenderness is gushing out while her blooming beauty and appeal once more evolved in her blush. It seems all of a sudden that Nature has participated in the reunion of these long estranged lovers.

Suddenly Hester realises that the minister should see Pearl with this resurrected spirit and with a new look. The minister has been afraid of children all these years and he is afraid of Pearl too. Pearl has been engrossed with the dark forest which haunts his mind full of guilt. Pearl, on the other hand is adrift in perfect harmony with nature. Pearl seems to have become a part of this nature so that the fauna and the flora are quite at ease when Pearl is among them. The various falcons like partridge and pigeon, the squirrel and the fox are less afraid and more cordial on Pearl's arrival. It is said that even one wolf came near Pearl and after smelling her, left her alone. The narrator believes that all these animals and birds must have located the wilderness of the wood in little Pearl. Like a little nymph, all decked up with flowers, Pearl seems to have increased the beauty of nature. When she heard her mother's voice, she gradually started moving towards the direction from where the sound is emanating.

Commentary

The title of the chapter explicitly hints at the hope of a life of illumination and togetherness in the life of Hester Prynne and Arthur Dimmesdale. The world of freedom beckons them almost as Hester finds an outlet. Ironically it refers to relief from painful existence and burden of life on earth. Still dwelling in the surrealistic world of imagination and speculation in the midst of the forest, Dimmesdale will start dwelling on false hope. The hope to reject destiny has germinated within him. The minister has never dared to breach of divine law but the narrator comments that this revolutionary spirit has stemmed from Hester Prynne because she has been a marginalised creature at the fringe of humanity. The beautiful analogy of Hester's mind and body with the untamed nature reminds us of Rossetti's Lilith who represents "the perilous principle in the world."[37] She emulates fear and joy of violation and deviations. Hawthorne writes Hester Prynne has "wandered, without rule or guidance, in a moral wilderness, as vast, as intricate, and shadowy as the untamed forest, amid the gloom of which they were now holding a colloquy" (*SL* 299).

The minister confined within the Puritanical religious codes remained ignorant while Hester Prynne has irrevocably explored the world and acquired knowledge in the course of her suffering. Nathaniel Hawthorne has mocked at knowledge that is pedantic and abstruse whether it is Dimmesdale's theological knowledge or Chillingworth's empirical knowledge. In contrast, Hester has enriched herself with knowledge of this world through her experience and agony. For a moment it seems that Hawthorne has revived once more the burning passion in his hero and heroine as Dimmesdale pines:

> Neither can I any longer live without her companionship; so powerful is she to sustain,—so tender to soothe! O Thou to whom I dare not lift mine eyes, wilt Thou yet pardon me! (*SL* 302)

Such vehemence of passion in Dimmesdale is witnessed in his oration and physical torture. But this renunciation is both corporal and spiritual. We see two conflicting urges within Dimmesdale—to hide and to expose and hence he requires an individual personality like Hester to support him. He needs to be endorsed and approved which only Hester can do.

Another significant aspect in this chapter is Hester's futile attempt to remove the stigma of the scarlet letter from her bosom. Taking off the scarlet letter, Hester seems to release her own body and spirit from the burden of guilt and shame the moment she threw away the letter. The gesture of refusal of the scarlet letter is her attempt to reject the Puritan tenet of guilt leading to repentance. This is her wilful spirit; her freedom of choice and a desperate effort to encourage Dimmesdale to participate in her plan. She has always defied the society by adoring the letter as an ornament, by being reluctant to give away the symbol when the Puritanical authority wanted it back and now she is discarding it by her choice.

In this chapter, Hawthorne once more reinforces the natural wild energy in Pearl. Her mystery and ethereal nature is captivating as she plays with the sunlight, the fauna and the flora like partridge, a squirrel, a fox, and even a wolf. The flowers communicate in their silent language with Pearl who seems to be like some heathen princess in the midst of nature. Pearl's wild ecstasies among the chattering squirrel who threw nut upon her head are complementary to her unbridled reactions and behaviours. In the uncontaminated communion between the child and nature, religion that the Puritanical world indoctrinated seems to be a threat and an intrusion. Hawthorne reflects that Pearl has orchestrated herself in the rhythm of nature: "The truth seems to be, however, that the mother-forest, and these wild things which it nourished, all recognised a kindred wilderness in the human child" (*SL* 307). Such union is divine when she dyed her body and mind with flowers and leaves like violets, columbine and anemones so that she appears a supernatural creature like the nymph or dryad. Pearl's verbal exhortation or her assortment of flowers reflects the purest moment of simplicity and the quintessence of life force in the deluge of primitive coherence between man and nature.

CHAPTER NINETEEN—THE CHILD AT THE BROOKSIDE

Hester mesmerised to see the primitive beauty of little Pearl decked in wild flowers recognises how pure and innocent the child is and hence she assures Dimmesdale that in future he will soon discover Pearl to be adorable. Dimmesdale acknowledges his fear that he has always anticipated that the people of Salem will soon recognise the child's father from Pearl's countenance because she strongly resembles him. It seems for the first time, they are enjoying the company of togetherness and parenthood of this beautiful child who carry the traits of both her parents. The narrator at this point observes how a magician or a prophet can easily discern the parentage of the child. Hester consoles that Dimmesdale must get rid of his fear since she can see her dream of their family consisting of the father, mother and the child to be soon materialised. She warns the minister that Pearl's life of isolation has a strange influence on her and so she is not easily accustomed to strange human emotions like excess of eagerness or passion but she is confident that Pearl will love her father with heightened intensity, the way she loves her mother. She recalls that from the earlier two interactions of the child and the father, Pearl has shown signs that she is strangely attracted towards Dimmesdale.

The incredulous minister full of self-doubt is still afraid of this preposterous plan of Hester and he explains that the brook appears to him like the gulf between two worlds. Pearl being an elf-child with supernatural power can cross the river and he fears that if Hester is not quick enough, she may lose her child. Hester encourages Pearl in her gambolling and mirth and the child looks like a deer leaping and bouncing. She explains Pearl about this new friend of the mother and the daughter who is awaiting to meet little Pearl. Pearl behaving in a strange way wonders at her mother and the minister who at this point spontaneously has kept his hand on his chest is tensed and anxious. Staring at her mother and the minister, she suddenly refuses to come and only raises her hand towards Hester's bosom. Hester unable to understand sudden arrogance of Pearl scolds her that provokes strange outburst of the child who in a fit of passion seems to be full of rage. Stamping her foot and wildly screaming with her index finger pointing towards Hester, it seems the entire wild forest has precipitated in Pearl's anger and anguish. Hester soon realises that Pearl cannot identify her mother without the scarlet letter while Dimmesdale, afraid at this sight, requests Hester to pacify the child since he cannot withstand any violent scene except Mistress Hibbin's gambolling in the midst of the wood. Hester Prynne requests the child to pick up the scarlet letter beside her but the child refuses. Hester enjoyed the freedom of being free from social stigma for an hour but it seems that Fate has impinged the letter eternally for her. She pinned it again with the determination to fling it into the sea very soon.

Little Pearl now recognising her mother embraces her and with abundance of love kissed her. She soon queries about the minister's presence and her mother explains that Arthur is waiting to welcome and bless her. Pearl interestingly asks whether the minister will love them and hold their hands in the town. Her mother explains that if not now, this will soon happen when in their own home; the child sitting on the minister's lap will learn new lessons with love and care. Pearl seems to be jealous of the attention that her mother has given to the minister or may be out of her strange whims; she rejects to come close to the minister. When Arthur attempts to kiss the child's forehead, she escapes and washes her forehead. From the distance, she watches her mother and the minister conversing.

Commentary

This chapter shows how Pearl is the moral guardian of her parents. Pearl is the key motivator and the actor in this scene. Her bizarre reactions to Hester and Dimmesdale suggest that she does not anticipate a promising future to the couple. She is almost messianic in conveying the message to Hester that her dream is futile and illusive. Just like nature, she is whimsical, beyond control and cannot be governed by any human laws. Her impulses are strange and in this chapter we get glimpses of such rare impulses. But such mystic behaviour of Pearl is not designless, on the contrary she provides the prognosis that destiny cannot be altered. Hester and Dimmesdale ponder about their child's feature and try to discern her resemblance with them in physique and nature. Being an intelligent mother Hester is quick to recognise the attractive spirit within her gorgeous child. She tries to explain Dimmesdale about her natural beauty, her artistic bent of mind and how she is like an angel in their lives. With her maternal adoration she is confident that Pearl will love her father with same intensity as she loves her mother. Hawthorne defines her as 'the living hieroglyphic' and the 'character of flame' who embodies Hester's wild spirit of defiance. Pearl's innocence also reflects the potential goodness in her parents and her adornment with flowers is the inherited artistic genius from her mother. In contrast Dimmesdale's concern is not for Pearl but for himself. He confesses that the child is a reminder of his sin and is afraid that people may discern Dimmesdale as the child's father. The narrator focuses how this sudden intimacy of the father, mother and the child makes Hester forget about the world but Dimmesdale is incompetent to have faith in this togetherness. He lacks self-confidence, love and responsibility for the child and her mother.

Pearl's complete image reflected perfectly in the brook seems to have separated her from Hester and the minister. She fails to recognise Hester without her scarlet letter and this ensures that the scarlet letter is the personification for her mother. She refuses to cross the brook and we can anticipate that Pearl in her later life will be an individual spirit. She encodes the complexities in Hester and Dimmesdale's lives by suggesting that honesty and clarity are the best principles to live a life of happiness. Pearl being the child of nature cannot condone human sedition, treason and conspiracy. She is that unbounded spirit who stands for unostentatious and prosaic style of living. Her sudden passionate outburst at the distortion of the image of her mother is unbearable to Dimmesdale which shows how inwardly weak and fragile the man has become who is vivified at her own child. Pearl's budding heroic individuality is fearful to Dimmesdale because he is a part of the Puritanical chauvinist world. It horrifies his consciousness and his masculinity that otherwise is afraid to accept the responsibility of Pearl. Pearl's aberrant behaviour reminds him that she is the living testimony of her sin. By not allowing Hester to reject the scarlet letter so easily and by denying kiss to Dimmesdale, Pearl imparts respective messages to her parents. She reminds Hester that denying the scarlet letter is a way of denial of the consequence of her love which is Pearl. Her rejection of Dimmesdale is the rejection of his hypocrisy and cowardice nature to accept his fatherhood.

CHAPTER TWENTY—THE MINISTER IN A MAZE

Dimmesdale departs while Hester and little Pearl watch him from the wood beside the mossy trunk covered in darkness that seems to have been preserved for the secret union of these two forbidden souls. His mind is now pondering on the dream that Hester has adumbrated. The concept of home and togetherness in the Old World seems endearing to the minister. All his reasons seem to be supporting this proposition that Hester has proffered. His deteriorating physical condition is incapable of withstanding the severity of winter of North America. Moreover, it seems that his scholarship and elevated religious preaching will be pertinent and satisfying to a learned cultured community than the brutal world of the new found land. Hester as a Sister of Charity has gathered the knowledge that a ship has arrived from Spain and within four days will depart for Bristol. She knows the captain and the crew personally and can easily manage to reserve passes for the three without disclosing their identity. Hester has also preserved money to buy tickets for them.

The Massachusetts Bay Colony will soon celebrate the only holiday of the Puritans, the Election Day which happens in May, around the fifth day after Easter. The day is meant for the selection of the new governor and his inauguration to the system for one year term. This year Dimmesdale has been selected to deliver the Election Sermon. As the ship will depart on the fourth day, it appears to Dimmesdale that he will also be able to perform his last duty as the minister in Boston. It is considered as one of the remarkable days when special guests from other native villages, colonies and England will congregate to become a part of history. Hence Dimmesdale planned to complete his responsibilities and depart next day so that no one can blame that he left his social duties unperformed. His encounter with Hester Prynne in the wood and the consequent planning has induced some diabolic energy in this man evident in his speedy gesture and his sense of detachment with the surrounding town people. Strange mischievous joys occurred in his mind so that at one point he feels like passing some humorous comments to his parishioners and see their reactions but he finally controlled his temptations.

His sudden meeting with an aged deacon spurred in his mind some mischievous spoofs so that in his excitement he feels like shouting blasphemies at him but his anarchistic spirit is restrained immediately. He enjoyed this sudden spark in his mind as if a fresh new air breathed in new essence. Another old pious woman who is always replete with warm memories about her dead husband and her children has been replenished with religious words of the minister ever since she came under his influence. The minister's mesmerising words from Gospel seem to be rejuvenating for the lady but this time when Arthur whispered in her ears, some confused utterance appeared as he could not recall anything from the Gospel. At the end, the minister's blissful shinning face appears to be emitting glorious light of heaven and it immediately created an impact on her. Lastly, a youngest woman who seems to be in the prime of her beauty and youth appears like a freshly blossomed lily and she came across the minister who has won religious faith in her through his sermons. Arthur for a second is tempted to destroy her innocence and faith in the minister by giving a wicked look and thereby nourish her lust. When the minister has come across a group of Puritan toddlers who have just learned to utter few words, he is tempted to whisper in their ears some vulgar shameful words. When he has seen a crewman from a Spanish ship who generally happens to be an atheist, he wishes to shake his hand with the crewman to hear some bawdy jokes and anti-god statements.

All these frightened the minister and he doubts that he has signed the bond of Satan with his blood in the forest. He fears that Satan is provoking him to corrupt his soul and perform as many evil deeds as possible. When Dimmesdale is lost in such apprehensions and striking his forehead with his hand, old Mistress Hibbins passes him and confirms that the minister must be coming from the wood. She assures that she can help her to get in touch with the Black Man in the forest. The minister explains that his purpose has been to pay a visit to his friend Apostle Eliot but the lady crackles and as if she knows some dark secret, summons him through her silent language to participate in the supernatural revelry at midnight in the forest. The minister ponders that lured by personal happiness; he seems to have sold his soul to the Devil, whom this old lady worships. He suffers from guilt conscience for his weird desire to mock everything that is holy. When he reaches home, he is relieved that his erratic desires have not materialised in the street and he has been able to hide them but the same home which has been so familiar for his meditative contemplation on God, for his religious pre-occupations and for his study of Bible, now appears anonymous and strange. He can clearly distinguish the two different selves of him—the former, who has been writing the Election Sermon plucked from the suffering and contrition in his own life, and the latter returned from the forest, completely metamorphosed into a wise man with hidden mysteries and secret intentions.

When Dimmesdale is contemplating on these transformations, Chillingworth enters in his room. The sudden confrontation with the physician turned the minister pale with one hand on the Holy Scriptures and the other on his chest. When the doctor suggests that Arthur requires his treatment as he appears extremely pale sickly after his visit from Apostle Eliot, Arthur with humbleness and yet with indignation eliminates the requirement of medicine. In their silent exchange of gazes, it is evident that the doctor with his introspective observation is confident that the minister has already recognised him as his enemy while Arthur apprehends that Chillingworth has already comprehended his meeting with Hester. Both of them are eager to confront each other directly and with enough provocation the physician asserts that he must take care of his patient so that he is strong enough to deliver his precious sermons which the people of Salem may miss next year in the absence of Dimmesdale. The minister claims that the possibility of such absence is due to his soul's departure from his body but still he does not require any more medication, instead he blesses with prayers to the doctor for being so kind of him. The doctor left and the minister after ravenously eating some food burnt those earlier compositions for the Sermons and set forth to write a new one with his mind full of revolutionary zeal till the dawn breaks in.

Commentary

This chapter is about the spiritual battle of Arthur Dimmesdale with his passionate self. This conflict is the dramatic locus of the novel and also reflects the dilemma in the life of the author of *The Scarlet Letter*. It suggests thraldom is too profound to break or demolish. Hester's enticement is a call for a new Dimmesdale and therefore a new nation that represents individuality and freedom. For Dimmesdale it may appear a conflict between sin and salvation but Hawthorne suggests the conflict between the individual and the traditional or the conventional. He has been so much pre-occupied within his own narcissistic world that even Hester's plan to elope appears as a relief from the burden of sin rather than a reunion of a happy family life. He knows his daring dream is another act of transgression but it entails incarnation of another Dimmesdale. The conflict of identities is mocked at by the author when he comments

> No man, for any considerable period, can wear one face to himself, and another to the multitude, without finally getting bewildered as to which may be true. (*SL* 322)

Dimmesdale's hallucination regarding his transformation from a suffering soul to a rejuvenated spirit is Hawthorne's attempt to introspect the psychology of the minister. This psychology reflects the Calvinist distinction between man's propensities to sin and actual sinning. He suddenly seems to be a man of fire surcharged with the irrational wild desires intending to do wicked tricks with strangers and members of his congregation. He can scarcely refrain from mocking the Communion supper, feels the irresistible desire to join a group of dissolute sailors or whispers against the Holy Scripture. We witness some Dionysian spirit within him leaping and bouncing for some weird expression and mockery of the system. But this transformation is his repressed desire which he dare not aspire until Hester Prynne provoked him. We can call this a parasitic element in his character as he hardly decided to take the initiative. Even the possible arrangements and the ways are pragmatically devised by Hester Prynne.

This bounteous energy is also revealed in his preparation for Election Sermon. Mistress Hibbins, the witch with her supernatural power recognised the kindred spirit within the minister and Chillingworth senses the pulsation of energy within him who seems to be preparing for another world. The tragic dilemma in his character is his indecision, the eternal maze where he can hardly rationalise. In his conflicting condition the five temptations or impulses refer to Biblical analogies. The first temptation is to blaspheme the sacrament of the Lord's Supper with an old gentleman who speaks with paternal affection. The supper refers to the body and the blood of the Saviour and Arthur's blasphemy will therefore relate to a symbolical crucifying of Christ. The second temptation to whisper about the immorality of the soul is to hurt the creator and speak of devil's words. The third temptation to destroy the soul of a virgin sister by sexual impure gaze refers to the sin of the flesh. The fourth temptation to corrupt the soul of the children is a satanic act which the Fallen Angel performed out of jealousy and revenge.

This madness indicates a failure of the rational mind which controls the upheavaled emotions. It is difficult to expect a balanced mind in this man any more especially when he has realised how Chillingworth, the disguised physician has psychologically raped him with eternal blisters, wounds and shame. He therefore does not want to confront the man but concentrate on the sermon. The despondent Romantic spirit of Dimmesdale is ironically preparing for its tragic doom while his morbid artistic genius prepares for the final rendering of speech. There is a duality of feeling within him—a depressed sense of debasement and the elevated sense of prophetic power. He reminds us of Milton's *Il Penseroso*:

> There let the pealing organ blow,
> To the full-voiced choir below,
> In service high, and anthems clear,
> As may with sweetness, through mine ear,
> Dissolve me into ecstasies,
> And bring all heaven before my eyes.[38]

It seems all of a sudden that Dimmesdale is too harsh about the Puritanical world. Obviously Hawthorne is interrogating issues like freedom, predestination, reprobation, damnation and sin. Dimmesdale's intense desire to transgress at Hester's inspiration has the element of hedonism which of course the Puritanical society prohibits. The fear in Dimmesdale reminds us of the conflict between Renaissance Humanism and Calvinism in Doctor Faustus of Christopher Marlow. Dimmesdale cannot reconcile with any of his uncongenial sides—religious Puritanical self and the sensual passionate self. We have to remember that Hawthorne, along with other transcendentalist writers, has already started reflecting on the concept of the American frontier beyond the ethereal power of myth, religion and ideals. Dimmesdale's transformation just after his return from the wilderness of New England reflects how the wild land itself shapes a revolutionary spirit in humanity. The frontier men of America have already started to deconstruct the age old hackneyed customs and traditions of England. In "Earth's Holocaust" Hawthorne reflects on this emerging spirit "to escape from every existing mode of organising and explaining experiences, in order to confront life on entirely original terms."[39] His difficulty lies in his excess of narcissistic nature and hence even after suffering from a sudden sense of levity he wonders:

> Am I mad? or Am I given over utterly to the fiend? Did I make a contract with him in the forest, and sign it with my blood? And does he now summon me to its fulfilment, by suggesting the performance of every wickedness which his most foul imagination can conceive? (*SL* 330)

Dimmesdale cannot break away the bonds of custom and religion. Though Hawthorne along with Thoreau has sensed the American impulse to "purgatorial action—preceding, as it were, the life of the new Adam in a new earthly paradise",[40] yet such triumphant individualism is too much to expect in a man like Dimmesdale because he lacks aggressiveness and daunting pioneering spirit.

Apart from Dimmesdale's split personality that the chapter mainly tries to highlight, the brief little intervention of the physician in his patient's room is also noteworthy. Chillingworth is the prototype of a modern psychiatrist who is quick and prudent enough to understand that Dimmesdale has already come out of the illusion of his friendly pretension and has recognised the bitterest enemy in him. Their conversation and exchange of words are full of irony as Dimmesdale addresses his physician as "most watchful friend" (*SL* 336). This is for the first time we see both the characters confronting each other without any mask. When both are referring to 'another world' that Dimmesdale may visit, we can understand that the physician is much ahead of the minister in terms of shrewdness and play of words. Though apparently he refers to life after death, but the astute physician is also an ingenious psychiatrist who can anticipate Hester and Dimmesdale's plan to escape from New England. The concealed meanings, tart sarcasm and repressed hatred are now clear although none of them are direct in their attacks. Author Steven Poole calls such playful use of words as 'Unspeak' in the book *Unspeak*. 'Unspeak' represents an attempt to say something without saying it, without getting into an argument and so having to justify itself. At the same time, it tries to unspeak—in the sense of erasing or silencing—any possible opposing point of view by laying a claim right at the start to only one way of looking at a problem. It saturates the mind with one viewpoint while simultaneously makes an opposing view ever more difficult to enunciate. Chillingworth's weapon is his language; its power is so strong that is can be both a medication and a poison. Hence, Arthur Dimmesdale finds Chillingworth's words extremely unbearable and he rushes outside the room. Chillingworth dissipates language and yet hits the meaning. Chillingworth has recognised this play of words as the tool of his revenge and oppression and therefore his language invades the secret heart of his patient.

CHAPTER TWENTY ONE—THE NEW ENGLAND HOLIDAY

On the day of appointment of new governor, the entire Salem community gathered in the town. Hester Prynne is wearing the coarsest faded attire as she wears every time to remain in oblivion in the midst of the crowd. She appeared with Pearl among many other people. Her scarlet letter stands in contrast to her dress and her solemn emotionless face. She seems like a dead being walking in the midst of the living, and yet some subtle hidden feeling is there which only a psychologist can read. It seems that her penance of enduring public resentment has come to its end and she voluntarily chooses to bear it for the last time before her agony is converted into her triumph. The narrator explains beautifully that it seems that Hester Prynne is consuming the last bitter sip of her life before she begins drinking the wine of life. Pearl in her vibrant dress seems like a butterfly whose dress reflects her character. She stands in contrast to her mother's attire and mood. For the rest of the world Pearl's sprightful dazzling look can betray some hidden storm inside her but her mother can sense Pearl's super sensitivity in anticipating some sinister. Pearl's abundant energy and wilderness becomes heightened in the market place when she is amazed to see the animation in the growing crowd of Salem.

Pearl's inquisitive mind is in constant interrogation as she hovers on the well-dressed cleaned blacksmith, the nodding smiling jailer Master Brackett, or the strange minister who holds their hands in the midnight on the scaffold or in the forest and attempted to kiss little Pearl but refuses the same action in the day light in the town. To divert Pearl's query, Hester explains the significance of the day to her little daughter, how the people have withdrawn from their daily chores of work and wait with great enthusiasm for the newly elected governor to walk along with the ministers. Continuing Hester's description about the significance of the day, the narrator reflects upon the divergent manners of celebration between England during the reign of Queen Elizabeth and the Puritanical restrictions to jubilance and mirth. Most of the people thronged at the market place happen to be from England whose forefathers have witnessed such gala celebrations during the Queen's empire. The nostalgia of theatrical performances, ballad, jugglers, jesters and dancing apes are no more found but the simplicity and smiling faces are enough to gauge their contentment and happiness. The Puritanical settlers are hardly decked up in gorgeous dresses and they prefer to stick to Puritanical ideals but some of the natives are ablaze in their best attires. With their colourful appearances, grave faces, bow and arrows, they stand separately from the rest of the crowd and the narrator describes them as savage wild barbarians with the ferocity of the animals in the wood. Besides these Indians, another belligerent group consisted of sailors also gathered. These sailors always drunk or smoking tobacco seem like pirates as they carry knife, wear gold plated short trousers and indulge in stealing. These sailors are not disturbed by the Puritanical society as they deal with that part of nature which cannot be controlled by humanity.

One of the commanders of the ship with dazzling gold laces and ribbons on his dress, sword and sword scar on his forehead is seen to be in conversation with the Physician. Soon he meets Mistress Prynne for some conversation. Previously when Hester has been the cynosure of curses and abuses, it would have been difficult for anyone to communicate personally but since her scarlet alphabet has undergone transformation from adulteress to Abel, it has become easy for her. Hester is startled to know that beside Pearl, Dimmesdale and herself, Chillingworth is also accompanying them to England and has already introduced himself as a good friend of Dimmesdale. Though Hester controlled her consternation but through her silent exchange of glances with her previous old physician husband, she feared a secretive revengeful smile on his face.

Commentary

This chapter anticipates the third scaffold scene in the novel that prepares the readers for the climax of the plot. Hawthorne makes satirical comment on the Puritanical society and the hypocrisy of the community in relation to the significance of the day. On the other hand, the tension in Hester's mind is so intense that the readers are left in suspense about the final move of the lovers. Hawthorne has perfectly woven the Puritanical history of New England with Hester Prynne's microcosmic world of struggle.

Hawthorne makes a distinction between public and private by placing Hester's struggle on the eve of New England Holiday. Hawthorne's scathing criticism about the socio-political and religious ideology of the Puritans reflects that the private life is being mocked and concealed by the public life. He reflects back on those days in England when celebration involved cultural proliferations and amusement. The reference to music, jugglers and jests, is replaced by a gloomy sombre atmosphere. There is a strange nostalgia for a glorious royal life of England. One can detect traces of grotesquery in the "sadcolored" and "gray," clothes of the towns people portraying the Puritans' refusal of anything merry or colourful. It seems as if the contiguity of prison and cemetery has a significant impact upon the inhabitants of the city. Hawthorne's nostalgic account of the old festivities also indicates that the carnivalesque spirit cannot be totally erased since the lingering memory still makes them compare between the past and the present. Nathaniel Hawthorne deftly addresses the Puritan culture of the seventeenth-century America as, a "monological culture", a term used by Mikhail Bakhtin. By monologic culture Bakhtin meant a culture which is isolated, divorced and passive. Bakhtin has primarily introduced the concept of monologic in opposition to dialogic which has the openness for interpretation and interaction of everyone. Hawthorne wants to reflect here that laughter and the spirit of carnival cannot be totally repressed even in the most ideological and monological cultures.

Apart from settlers of New England who strictly follow the Puritanical ideals, however, Hawthorne has reflected upon those transgressed figures who are either not worthy to be considered within the Puritanical ideals or bold enough to deviate the rules. The first category refers to the native Indians who in their savage "embroidered deerskin robes" represent the Barbarian while the second category is represented by the 'rough-looking desperadoes' mariners. Hawthorne explains that:

> They transgressed without fear or scruple, the rules of behaviour that were binding on all others.... It remarkably characterised the incomplete morality of the age, rigid as we call it, that a license was allowed the seafaring class, not merely for their freaks on shore, but for far more desperate deeds on their proper element.

Why are the seafarer excluded from the Puritanical world of morality and strictness? These seamen are close to nature than to society. For, Hawthorne explains that

> the sea, in those old times, heaved, swelled, and foamed very much at its own will, or subject only to the tempestuous wind, with hardly any attempts at regulation by human law. (*SL* 348)

What Hawthorne wants to emphasise is that nature is one such basic truth which cannot be controlled, altered, denied or transformed. Hawthorne being influenced by the spirit of 'Transcendentalism' tried to reflect the same philosophy. For the transcendentalists like Emerson, Jones Very, nature is the primary force and it is the predominant source to understand humanity. For Emerson the richness and complexities of the world can be seen in humanity. To understand the self, one must understand nature. Emerson in his 1836 book, entitled *Nature* explains that each individual is a manifestation of nature and contains the key to unlock the mysteries of the universe. For him, *Nature* is an expression of the divinity.

Emerson exemplifies beautifully that when a man gazes at the stars, he becomes aware of his aliention from the material world. Similarly, Hawthorne explains that the spirit of the unbounded untamed sea is reflected among the mariners. They are wild and live their lives according to their whims. Hawthorne is ironical and explains that nature is a part of man, and all aspects of nature correspond to some state of human mind. The Puritans failed to realise this special bonding between nature and man.

The Puritans believe that men if they idealise the future, then they depreciate the present. The concept of holidays, mirth and jubilation are unknown to the Salem community. Abstinence is the motive of life and on any such rare holidays like New England Election Day, the people are always more controlled and grave fearing that they should not cross the legitimate boundary of social parameters. The Puritans are supposed to have come to America to form the Massachusetts Bay Colony on a sacred mission, ordained by God, to create a model community and thereby fulfil a divine covenant. The Puritanical maxim says that "They for whom all days are holy can have no holiday" and hence they were contemptuous of celebration and deviation from duties and responsibilities in life. They renounced material wealth, decoration and gift in order to prevent corruption of the soul but in that way they also denied human emotions. Such impossible strict moral code is satirised by Hawthorne because it is against the law of nature to lead a life of absolute abstinence:

> Into this festal season of the year—as it already was, and continued to be during the greater part of two centuries—the Puritans compressed whatever mirth and public joy they deemed allowable to human infirmity; thereby so far dispelling the customary cloud, that, for the space of a single holiday, they appeared scarcely more grave than most other communities at a period of general affliction. (*SL* 343-44)

The purpose is to control and sublimate the natural instinct of humanity forcibly by extirpation. The result of such repression, fear, sin, taboo and abstinence is bound to end in hypocrisy and secret gratifications. Such repressed gratification is noted when Hester Prynne adorned Pearl colourfully in bright gorgeous dress. The gloomy life of restriction and control is noted in her grey shabby dress while her inward excitement of her dream about a life of togetherness and a relief from the claustrophobic world of the Puritans is reflected in Pearl's dress. In Pearl, we can see that nature has reinvigorated bounty of energy. Through Pearl,

Hawthorne wants to offer insight that Nature and Pearl are synonymous. Hester Prynne and Dimmesdale are the microcosmic reflection of such restraints that result in hysteria, neurosis, morbid fears and suicide. With strict Calvinist principles in mind, the Puritanical authoritative people believe that any chance of expression of emotion is a way to lascivious behaviour.

But the narrator comments one who has got an introspective vision can see the inevitable superabundant excitement in Hester Prynne behind the mask of coldness and frigidity. That is why D.H. Lawrence has said that—

> *The Scarlet Letter* isn't a pleasant, pretty romance. It is a sort of parable, an earthly story with a hellish meaning.... That blue-eyed darling Nathaniel knew disagreeable things in his inner soul. He was careful to send them out in disguise.... Nowadays men do hate the idea of dualism. It's no good, dual we are. The cross. If we accept the symbol, then, virtually, we accept the fact. We are divided against ourselves. For instance, the blood hates being KNOWN. Hence the profound instinct of privacy. And on the other hand, the mind and the spiritual consciousness of man simply hates the dark potency of blood-acts: hates the genuine dark sensual orgasms, which do, for the time being, actually obliterate the mind and the spiritual consciousness, plunge them in a suffocating flood of darkness.[41]

The duality that Lawrence has detected at the centre of the novel can be traced back in the character of Dimmesdale primarily as well as in Hester Prynne. Hester is forcibly reduced to "marble quietude" that is "like the frozen calmness of a dead woman's features" (*SL* 339-40) but Hawthorne also reflects the "wine of life" that Hester possessed that could have enriched her life. This duality is contrasted against Hester's doleful shady attire and Pearl's burning lustrous dress. To think that Hawthorne is only criticising the gruesome Puritanical society is not enough. Even in "Endicott and the Red Cross", he exposes visceral images of horror:

> But among the crowd were several whose punishment would be life-long; some, whose ears had been cropped,

> like those of puppy-dogs; others, whose cheeks had been branded with the initials of their misdemeanors; one, with his nostrils slit and seared.[42]

What Hawthorne wants to ponder is the germination of the spirit of rebellion as we see in Hester Prynne. She reveals that human intellect cannot be constricted by law. Her intellectual and passionate self is emancipated in Pearl who assumed a freedom of speculation, the freedom of choice and a life to live by one's own will. That is why Hawthorne explains that Pearl's dress—

> seemed an effluence, or inevitable development and outward manifestation of her character, no more to be separated from her than the many-hued brilliance from a butterfly's wing, or the painted glory from the leaf of a bright flower. (*SL* 340)

Pearl on this very day extraordinarily represents the rare spirit of liberalism. The butterfly or the bird with which she is compared to by the narrator symbolises freedom which does not lead to self-distortion as the Puritans believed in but reflects the essential nature, self-expression and self-government. But Pearl's strange overzealous behaviour also created doubt in Hester's mind as she anticipated some catastrophic end. Hester may dream that her purgative womanhood is coming to an end and now she hopes for a life of solace and happiness but in Pearl, Hester can see the premonition of a storm. Pearl represents both rebellious impulses toward and aggressive impulses to detect and accuse. Pearl seems to be always in motion, never static but some natural grace and energy always acting within her. Her unflagging spirit is unacceptable in the Puritanical society but Pearl's eldritch shriek is a protest against any attempt to tame her. She is the microcosm of the chaos in Hester's mind. Her spirit of inquisition is unending and it is this thirsty spirit to know the world which is dangerous. In this chapter also we find that Pearl's incessant questions are sometimes difficult for Hester to answer. It reflects her creative mind and her extra ordinary awareness. Hence, Hawthorne has revealed how her innocent spirit can perceive truth as she mutters:

> In the dark night-time, he calls us to him, and holds thy hand and mine, as when we stood with him on the scaffold

> yonder! And in the deep forest, where only the old trees can hear, and the strip of sky see it, he talks with thee, sitting on a heap of moss! And he kisses my forehead, too, that the little brook would hardly wash it off! But here in the sunny day, and among all the people, he knows us not; nor must we know him! A strange, sad man is he, with his hand always over his heart! (*SL* 343)

It is difficult to believe such words from a seven years old child like Pearl. But what Hawthorne wants to reflect here is that the innocent spirit of the child dictates her to act and hence her words and actions are the outcome of her intuition and instinct. Although Pearl is immature to recognise the relationship between Dimmesdale and Hester yet she can perceive some strangeness in the minister and also can sense some undefined relationship between the two. Hester's explanation about the significance of the day to Pearl is reminiscent of the parable of the prodigal son:

> The children have come from their schools, and the grown people from their workshops and their fields, on purpose to be happy. For, to-day, a new man is beginning to rule over them; and so...they make merry and rejoice; as if a good and golden year were at length to pass over the poor old world! (V, 274)

The conclusion of this chapter is interesting as it deals with Hester's discovery of Chillingworth as the co-passenger in their voyage from New England to Bristol. Hester is not merely shocked but she anticipates Dimmesdale's doom because she realised that it is difficult to separate the physician from him. One can anticipate the impending catastrophe that Hester can foresee. In Chillingworth, Dimmesdale and Hester, Hawthorne tries to expose the fragmented modern sensibility and one cannot escape the doom. Chillingworth represents the detached scientific intelligence whose reason for survival in this world is Dimmesdale. After all he is the leech as Hawthorne has already suggested in Chapter Nine who has developed the parasitic relationship and hence Dimmesdale's anguish is his source of nourishment. When Hester saw Chillingworth in the midst of the crowd, she is vivified to witness the evil spirit in his smile. Hester has completely understood that perhaps it is too late to separate the parasite from the host especially when volatile hatred is the source of parasitic existence.

CHAPTER TWENTY TWO—THE PROCESSION

Even before Hester can resolve the newly discovered anxiety and ponder over the matter, the commencement of the marching procession of magistrate and ministers towards the meeting house is declared where the sermon will be delivered. The procession consisted of incongruous musical instruments without any harmony but the effect seems impressive. The musical band is followed by arm of British soldiers thrillingly attired in colourful military outfit and experiences of various European battlefields. The narrator gives a detail description of the army. The eminent statesmen behind the army are also significant to note. Their excessive majestic appearance can cast a dull impact on the militant. The reason behind all these is reverence and although the Puritanical settlers in the New England have left back the grandeur and royalty with kings and emperors, yet the legacy still continues. The narrator comments that grey haired people of wisdom, solemnness, and sobriety deserve reverence during those days than actual intellectual stimulated mind. The appearance is of immense significance than the reality and these statesmen in terms of their appearance can rank to English Lords and king's councils.

After the magistrates arrive, the young minister Arthur Dimmesdale is seen, ready to deliver sermon to the community that exclusively admires this man. The narrator comments on the potential power of a beloved minister of a community and his elevated divine status. Arthur seems to be unconventionally charged with mysterious energy. His hand is not on his chest, the body does not appear lean and fragile and his mind seems to be preoccupied in some other worldly affairs. Whether the source is some spiritual power, some effusion of joy or is it the music of the band, Dimmesdale is hardly in this world and is aware of this surroundings. When Hester spotted the minister coming forward, she foreshadows some strange impending disaster but cannot locate the cause. The minister and Hester exchanged their glance and Hester can feel the smile at the corner of his eyes.

The previous night meeting in the forest, their exchange of love, promises and the proposition of a new life all seem to be alien and remote as the minister with his bold and steady steps move forward. Pearl is excited to see the transformed minister who kissed her in the forest and unable to control her excitement, she exclaims to her mother to ensure if he is the same minister. Admonishing her daughter, Hester alerts Pearl that she should not repeat anything about the forest incident in that special occasion. While the procession has progressed towards the building where the sermon will be delivered, another spectator, famous for her oddness and insanity, has also noticed the change in the minister's appearance. She is none other than Mistress Hibbins who most brightly attired in fanciful embroidery approached Hester Prynne.

Mistress Hibbins, famous for her witch-like identity is always avoided by the community of Salem as the Puritan society believed that to get in touch with an evil spirit like Mistress Hibbins will cast them into eternal damnation. As a result even in the midst of the crowd, a natural spontaneous passage is created since the people are cautious that they should not even brush against her body. This fear of the community is intensified especially when one ostracised damned soul intends to meet another like Hester. She asserts Hester that she has always been in the forest and one cannot fool her as she knows other visitors in the forest as well. Hinting at Hester's Scarlet alphabet, she vociferates that Hester has chosen to wear it in public but the minister hides the same alphabet in his chest where he keeps his hand. She warns that the Black Man whose bond the minister has signed, knows the ways and the means to make the minister publicly confess about the hidden alphabet on his chest. At this point Pearl intervenes and Mistress Hibbins explains to the child that she is the daughter of the Prince of Air and she must come for a wild ride with her in the full moon in the forest.

By this time, the sermon has already started and Hester prefers to remain outside the hall because it is so crowded, that she cannot penetrate along with little Pearl inside the hall. The minister's voice can be heard as it rises and falls with passion and zeal. Hester wonders that even if there would have been rooms and space inside she would not have been able to move forward any further as she is drowned in her nostalgia about the several scaffold scenes that relate the story of her life of infamy for last seven years. This forbidden spot seems to have connected her entire life, past, present and future. In the meantime, Pearl absorbed in her fun and frolic in the market place is bewitched by fanciful stuff which she hardly comes across in the secluded part of her cottage. The Spanish ship captain captivated by little Pearl's charming beauty tried to kiss her but Pearl, like a humming bird, is lost in her own world. In order to draw her attention, the captain tossed a golden chain from his hat in the air and when Pearl grasps it, he whispers into her ear to deliver his message to her mother. Addressing the child as witch-child, he confides in her ear that she should pass the message to Hester about the hump-backed doctor who has ensured about the minister's secret boarding of the ship tomorrow. He further adds that Hester should contemplate on Pearl and her escape only since the doctor as the close friend of the minister has assured that nothing is to be worried about. Pearl annoyed, admonishes the captain that she is the child of Prince of Air which Mistress Hibbins has confirmed and therefore if she is addressed as witch-child, she will tell her father to sink the captain's ship during some tempest. When Hester hears from Pearl the captain's message, her heart sinks in some insurmountable misery and her dream seems illusions and unachievable.

People from various towns outside Salem thronged all around Hester Prynne to watch the living woman about whom they have heard so many exaggerated stories. The Indians also joined the settlers and all their eyes focused on the alphabet on Hester's bosom. Hester's torment is revived once more as the people of Salem joined these outsiders to watch the woman of shame. When Hester Prynne has decided to shade off the scarlet letter, it seems once more the letter has started burning with the same intensity as it burnt seven years back when she came out of the prison door. The people gathered round her in circle and Hester seems to be burning in the magic circle of shame. No one among the crowd can ever imagine that the minister in the church delivering such divine sermon shares the same scarlet letter which burns in Hester's Prynne's bosom.

Commentary

It is believed that Nathaniel Hawthorne (1804-64) brought widespread attention to America's Puritan past and its military force by setting many of his works in seventeenth-century New England and by showing its lingering impact on America of his time. Though Nathaniel Hawthorne self-proclaimed about himself as "the obscurest man in American letters," yet Hawthorne has been actively involved in the contemporary politics. In this chapter, Hawthorne comments on the politics and the politicians of the seventeenth century. Hawthorne is pondering also on the question of American history and progress. The Puritanical view of America as the newly promised land is explored. For him, these early politicians lack mental brilliance but full of "ponderous sobriety." He admires their great fortitude and inner strength and their capability to take wise decisions in moment of emergency. The description of the military force which has always been the glory of England is still described by Hawthorne with great pride. The power of the Boston military theocracy is exemplified. The attempt of the Puritanical religious government is to produce a unified community. The procession at this juncture also suggests that the main characters are almost in transitional state of being. Hester Prynne standing in the midst of uproarious procession, is confused between past, present and future. She has dreamt that this day of New England holiday will be her last day when she will be standing on the threshold of a new life. So the procession with its military parade, music and grandeur is used as a narrative device to represent the internal turmoil of the characters when they are supposed to take the most crucial decisions in their lives. It is almost a 'carnivalesque' atmosphere, a term used by Mikhail Bakhtin that represents the possibility of the ultimate involvement of the self with the flow of life. Mikhail Bakhtin in his famous discourse "Carnival and Carnivalesque" in the book *Cultural Theory and Popular Culture* explains that the carnival is a celebration where both the spectators and the performer are on the same platform. It is an upside-down world where all the rules, regulations, inhibitions and restrictions of the society are restricted. Bakhtin finds this as the scope to express the hidden repressed desires and behaviour of humanity which otherwise is illegitimate and unacceptable. It is an opportunity to unite tradition and modernity, sacred and pleasurable, old and new. Hawthorne's description of the New England Holiday anticipates such reversal when the adorable minister of respect and reverence will confess his sin. With enough irony Hawthorne hints at Dimmesdale's final involvement with the society by confessing his repressed guilt. According to Bakhtin, the core of the carnivalsque sense of the world lies in the pathos of changes and renewal, of death and rebirth. While Dimmesdale will meet the end of his life, Pearl will gain a new identity with the acknowledgement of her father. It is this excess of significance that will heighten the carnivalesque element in this chapter. The strong military presence "which still sustains a corporate existence, and marches down from past ages with an ancient and honourable fame" (*SL* 354) ironically suggests that even on the day of the occasion, the society is under control and surveillance. The military then represents the mere vanity and illusory aspect of the contemporary life much like Dimmesdale and Hester Prynne's dream to escape from New England. Hawthorne in his tale "The May-Pole of Merry Mount" suggests similar ubiquitous power of the military force. The evil manoeuvring of Chillingworth is just a predicament to remind Hester that freedom is a far-fetched dream. The deep sense of foreboding and gloom hang large behind the festive mood. The mirthful dream is soon to be shattered.

After commenting on the socio-political scenario, the narrator concentrates on Hester's psychological turmoil at the appearance of Dimmesdale. Even before Hester can resolute firmly and get a grasp to contemplate on Chillingworth's plan, the music and the procession of ministers almost defuses her every attempt. It is as if fate has not decided to favour her and the entire world seems to be conspiring against her futile attempt. Hester's trouble lies in the fact that she can neither reaffirm with complete assurance her bold deviating love nor disavows it completely. There is a dualism in Hester's spirit to bridge memory and hope, self and society, nature and culture, past, present and future—all of which are not reconcilable and is antagonist to each other. We can say that there are two selves in Hester Prynne—the antinomian and the other is American. The antinomian Hester makes her feel that she is the maker of her own destiny, while the American self allows her to be patient and to conform to the society. To reconcile the conflict between the self and the society is a vain attempt and her world of happiness with Dimmesdale and Pearl is therefore utopian. Hence though towards the end of the novel the readers may expect reconciliation, one cannot forget that there is no coherent pattern in any of the characters aiming for reconciliation. The ambiguity and ironies are inherent in each of these characters as these characters are part of social cohesion. The minister now appears to her to be dwelling in some another world and her dream of union is remote. The forest rendezvous seems obscure and illusionary and Hester suddenly realises that Dimmesdale is detached from her. There is a strange sense of betrayal in Hester as she feels the pang of Dimmesdale's willing separation. She has always suffered and felt the anguish of the father of her child but now she realises that it has not been mutual reciprocal suffering.

The intervention of the character of Mistress Hibbins foreshadows the tragic ending and the intuitive understanding of human hearts. The premonition of the old witch is like a warning that explains that the minister's sin will soon be publicly acknowledged. She further reminds that humanity cannot trifle against nature so that the forest keeps a record of all the secrets of humanity. Just like dried leaves and twigs that are left on one's body as a trail, similarly the forest has some strange impact on human soul to be pure and transparent. The reference is to human sin, temptation, frailty and emotions. The world may remain unaware, but here the narrator is trying to intertwine neatly the plot of the novel by bringing Hester, Dimmesdale and Pearl together. As Dimmesdale moves closer to his end of his life, conventions come into firm accord with nature. The introduction of the figure of mysterious Mistress Hibbins "who, arrayed in great magnificence, with a triple ruff, a broidered stomacher, a gown of rich velvet, and a gold-headed cane" (*SL* 360) is interesting as Hawthorne wants to suggest the struggle between the evil and good force over the possession of the soul. The reference is to destiny of humanity in Christian theology about the choice of good and evil. Mistress Hibbins represents those outcast legions who belong to the darker world propounded by the Puritanical religious dictators. Her voice seems to be like Satan's voice reminding Hester about the hidden secrets and dark wishes cherished by the two lovers.

New England Congregationalists inherited this tradition of good Election Sermon long time back and is considered to be the most essential part of the ceremony to inform and convince the community about the leader. In colonial New England, the words of the preacher are of great influence especially because of the Calvinist belief that all humanity should remain within the jurisdiction of God's words. In Massachusetts, Election Day was a colony-wide holiday. Although the ceremony is initiated with music, military exercises and procession of government officials from the seat of government to a nearby church, but the most important aspect of it is the sermon. The sermon is meant not only for common men but also for the most politically and socially important members of community. Dimmesdale's sermon is expected to be extraordinarily electrifying because of his already proven oratorical flair. His Election Day Sermon will be the jeremiad that will insinuate the hope of a Promised Land. The term jeremiad is extremely significant in the context of New England Election Sermon as it refers to the Old Testament prophet Jeremiah, who in the seventh century B.C. attributed the calamities of Israel to its abandonment of the covenant with Jehovah and its return to pagan idolatry. He reflected upon religious and moral iniquities, and summoned the people to repent so that Jehovah might restore them and renew the ancient covenant. This Election Sermon which is a jeremiad is defined by Sacvan Bercovitch as—

> a mode of public exhortation that originated in the European pulpit, was transformed in both form and content by the New England Puritans, persisted through the eighteenth century, and helped sustain a national dream through two hundred years of turbulence and change.[43]

Dimmesdale's jeremiad is full of ironies because though the sermon is meant as a social criticism about the sin and evil of the community in the past, he will speak also about his own sin and deviation from Christian righteousness. Dimmesdale as the chosen minister to deliver the sermon is supposed to be like an Old Testament prophet. The sermon is an opportunity to mark the commencement of a new political year but on the contrary it marks the end of his life. Hawthorne describes with such gravity the appearance of Arthur Dimmesdale like a divine presence:

> Next in order to the magistrates came the young and eminently distinguished divine, from whose lips the religious discourse of the anniversary was expected. (*SL* 356)

People are shocked to see the extravagant energy in the same man who appeared always to be on the brink of death. His sermon is an allegorical embodiment of his own life and his impending death. Hawthorne's narrator comments that the source of such unbounded energy in Dimmesdale is not from his body but some remotest corner of his mind. His sermon has the strange confluence of passion, love, catechism, pathos, tenderness, repentance and the hope of resurrection. The flame in his speech is of love and passion of suffering. He is almost enshrined with a divine spirit. The spectrum of humanity witnesses already a transmogrification in Dimmesdale. Though his body is the same pale weak one, yet he carries a resurrected spirit that is hardly aware of anything earthly in his surroundings. This change foreshadows the ending. Such oblivious aspect is no longer ruled by his speculative rational self but by some 'preternatural' force. Dimmesdale's unwillingness to recognise Hester by glancing towards her is only to recognise her more dramatically at the final moment of his confession. Hawthorne wants to reflect on the question of will of the mind over the body. The body of flesh and blood which is the medium of his sin is decrepit and is full of morbid hatred of the minister himself. It seems as if he is now heightened with intense will to destroy completely this living epitome of sin. But unlike his fatal imbecile body, his mind is in full vigour to perform the last ritual. It is the time when the soul must transcend the sensual body by disintegration of the soul from the abject body.

Interestingly Hawthorne never elucidates and includes the exact sermon of Dimmesdale in the text. A sermon is always didactic in nature but this time Dimmesdale's mesmeric sermon has a personal tone in it. His elocution appears to be like music so that his—

> vocal organ was itself a rich endowment, insomuch that a listener, comprehending nothing of the language in which the preacher spoke, might still have been swayed to and fro by the mere tone and cadence. (*SL* 363)

The sermon has the immense power to absorb the listener but will never allow any intervention by any one of them. Whether this spectacular oratory power stems from his weakness or strength to confront his sin publicly is not so clear but it appeared to Hester that the sermon was especially meant for her. Hawthorne has emphasised that Dimmesdale's weakness is his power and the sermon on the Election Day unites his divided two selves—private and public.

Lastly Pearl's interaction with the mariner of the ship and her bullying that she is the child of a Prince and not of a witch is intriguing at this point. Since Pearl's father will soon be reckoned and Dimmesdale for the first time will acknowledge his own daughter, Pearl seems to be supernaturally confident and is not afraid to confront the crowd of Salem.

CHAPTER TWENTY THREE—THE REVELATION OF *THE SCARLET LETTER*

The long enchanting phase of the Election Sermon is now over. The minister's heavenly majestic voice has become silent and incoherent. The people have come out of a long enamouring spell and when the crowd disperses from the church, it seems that they are released from a fiery atmosphere surcharged with addictive perfume. The approbation about the minister's breathless sermon and his captivating personality have created a magical effect which can be felt in the air of the market place where everyone is bursting with their gushing praise about the Reverend Arthur Dimmesdale. Such beatific oracle appears to them as someone possessed with divine spirit. They are impressed as the minister concentrated on the relationship between God and humanity in the wilderness of New England. He sounds like a prophet but his melancholic tone always floated in the air which cannot be overlooked. They sense this as a kind of forlorn of a man shortly departing from this earth so that the angels from heaven have showered him with divine words which he uttered as the ultimate message from God.

The sound of the band continues as the militia proceeds towards the town hall where a banquet will bring in conclusion of this great ceremony. As the procession moves forward, the over enthusiastic people shouted in praise of the minister and his spectacular speech. Perhaps this is the first time in the history of New England; a man is being honoured with such high gratitude. It seems an imaginary sparkling halo round the man's head as his high spirit descends to the ground in the midst of the Salem community. They wonder at the pale man whose fire seems to have extinguished into a dying ember. Reverend John Wilson watching the decrepit pale condition of the minister extended his hand to support him but the minister refused and in trembling steps, he moved forward as if like a little toddler in wavering steps he is approaching his destination. The band proceeded forward but the minister stopped at the platform where Hester with her little baby has been punished seven years back. Governor Bellingham who has been keeping an eye on Arthur because of his excessive physical weakness and decline of health, suddenly felt the impulse to help him but something in the minister's expression prevented him. The entire crowd of Salem is taken aback and all their focus turns to Arthur Dimmesdale.

Taking the names of Hester and Pearl, Dimmesdale called them loudly in front of the crowd. Pearl, like a flying bird immediately ran and embraced the minister's knee with great affection. Slowly against her will, Hester Prynne moved forward anticipating the impending doom. All of a sudden, the old malicious physician Roger Chillingworth, as if emerging from hell, rushed in and whispered in the minister's ear in order to prevent him from his anticipated action. He suggests him not to ruin his fame and die in dishonour. Arthur boldly answers the doctor saying that he is powerful enough to overcome the physician's evil power. Dauntlessly, he approaches Hester

Prynne repeating her name and exclaiming that he has gathered his strength to proclaim what he should have done seven years back. He publicly dismissed the physician's attempt to hold him back and pines for Hester's strength and support in this last and crucial hour of his life. The entire crowd of Salem seems to be completely lost in some frenzy including the men of status and rank. They are awe stricken, numbed and passive watching the inconceivable scene. They are in an inconceivable condition to witness the scene where the minister leaning on Hester's shoulder and holding the hand of the illegitimate Pearl is moving forward. The physician also followed them since he has also been an active player in this drama and should be there in the concluding scene.

Arthur in the presence of the entire community clarifies to Hester that perhaps this is better than what they had planned in the forest. He proclaims that he has received the indication from the Almighty to execute this final action before death comes in as he can sense that he is near the end of life. With his solemn majestic voice he addresses the people of New England who seem to be flooded in a mixed emotion of fear and sympathy for the man of high reverence who now seems to be ready for redemption. He confesses that he is the greatest sinner in the world whom they have mistakenly admired and cherished. He asserts that they have impugned Hester Prynne with her burning scarlet letter as an outcast but failed to shudder at the sinful man in disguise among them. He affirms that when his strength seems to be ebbing away, Hester's arms provide him with immeasurable strength for the divine justice. For a moment it seems that the minister is not left with enough life to complete his pledge but with all his last vestige of strength, he avows to the world that he is the man who has been constantly under the vigilance of angel and the evil spirit because of his sin which he should have confessed seven years back. People have seen only the scarlet letter burning on Hester's bosom but he declares that they have not seen the same hidden letter which he wears on secretly his bosom. He exemplifies himself as the living example of God's punishment upon a sinner. As the minister reaped of his garment to reveal the scarlet letter, he crumbled on the stage and reclining on Hester's bosom he addresses the doctor for God's mercy who has equally sinned in the whole act. Chillingworth is shattered and seeing his object of prey perishing, his entire life force is drained away. With abundant love, the minister asks Pearl for her precious kiss which she denied in the forest. As Pearl kissed her father, her drops of tears on her father's cheek symbolise that she is no more an object of shame but achieved a new dimension in her character in order to evolve from wild infant to a beautiful woman of joy and sorrow.

Hester abandoned in boundless pain asks for eternal reunion in heaven as they have survived the misery in this world. The minister bidding final goodbye to Hester feels hardly any such hope as he recalls the burning torture that he has been bearing all these years aggravated further by the arrival of the evil physician and finally the shameful death which he meets at the end. Arthur Dimmesdale's soul departs and the entire crowd shocked and bewildered whispers among themselves that hushed in the entire atmosphere where their beloved minister's soul has sublimated.

Commentary

All the principal characters are brought in together to mark the climactic end. It marks the triumph of Dimmesdale even at the end of his life because he succeeds in preserving his elevated self-image through his miraculous oration. Arthur Dimmesdale's ironical speech is often seen as reflection of the speech of William Arthur in 1850, the year when *The Scarlet Letter* is published. Dimmesdale's personality is immersed in his speech. What the minister utters is not as important as the way he delivers the speech. Hawthorne explains the effect of such speech as a kind of passionate absorption and hypnotization of the listeners:

> In a moment more the crowd began to gush forth from the doors of the church. Now that there was an end, they needed more breath, more fit to support the gross and earthly life into which they relapsed, than that atmosphere which the preacher had converted into words of flame, and had burdened with the rich fragrance of his thought. (*SL* 370)

It seems that during the outpouring of speech, the audience is held back with some cosmological force. As if there is some transformative magical power in the minister which transfixed the audience but perhaps Hawthorne is trying to hint that if someone has this power of rhetoric in oration, then it is easy to drive the audience to any kind of persuasion. The magical power of human language can be so strong that the residual impact can transform or withhold one's thought process. The Neoplatonic philosopher of Italian Renaissance Marsilio Ficino explained that an orator and a magus are similar. A perfect orator accommodates his discourse to the multiplicity of human soul while a magus accommodates invocation to the movement of the stars. Ficino believed that man's imagination is the primary faculty which utilises the corporeal objects and the incorporeal subject in speech. Human mind exists in matter and language invokes those matters to affect the mind. Each word of Dimmesdale therefore acts like a talisman, magic power that induces belief in the way he wants. The great avalanche is poetically described by Hawthorne:

> It was as if an angel, in his passage to the skies, had shaken his bright wings over the people for an instant—at once a shadow and a splendour—and had shed down a shower of golden truths upon them. (*SL* 372)

This is Dimmesdale's not only oratorical triumph but also a paean of triumph of his forging reputation. In his sense of repentance and guilt, actually he has developed an alliance and intimacy between himself and the listeners. They are caught up in the spell of same powerful emotions as the minister himself. The overflowing emotion is both personal communication as well as general comment on the election and god's decision.

One can get confused at the singular power of Dimmesdale's speech about his role as an orator or a leader. His linguistic ingenuity and deep seated desire for worldly fame have erased the line between orator and leader. His "Tongue of Flame" among magistrates and other ministers who could hardly make a distinction between intellectual and literary acumen appeared divinely. Therefore, even at the penultimate moment of his life, his confession is evasive and ambiguous. The crowd has not received anything substantial about religion, god, faith or government from Dimmesdale's speech yet the entire space seems to be 'babbled' under the effect of the 'eloquent voice' of the minister. Hawthorne is posing doubt and distrust about the power of speech and discourse which need not be always truthful. He is reflecting upon the power of words and the danger of double edged words. Dimmesdale's speech is not merely a reflection of the power of the ministers over the community but it also shows the multi-faceted potentialities and deceptiveness of words. It is self-satisfactory as well as open ended for the audience to draw their own conclusions. Dimmesdale with his extraordinary play of words continued his hypocrisy till the last moment of his life. If Chillingworth has used words as the alchemy of his malice and revenge, so also Dimmesdale has used the same words as his weapon to defeat him. At the same time in his speech Dimmesdale has ventriloquized with Hester and Pearl. The end of Dimmesdale can be seen as a day of triumph but his affectation is so strong that even in the name of divinity he remained an imposter. Hawthorne compares him to an angel who in his oration seems to be lavishing shower of golden truths from his wings.

The minister soon chooses to discard all support while walking towards the scaffold. He rejects support of John Wilson, Bellingham and others because he wants to bear the burden of his own sin. He only summoned Hester and Pearl for the final acknowledgement of his sin in the company of his joint sinners. Actually Dimmesdale has chosen to break his personal covenant with Hester and chose public confession as a way to his repentance. By inviting Hester and Pearl, he does not intend to embrace them proudly but his purpose is to compel the woman and her child to accept socially sanctioned public shame along with him. But for Hester Prynne public judgement, forgiveness and sanctity are not required of as long as both she and Dimmesdale consider their love to be true. As a result she remained unconvinced as she expressed "I know not! I know not" (*SL* 379).

When Dimmesdale tears of his robe to expose the scarlet letter on his breast, it still appeared an evasive disclosure. Hawthorne perhaps hints that the art of disclosure sometimes conceals more than what is displays. The narrator comments that the multitude is "exceedingly apt to be deceived" and so the interpretations of the inscription on his chest varied. One has to note that Dimmesdale has shown rather than spoke of his secret relationship with Hester Prynne. His art of public obfuscation is heightened as his actions lack clarity of his words. If the audience is unwilling to accept the truth, then Hawthorne is suggesting that it is the blindness of the people. What Hawthorne wants to hint is that the people of the Puritanical society are incapable to discern the truth because they are blinded by their own guilt. They see those words with their idiosyncratic limitations. Their conclusion about the character of Dimmesdale and Hester is the outcome of their repression of their own desires and denial of their passions. This art of reader's choice is seen in Hawthorne himself who has never transparently opined or supported the controversies of his age. Even the readers cannot assert fully whether Hawthorne has supported Hester Prynne's act of violation of the Puritanical ethics or criticised it with premonition of destruction. So both Dimmesdale and his creator have avoided direct affirmation. The trick is captured when Dimmesdale unbuttons and just utters "it were irreverent to describe that revelation". Hence, we cannot conclude that Dimmesdale is lying because of the ambiguity with which he ends. He has now refused to continue his conscious life as a hypocrite in contrast to Hester Prynne who remained as the glaring example of Thoreau-like possibility of truthfulness. Arthur Dimmesdale therefore represents everyman who transgresses and throws the first stone of hypocrisy.

There is however, a calm recognition in the man that escapism is not the route of survival. He therefore asserts Hester that his final decision to confess and repent is better than escaping from New England. Though Arthur abandons Hester's plan of elopement yet he requires Hester's strength and support till the end. His tormenting soul is relieved because he seems to have realised his victory over Chillingworth by relieving himself from the bondage of his over caring physician. Dimmesdale has always been self-seeking and hence he can be self-justifying by asking Hester whether confession is better than escape but unlikely Hester's comment is more realistic when she expresses her loneliness and Pearl's fatherless identity in absence of

Dimmesdale. Hester Prynne has always been hopeful and faithful in her burden of shame but now at this penultimate point of union, she realises that her dream of reunion is illusion and in reality she is far away from the minister. When Hester pledges the minister for a life of togetherness in eternity, Dimmesdale tries to reinforce the sin that they have committed which society perceives as the violation of sanctity of relationship. When he hushed up Hester by reminding her that the past cannot be erased from the memory but exists in the present, the minister is more self-centred and least concerned about Hester and her daughter. He is aware of Hester's revolutionary spirit but refuses to ally with her especially in supporting a woman transgressing social restrictions. Dimmesdale thus reinforces that no one can escape the moral physics of the Puritanical world. This is the cultural strategy of control where the most difficult task is to escape the narrow essentialism of the society.

Strangely for the first time we also witness that Pearl with her innocent instinct kissed her father as he dares to recognise his child. The filial affection between the father and the child is so pure that Hawthorne explains that the spell is now broken and the milk of humanity will be in abundant in Pearl. Pearl's life has always been marked by the absent of the father figure. Dimmesdale's acknowledgement of Pearl is a step to give relief to Pearl's psychological turmoil about the mysterious identity of her father. It is as if she is legitimated by Dimmesdale's tears and confession which will further be completed by Chillingworth at the end by declaring Pearl as his heir. Dimmesdale though finally provides redemptive grace to Pearl but never with simplicity proclaimed that he is the father of the child. Definitely Hawthorne at this point enriches the sentimental culture of nineteenth century:

> Pearl kissed his lips. A spell was broken. The great scene of grief, in which the wild infant bore a part, had developed all her sympathies; and as her tears fell upon her father's cheek, they were the pledge that she would grow up amid human joy and sorrow, nor for ever do battle with the world, but be a woman in it. Towards her mother, too,

> Pearl's errand as a messenger of anguish was all fulfilled. (*SL* 382)

Chillingworth on the other hand ends with motiveless life as he once more becomes a loser. The hunter has lost his object of hunting with the demise of Dimmesdale. His incessant torture inflicted upon the minister has always been his life force and his medication to his affronted shameful heart. Above all, the dying minister has blessed him retaining his reverence and his kindness by asking God's forgiveness for Chillingworth. His superiority became the reason of his victorious end while the physician failed to withhold him. The physician thus remained a social ineptitude so that the reason of his resentment is now his existence without the person to be avenged. He is sabotaged when the object of his rage is gone. Having lost the body on which he has preyed, he has lost his own soul and now his potency is vanquished.

It seems that during the outpouring of speech the audience is held back with some cosmological force. As if there is some transformative magical power in the minister but perhaps Hawthorne is trying to hint that if someone has this power of rhetoric in oration, then it is easy to drive the audience to any kind of persuasion. The magical power of human language can be so strong that the residual impact can transform or withhold one's thought process. The Neoplatonic philosopher of Italian Renaissance Marsilio Ficino explained that an orator and a magus are similar. A perfect orator accommodates his discourse to the multiplicity of human soul while a magus accommodates invocation to the movement of the stars. Ficino believed that man's imagination is the primary faculty which utilises the corporeal objects and the incorporeal subject in speech. That is human mind exists in matter and language invokes those matters to affect the mind. Each word of Dimmesdale therefore acts like a talisman, magic power that induces belief in the way he wants. The great avalanche is poetically described by Hawthorne:

> It was as if an angel, in his passage to the skies, had shaken his bright wings over the people for an instant—at once a shadow and a splendour—and had shed down a shower of golden truths upon them. (*SL* 372)

This is Dimmesdale's not only oratorical triumph but also a paean of triumph of his forging reputation. In his sense of repentance and guilt, actually he has developed an alliance and intimacy between himself and the listeners. They are caught up in the spell of same powerful emotions as the minister himself. The overflowing emotion is both personal communication as well as general comment on the election and god's decision.

CHAPTER TWENTY FOUR—CONCLUSION

Several days passed and it took time for the community to recover from the shock that they have withstood on the Election Day. Rumours are heard all through the town regarding the mysterious symbol on the minister's chest. Some assert that they have witnessed the burning scarlet letter on the minister's breast; some believe that minister's scarlet letter is visible once old Chillingworth applied some magical power on Dimmesdale and many people also assert that the minister inflicted himself with torture from the day when Hester Prynne has started wearing the scarlet letter on her bosom. Another version of the story is that the alphabet is a natural heavenly rendition of the minister's constant remorse and guilt conscience. On the other hand, the ministerial group explains that they have not seen any mark on the minister's body but it was as bare as a new born babe. They feel that there is no connection between the ministers's dying words and Hester Prynne. They justify it as the minister's humbleness to die in the arms of the most sinful woman since the entire community treated him as divine incarnation. His sensational death has become a parable in Salem and the people believe that the minister wants to preach a lesson to the human race about sin and purgation.

In the meanwhile after the death of the minister, the physician underwent a terrible change in his appearance and all his intelligence seem to have lost in oblivion. He appears shrivelled, wearied and all his strength and power seem to have drained away. He vanished into oblivion after his game of revenge is over. The narrator comments that after the death of the physician, it can be that their hatred for each other is transmogrified into love. The narrator contemplates on the binary opposite human emotions—love and hate which are intrinsically related to each other and are remarkably same as they are directed toward humanity.

The narrator provides some significant concluding information at the end of the story. Roger Chillingworth died within one year after the minister's death. His great property in Boston and England are left in the name of Pearl. Pearl's inheritance of the enormous property turned her status from elf-child to the richest heiress in the New World and if they would have continued to stay in New England, she could have been wife of the most devout Puritan. After the physician's death, Hester and Pearl disappeared all of a sudden and rumours are only heard in the air. The story of the scarlet letter has been transformed into a legend as people recollect with awe the platform where the minister breathed last time and also Hester's cottage by the seashore where the most aberrant woman of Salem lived. Several years later, one afternoon Hester Prynne once more appeared in her cottage to re-live her life of shame. She is wearing the same grey robe with the scarlet letter embroidered on it. Hester is now afraid to enter alone the same cottage where she lived for several years. No one knows whether Pearl is alive or her wild aberrant nature has transformed into womanhood of beauty and gentility. The only thing that one knows is that there is someone in England who cares about old Hester Prynne as it is evident in the letters affixed with stamp of nobility that Hester received and the also in the expensive luxurious gifts that decorated her cottage but never used by the old lady. It is believed that Hester is once seen making a baby's dress with such prettiest and costly embroidery that no child in the Salem community has ever seen to be wearing.

The narrator asserts that Mr. Surveyor Prue, from whose manuscript he revived the anecdote of Hester Prynne has assured that Pearl is alive and happily married. She is extremely caring of her mother but Hester has chosen the land of penitence where love, sin and repentance have given a new dimension to her life. Till her last day, the scarlet letter never parts from her body. Hester till the end, lived for the interest of humanity and rescuing those fallen souls who suffer from trials of their passion or burden of being unloved by the world. She believes that being stained with sin, no mission of divinity can come to her. When Hester died, she is being buried beside Arthur Dimmesdale and in later days, the King's Chapel is being built beside their grave. On the tombstone one message is engraved which says "On a field of black, the letter A in scarlet."

Commentary

After tumultuous demise of Dimmesdale, this last chapter provides the conclusion to well-knit the plot. But Hawthorne never makes assertive conclusion and purposeful vagueness is left for reader's own decision. The gossip and confusion about the inscription on Dimmesdale's chest is open ended just to emphasise how difficult it is for the community to deconstruct their beloved minister's image. Though the author emphasised on 'Truth' but he never elucidated the ways to express the truth. The ambiguity surrounding the scarlet letter is heightened because the people of New England cannot destroy their faith in the integrity of the minister. No doubt that Dimmesdale feared to confess the truth since he was aware of the community's deep rooted faith in him. For some there has not been any inscription while for others it is due to some evil impact of the physician on the minister. Dimmesdale himself is the ambiguous representative of the Puritanical world and his words and their meanings are extrapolated with mystery. The ultimate message is about the delusion in the mind of the people of the age and their all-pervasive irrational belief. The exaggerated faith of the people in this minister reflects their illiteracy and blind faith in religion. Hawthorne with his psychological insight is sceptical about the role of religion that Puritanical society indoctrinated rigorously. Truth is a moral imperative for them. They fail to understand that like Dimmesdale they are caught in the same dilemma between reason and passion, mind and body. One cannot blame the community for their lack of rational analysis but it is the outcome of blind adherence to Puritanical views. Instead of understanding the subtle hypocrisy of the minister; it is easy for them to discern that Chillingworth is the necromancer who caused some evil impact on the minister. Dimmesdale is seen in the light of celibacy and hence they cannot think him as Hester's secret lover or Pearl's illegitimate father. So when Dimmesdale has uttered:—'Be true! Be true! Be true!', there lies endless irony. Truth is psychological and there is no universal truth. The emotional confusion, the psychological fragmentation, condemnation of Chillingworth and rejection to believe one's own eye all reflect that it is psychological and that these people are imprisoned within the fragile Puritanical limitations.

Chillingworth's demise is inevitable after the death of the minister. In his revenge scheme, Hester does not count and hence he is barren. In the chauvinist power grid, male envy and revenge is alive as long as the opposition remains. The physician vanished unknowingly just like the way he appeared on the day of the first scaffold scene. Hawthorne perhaps tried to reflect on the mystic conflict between nature and culture. Dimmesdale's self-imposed penance was as hypocritical as Chillingworth's meaningless revenge for Dimmesdale. It is a mockery of futility of human punishment where in the process each of them is eroded and perished. It seems that all the power of the old physician is dissolved and robbed by Dimmesdale at his death bed. Hawthorne's philosophy of love and hatred is interesting as it primarily focuses on the psychology of man. The emanation of love and hatred are same and Hawthorne equates them in the scale of human emotions. For him, love and hatred are alterable and hence destabilising. In Hawthorne's psychological introspection, he explains that if Hester Prynne in absence of Dimmesdale has lost the purpose of living, so is Roger Chillingworth's life has become meaningless without the minister. Such polarisations like love and hate, good and evil or beautiful and monstrous are all psychological extension of the human mind. He undermines such easy dualistic simple equations of life in terms of binary oppositions. His bold equation of love and hatred is justified when he entitled Pearl as the heir of his property in England and New England. So Hawthorne writes:

> ...the two passions seem essentially the same, except that one happens to be seen in a celestial radiance, and the other in a dusky and lurid glow. (*SL* 389)

Hester left New England after the death of the physician. This perhaps suggests that she cannot avoid her ennobling recognition or her responsibility towards her husband. Chillingworth's decision to entrust Pearl, the child of his enemy is unresolved by Hawthorne. We cannot forget that Chillingworth pacified the baby Pearl in the prison from unbearable pain. Dimmesdale has induced humanity in Pearl by announcing him as his earthly father in an implicit way. If Dimmesdale has usurped the position of being Hester's man of love, then Chillingworth has also usurped the role of the father of Pearl by entitling her as the owner of her property. There is a mysterious relationship between Pearl and her surrogate father. Pearl has always represented the sin that has tormented Hester while Chillingworth has represented the sin that has tormented Dimmesdale. Both appear at times mysterious and semi human. The physician's victory remains in embracing paternity when he bequeathed Pearl his properties. Dimmesdale throughout his life struggled and hesitated to claim his own flesh and blood as his own but Chillingworth easily claimed his paternity when Pearl's existence is actually a continuation of his own existence as Pearl is recognised as Pearl Prynne.

The ambiguity of Pearl's adult life is purposely left unresolved by Hawthorne. Pearl's later life after marriage remained in oblivion and the readers are informed that she lived a long happy married life. Her elevation in economic status is significant. Pearl has deviated from the restrictions of the Puritans by not marrying a Puritan and Hawthorne notes that her life is completely untouched by all the past hazards. Pearl carrying the same spirit of rejection of Puritanical belief remained away from the life of New England. What Hester dreamt in her life is perhaps fulfilled by Pearl in her choice to live a life of freedom and happiness. She carried within her the seed of emancipation. She is no more an 'elf-child' but has undergone complete transmutation as the alchemy of love is evident in her care for her mother.

Hester once more has the opportunity of not returning back to New England once she left it after Chillingworth's death but as ambiguity is the idiosyncrasy of Hawthorne's writing, no clear reason is given by the narrator why Hester chose to return in the cursed land. Whether it is the pang of unrequited love or the desire to cling to memories of her existence, it is left for the readers to decide. Even her individual choice to continue wearing the scarlet letter on her bosom is also unexplained. Throughout her life Hester with her individualism has chosen her own path. She decided to transgress by indulging in an unwanted relationship with Dimmesdale and giving birth to Pearl, she decided to keep away Pearl from the rigorous Puritanical upbringing, she chose to return back to the damned land and finally it was her choice to wear the scarlet letter proudly till the end of her life. If she wanted, she could have chosen to become the prophetess of enlightenment with a new philosophy of love but unlike Dimmesdale she is never bothered by the society. Dimmesdale always conveyed his ambiguous message through his speech but Hester speaks through her scarlet letter. After her death, the lovers cannot unite in their ashes of pain and suffering. Their graves are apart but they share common tombstone. Her scarlet letter at the end of her life became the object of love. While living at the fringe of the society, she has taught the society how to be a part of the community. She is the counsellor and articulator of emerging American values. Hawthorne ironically reflects that symbol is always in flux and is subjected to incessant interpretations. Life cannot fulfil Hester's dream but the symbol has reunited Hester and Dimmesdale as both of them lie under a single gravestone embellished with the scarlet alphabet 'A'. It is the symbol of their shame, guilt, torture, suffering, love but also the cause of their union. Nina Baym's essay, "Revisiting Hawthorne's Feminism," beautifully describes Hester Prynne as the new heroine of American Literature:

> In Hester Prynne, Hawthorne created the first true heroine of American fiction, as well as one of its enduring heroes. Hester is a heroine because she is deeply implicated in, and responsive to, the gender structure of her society, and because her story, turning on "love" is appropriate for a woman. She is a hero because she has qualities and actions that transcend their gender reference and lead to heroism as it can be understood for any one.[44]

Thus through his unique creation of an individualistic unparalleled heroine, Hawthorne has tried to represent an alternative world of existence.

NOTES

1. Nathaniel Hawthorne, *The Scarlet Letter*, Vol. I of *The Centenary Edition of the Worlds of Nathaniel Hawthorne*, ed. William Charvat et al. Ohio State Univ. Press, 1962, p. I.
2. Hawthorne, Nathaniel. *Twice-Told Tales*. American Stationers Co. 1837, p. 3.
3. James, Henry. *The Art of Criticism*. University of Chicago Press, 1986, p. 116.
4. Hawthorne, Nathaniel. *The House of Seven Cables: A Romance*. Routledge and Co. 1852, p. 185.
5. See notes at the end of the book.
6. Smith, Adam. *The Theory of Moral Sentiments*. Oxford University Press, 1976, p. 234.
7. Hawthorne, Nathaniel. *The American Notebook*. Ohio State University Press, 1972, p. 25.
8. Emerson, Everett. Ed. *Major Writers of Early American Literature* University of Wisconsin Press, 1976, p. 36.
9. Hawthorne, Nathaniel. *Selected Tales and Sketches (the Best Short Stories of Nathaniel Hawthorne)*. Digireads.com Publishing, 2007, p. 286.
10. A De Salvo, Louise. *Nathaniel Hawthorne: Feminist Readings*. Humanities Press International, 1987, p. 12.
11. Matriphobia is hatred and loathing for motherhood due to sexual fidelity.
12. Ralph Waldo Emerson has written an essay called "The Self-reliance". In this essay Emerson explains that self-trust is the most essential thing for individual spirit. The self-trust is the first things that society tries to dominate. In solitude the self-trust is evident as the individual voice is audible but it becomes faint and inaudible in the midst of the crowd. Emerson supported that every individual should discover onself even in the midst of the crowd and the cultivated self must confront the society with full confidence.
13. Bloom, Harold. Ed. *Hester Prynne*. Chelsa House, 2004, p. 23.
14. Scopophilia is the term derived from Sigmund Freud's concept of 'Schaulus'. The root is in the Greek meaning of deriving pleasure in looking. Freud has talked about the natural instinct, intense desire

and curiosity to see a woman's body. Otto Fenichel also discussed about the child's libidinous desire.

15. Stannard, E. David. Ed. *The Puritan Way in Death: A Study in Religion, Culture and Social Changes*. Oxford University Press, 1977, p. 49.
16. Winthrop, John. *The Journal of John Winthrop*. Harvard University Press, 1996, p. 254.
17. Goetz, Anne Rebecca. *The Baptism of Early Virginia: How Christianity Created Race*. JHU Press, 2012, p. 1623.
18. 'City Upon the Hills' is a phrase from the parable of Salt and Light in Jesus' Sermon of the Mount. This phrase was popularised by John Winthrop in his sermon to reflect that America as the emerging nation with the dream of a god's kingdom will be watched by the world. Winthrop's sermon gave popularised belief that United States of America is God's country because metaphorically it is a Shining City upon a Hill, an early example of American exceptionalism.
19. Foucault, Michel. *Power/Knwoledge. Selected Interviews and Other Writings*. 1972-77. Pantheon Books, 1985.
20. Turner, Jack. *A Political Companion to Henry David Thoreau*. University Press of Kentucky, 2009, p. 230.
21. Gibran, Khalil. *The Prophet*. The Floating Press, 2009, p. 37.
22. Herbert, T Walter. *Dearest Beloved: The Hawthornes and the Making of the Middle-Class Family*. University of California Press, 1995, p. 145.
23. Friedman, Lawrence. *Crime and Punishment in American History*. Basic Books, 1993, p. 32.
24. The term 'Moral Hospital' is Theodore Parker's tropes in his book *A Sermon of the Dangerous Classes in Society*, Preached, Jan. 31.
25. Dickens, Charles. *American notes For General Circulation*. Baudry's European Library, 1842, pp. 146-47.
26. Blake, William. *The Tyger*. Harcourt Brace & Company, 1993
27. Upham, Thomas. *The Interior Life*. Harper & Bros, 1843, p. 394.
28. Field, James. *The Atlantic Monthly*. Atlantic Monthly Company, 1871, p. 508.
29. Aquinas, Thomas. *Summa Theologica I-II*, trans. Father of the English Dominican Province. Mobile Reference, 2010, p. 32.
30. Whitman, Walt. *Leaves of Grass: First and Death-Bed Editions*. Spark Educational Publishing, 2004, p. 263.
31. Woolf, Virginia. *Mrs Dalloway*. Interactive Media, 2012, p. 64.
32. Littlewood, Ian. *Sultry Climates: Travel And Sex*. Da Capo Press, 2003, p. 68.

33. Myerson, Joel. *Fuller in Her Own Time: A Biographical Chronicle of Her Life*, Drawn from Recollections, Interviews, and Memoirs by Family, Friends, and Associates; University of Iowa Press, 2008, p. 173.
34. Grenville, Bruce. *The Uncanny: Experiments in Cyborg Culture*. Arsenal Pulp Press, 2002, p. 249.
35. Wordsworth, William. *Poems by William Wordsworth: Including Lyrical Ballads, and the Miscellaneous Pieces of the Author. With Additional Poems, a New Preface, and a Supplementary Essay*. Longman, 1815, p. 313.
36. American Dark Romanticism is a literary subgenre and it primarily reflects human fallibility to sin and self-destruction. The writers consisted of mainly Edgar Allan Poe, Nathaniel Hawthorne and Herman Melville. It relates to the grotesque, gloomy and morbid aspects of life. This group of writers explored the dark vision of human existence and emphasised on emotion, nature and individual. Violence and suspense are also part of the plot in Dark Romanticism.
37. Peattie, Roger W. Ed. *Selected Letters of William Michael Rossetti*. Penn State Press, 2010, p. 154.
38. Milton, John. *Il Penseroso*. Oxford University Press, 1876, p. 27.
39. Lewis, RWB. *The American Adam*. University of Chicago Press, 1955, p. 14.
40. *Ibid.*
41. Lawrence, D.H. *Studies in Classic American Literature*. Volume 2 Cambridge University Press, 2003, p. 81.
42. Hawthorne, Nathaniel. *Hawthorne's Short Stories*. Random House LLC, 2011, p. 168.
43. Bercovitch, Sacvan. *The American Jeremiad*. The University of Wisconsin Press, 1978, p. xi.
44. Baym, Nina. *The Scarlet Letter: A Reading*. Twayne, 1986, p. 98.

Chapter 4

HISTORICAL ECHOES AND PURITANICAL IDEALS IN *THE SCARLET LETTER*

The Scarlet Letter is often claimed to be a historical romance and the popularity of historical romance in American literature is unsurpassable in comparison to any other genres. Historical romance has been the most fashionable choice of readers for almost two centuries. The genesis of this popular genre in America can be traced back to nineteenth century when Walter Scott in Edinburgh published his Waverley reflecting on 1745 Jacobite rebellion.[1] Waverley novels provided a classic paradigm to show the freedom and advantages of novelists who can reflect on historical conflicts and transform the historical narrative into fictional form. Hawthorne could scarcely ignore the example of Scott or escape its influence. When Hawthorne decided to write *The Scarlet Letter*, he reconnoitred the advantages of a romance that suggests an unrealistic world and therefore with abounding freedom can criticise in ruminating America's ambiguous historicity, origin as well as contemporary politics. What does history mean to Nathaniel Hawthorne? For Hawthorne, history is not merely records and data of war, annexation or battles but for him history is a struggle between the authority and the tradition on the one hand and the desires for revolution and transformation on the other. *The Scarlet Letter* is a historical palimpsest where personal and universal histories converge. It reflects also simultaneously on transatlantic history relating to the English Civil War and rhetoric of native liberty. It underscores the cultural, political and religious origin of American national history. Besides, Hawthorne has also been aware of the various historical acts like the Indian Removal Acts,[2] the annexation of western territories and war with Mexico, the Fugitive Slave Law,[3] the 1848 Women's Convention in Seneca Falls,[4] History of the Quakers, the Married Women's Property Acts[5] and the spectre of the European revolutions of 1848[6]—all of which are echoed in the life of every individual Americans.

Hawthorne's desire to travel back into the ancient Puritanical world of New England is an anachronism if not an unjust assessment. Hawthorne has advocated a very modern approach to reinvestigate the past by examining it in the light of the present. Hawthorne has invented a fictional predecessor, Jonathan Prue, who inspired to unearth some intriguing history unnoticed and unknown to the world. Hawthorne reflects that the process of making history is a collection of personal and philosophical interpretation affected by the historian's ideologies. *The Scarlet Letter* is a novel that raises question about history and truth, judgment and punishments and the conflict between publicly trumpeted or imposed values and private decisions. By walking into history, he explored the definition of 'crime' and the authority to punish. Hawthorne's Puritanical New England reveals its townships, busy marketplaces, rustic dwellings, jagged coastline, and dark forests. For Hawthorne, the panorama of geographical description with its own distinct boundaries is also a part of cultural history of early America. The scaffold, the prison, the forest, the graveyard and the scarlet letter evoke a cycle of social and individual trauma, exposure and redemption. Invoking the biblical motif of the Eden, Hawthorne reflects on the history of immigration to the New World. The reason for immigration is to avoid temptation, vice, moral corruption and the contamination of a materialistic over populated society. The new found land with its dark wilderness inhabited by 'savages' is to be transformed, cultivated, and converted to a civilised world. In *The Blithedale Romance*, Hawthorne shows how Chillingworth's high-minded plans imposed upon the society ruined human lives and in *The Scarlet Letter* he protests against moralistic utopianism. Society cannot be a prison and such totalitarian attempt for utopian dream is evident in the production, disruption and reproduction of power. Emerging from the prison house and moving towards the scaffold, from secluded marginalised cabin at the outskirt of civilization, to city, market and finally to the cemetery, Hester Prynne has always been a threat to disrupt the pyramidal power structure of the society. The scaffold as a place of the pillory is invested with socio-political significance. Hester's bodily presence on the scaffold is immediately invested with significance of sin, crime and punishment. The baby within her folded arms becomes the physical symbol of sin. Tim Cresswell's notion of "appropriateness" in his book *In Place/Out of Place: Geography, Ideology, and Transgression*[7] is significant in this regard as Cresswell reveals how the "practice" of a particular behaviour in a particular place produces a set of cultural beliefs and gradually that cultural belief is appropriated. So Hester's presence on the scaffold is convincing enough that she is a sinful woman. Thus in this way, the Puritanical world initiated Hester into the hateful exciting gaze of the community where the discourse of sex, crime and women are coerced with new meanings. As an object of surveillance, Hester is banished at the societal fringe and yet subjected to derision when she entered the town. The margin and the borders between the town and the natural forest suggest the Puritanical stringent division between civilized and uncivilized, culture and nature and between control and uncontrolled savage world.

Hawthorne has always supported and believed in American federal union and supported enhancement of individual liberty and democracy. The Preface titled "Custom House" is invested with historical determinative ranging from autobiographical, ancestral to political and universal facets. Hawthorne's role as a governmental surveyor in the Salem Custom House reflects not only autobiographical elements but also his own implicit political rivalry and his role of a writer critically surveying his dusty heap of cultural histories, custom and ideologies of his race. He is a cultural theorist who has seen the emerging American culture under critical lens. With a self-critical perspective he also viewed history of his forefathers exploring beyond the ostensible ideological preferences and biasness. *The Scarlet Letter* reflects upon the history of Salem ranging from Puritanical settlement, religious bigotry, culture, habits, witch-hunting, slavery, unlawful displacement and genocide of the Indians to corruption of ecclesiastical life, social regulations and repressions and limitation of medical science. Hawthorne clearly mentions that the story of *The Scarlet Letter* is the product of "the period of hardly accomplished revolution, and still seething turmoil, in which the story shaped itself" (*SL* 68). The combative history of the Whigs and the Democrats and Hawthorne's political inclination is undeniable and irrefutable. The story starts from autobiographical meditation from contemporary present to seventeenth century past. The most controversial issue of Hawthorne losing his job with the rise of the Whigs and his opinion regarding the corrupt custom officers is an attempt to investigate the polemical context of the Whig's movement for moral reform in antebellum America. The Custom House is an autobiographical allegory that argues through the narrator's voice what Hester Prynne later desired for—a utopian gender free world. This utopian vision is seen as the narrator's desire for an ideal world of personal freedom and thereby criticizing the attempt of the Whigs to impose restrictive moral norms. As an open dialogue with the past, Hawthorne invokes a spiritual and moral critique of colonial America. His dream of democracy in the United States is analogous to his dream as a writer—the act of giving an egalitarian voice to the sublime.

Hawthorne' struggle to perceive his own identity and also to embody distinctively American national literature, lead him to trace the ancestral affiliations and roots of first settlement in the new found land. The journey involves travelling back from contemporary geographical and political boundaries to a collective national consciousness of history. This obviously leads him to the riddle of Puritanical settlement, its moral, religious and gender codes and the role of his ancestors. 'Puritan' is the name given in the sixteenth century to the more extreme Protestants within the Church of England. These Protestants thought that the English Reformation has not done enough in reforming the doctrines and structure of the church and hence they wanted to purify their church. In the seventeenth century, many Puritans immigrated to the New World, where they sought to find a holy

Commonwealth in new found land. In the Puritanical society, religion is the key semantic player in reformation of the society. The Puritanical religious doctrines emphasised that the soul has two parts, the immortal masculine half, and the mortal feminine half. Attending the church is a compulsion and any deviation to this rule is subjected to punishment. Primarily based on Protestantism, the church is the dominant legislative and governing body. The laws are established according to the Bible, since God is believed to be the supreme judge of the universe. The Puritans aimed at perfection and believed that without religious intervention, nothing is possible. Hence, the governor is not the sole person to take any decisive action but must decree in accordance to the reverend of the church. This immense power in the hands of the church has been the root of trouble which Hawthorne has emphasised again and again:

> There was a murmur among the dignified and reverend occupants of the balcony; and Governor Bellingham gave expression to its purport, speaking in an authoritative voice, although tempered with respect towards the youthful clergyman whom he addressed. "Good Master Dimmesdale," said he, "the responsibility of this woman's soul lies greatly with you. It behooves you, therefore to surround by the teachings of their religion and Puritanism itself...exhort her to repentance, and to confession, as a proof and consequence there of." (*SL* 100)

Governor Bellingham's immense faith and admiration for Dimmesdale in the novel also reveals to what extent the religious body influenced the socio-political subjects. The Governor replaced his authority over the life of Hester to reverend Dimmesdale and Dimmesdale's manipulation with his play of words again suggested that favouritism and nepotism cannot be obliterated from ecclesiastical life. In the Puritan theocracy, religion and state are absolutist forms and there is hardly any room for an independent civil society or democracy. By reflecting on the Puritans' authoritarianism, Hawthorne refers to the antebellum myth of the origin of American democracy. The image of the eagle and the reference to the childlike loyalty of the Puritan crowd to submit to its magistrates' rule suggest the need for democratic government.

Hawthorne is also critical of the theoretical hegemony as reflected in the solemnity of the community during the Election Day. The internal apathy and repressive laws are reflected when the community is forbidden to laugh and enjoy even on holidays. Hester becomes a living sermon and a glaring example of the deviants in the Puritanical world. Hawthorne reflects on the hypocrisy of religion and science where both the minister and the alchemist juggled with languages to dissemble their own identities. Hawthorne mocks at the democratic idealism of Arthur Dimmesdale. Both Dimmesdale and Chillingworth travel on the same existential path and fooled themselves. Like medieval morality plays, the story shows the tug of war between spiritual tussle and secular commitments. Morality and superstition have coalesced together to strengthen this conflict. Pearl is seen to be the demonic child and reminder of sin. The fear of damnation is always casting its shadow throughout the novel. Sexual escapades and outlet for repressed desires of young ministers and preachers have been sensational issues of the Puritanical world. Dimmesdale's character is not an individual portrayal of a man's struggle between morality and immorality but Hawthorne has reflected the hypocrisy in forcible incarceration of sexuality of the Puritanical ministers. Arthur Cleveland Coxe, declared that Hawthorne's tale of the "nauseous amour of a Puritan pastor" is a book "made for the market" like many popular seamy works, because, Coxe explained, "a running undertide of filth has become as requisite to a romance, as death in the fifth act of a tragedy."[8] One cannot deny that the antebellum public's special interest in sensational sex scandals and repressed desires. The story of Dimmesdale and his secret sexual liaison is another iconoclastic representation of widely disseminated rumour and stories that resonated in popular literature in relation to lecherous ministers and ecclesiastical figures. A devout Puritan Calvinist, Arthur becomes an ironical figure in juxtaposition to Puritanical hypocrisy. This is confluenced in Dimmesdale's character, who possessed both the profound convictions of the soul-searching Puritan and the lawless passions of a repressed man. Behind the veil of Puritanical soberness, Hawthorne questions about the natural 'id' that cannot be restrained in the name of morality. This is reflected in Dimmesdale's offspring, Pearl who exemplified anarchic, uncontrolled wild child of nature. The dilemma remains that Dimmesdale throughout his life suffered out of conscious attempt to cloak the sin in opposition to her lover's boastful brandishing of the sin. *The Scarlet Letter* acts as the mirror of Puritanical American culture and religion elucidating how specific religious and cultural images are socially over imposed in human mind. Hawthorne's exploration on the history of American ministers and Calvinist theology is crucial since the ministers ruled and served for two hundred years before American clergy emerged. Hawthorne has been aware of some of the fictional predecessors of Dimmesdale like Cooper's Meek Woolf. His scepticism in blind faith in religion assures that he has been a theological liberal.

When religion acts as an imperialist alibi, the result is duality and duplicity. This duality of life is shown by Hawthorne in the gap between appearance and reality. The hypocrisy of the magistrates, the governors and the ministers is shown in the mask they loved to wear. At the beginning of *The Scarlet Letter*, the narrator explains that to compose fiction based on history; one must speculate history and should not blindly believe in the facts of history. The act of blending "the Actual and the Imaginary" is not an easy thing for which Hawthorne's narrator recommends poetic licence and introspection. At the same time he also suggests that in this process of revisiting the past, there is a chance of rectifying truth which remained in oblivion. The symbolic figures in the novel like Hester Prynne, Pearl, Chillingworth and Dimmesdale—all reflect violation and disruption in the Althusserian "Repressed State Apparatuses" (RSA). Louis Althusser stated that Ideological State Apparatus or ISA is the method by which organisations propagate ideology. In contrast, "Repressive State Apparatus" or RSA which is mainly controlled by the ruling class, in this case the church, functions by means of repression and violence. These characters reflect Hawthorne's own feelings of claustrophobic social obligations and how the artistic individualistic spirits like him are discouraged to think, feel and act according to their choices. Therefore, the forest becomes the locus of liberty and acts as the mirror of the true self. For the Puritans, the forest is demonic, anti-Christian and obnoxious for human morality. The tantalising glimpses of proximity between Hester and Dimmesdale, the original self of Mistress Hibbins and the beauty of Pearl in the midst of unpretentious wilderness mock the veil of appearance. This is best exemplified in the words of Dimmesdale:

> I must stand up in my pulpit, and meet so many eyes turned upward to my face, as if the light of heaven were beaming from it!...and then look inward, and discern the black reality of what they idolize? (*SL* 287)

The power and art of language to conceal the real self is seen as a form of admirable art: "I should long ago have thrown off these garments of mock holiness, and have shown myself to mankind as they will see me at the judgment-seat" (*SL* 288). In contrast to Dimmesdale, Hester and Pearl are representatives of non-conformities but believe in clarity and honesty. Pearl emphasises the natural world free from pretension. In terms of her social appearance, Hester may be a fallen woman, disloyal, adulteress and violator of Puritan ethics but in reality she is endowed with individualistic spirit and is the emerging New Eve fighting for the space of her true love and passion. This recalls the infamous cruelty to the Quaker Ann Coleman,[9] who can be ascribed as a harlot but in reality, is the epitome of honesty. The physician Roger Chillingworth, who is supposed to be saviour of humanity is in reality a vengeful evil man whose doting medication is worse than poison to make the minister undergo the hellish psychological torment. Roger Chillingworth also provides the access to the perfect subconscious world of Dimmesdale's primordial self. Even the letter 'A' demands an imaginative power to interpret the reality behind the appearance. Hawthorne in *Endicott and the Red Cross* (1837) has written about the embroidered "fatal token" which is "Admirable, or anything rather than Adulteress".[10] Similarly when Dimmesdale stands at the verge of death and reveals his scarlet alphabet, Hawthorne writes "It was revealed! But it were irreverent to describe that revelation" (*SL* 381). The fear of reality is always insurmountable in Dimmesdale as he has been sceptical of Pearl's feature that may hint her biological father.

Hawthorne's delving into Puritanical history also relates to the question of citizenship in New England. When Hawthorne inserts the nineteenth-century term 'citizenship' into a seventeenth-century setting, he is also pondering on the history of the development of Puritanical settlement and US citizenship. Reflecting critically the perverse spirit of the ancestors, Hawthorne has hinted at the brutality and punishments meted out to the convicts. However, he has carefully avoided the issue of the Native Americans and the process of evacuation by his ancestors. Hawthorne's romance reflects and satirises his ancestor's efforts to begin a new chapter when already chapters after chapters of history existed. It starts with reflections on the Puritans' attempt to establish a fresh start in the New World:

> "the founders of a new colony, whatever Utopia of human virtue and happiness they might originally project, have invariably recognized it among their earliest practical necessities to allot a portion of the virgin soil as a cemetery, and another portion as the site of a prison". (*SL* 72)

However, he mocks at such attempt in the chapter "Another View of Hester" when Hester realises that the radical reforms she imagines would require "the whole system of society to be torn down, and built up anew". Finally when in the forest, Hester and Dimmesdale decided to elope, in a moment of heightened excitement they speak the truth: "Leave this wreck and ruin here where it hath happened! Meddle no more with it! Begin all anew!" (*SL* 297) Interestingly, John Winthrop, one of the Puritan leaders in New England compared marriage between man and woman to the relationship between the church and the community. For Winthrop, Puritanical political covenants are like marriages where husband and wife become one corporate body. The husband is granted the sole legal authority, and so Winthrop compares a woman's willing subjection in marriage to an individual's subjection to the magistrates who govern the political covenant and consents.

> The woman's own choice makes such a man her husband; yet being so chosen, he is her lord, and she is to be subject

> to him, yet in a way of liberty, not of bondage; and a true wife accounts her subjection her honor and her freedom.... Even so brethren, it will be between you and your magistrates". (*SL* 238-39)

Winthrop proclaims that a true Christian can achieve liberty only through total submission to Christ. The Puritans believe that just like a woman should completely surrender to her man, similarly the community should completely surrender to the political and religious institutions sanctioned by God. But Hawthorne never supported forcible submission in any relationship or civil or religious authorities. On the contrary, he believed in alternate possibilities like freedom for imagination, sympathy and love. Chillingworth's dark revenge is a threat to transform the land into a reign of terror while Hester dreams for a utopia with new social order and freedom for women are unrealistic.

The movement of Puritanism started in the 16th century with the aim to purify the Church of England which is primarily based on Roman Catholic orientation. Initially, the radical Puritans believed in return to primitive Christianity. Though the Puritan movement started in England, it gradually insinuated in New England in the 17th century where they sought to found a holy Commonwealth. The New England religious world is primarily based on Puritanism that emphasised on English Reformation. It primarily focused on four convictions. They believed that salvation is a personal thing that must happen between the individual and God. Secondly, Bible is considered as guiding force in life. Thirdly, the role of the church is to guide humanity with preaching and morals of the holy Bible. Finally, society is being given more importance that individualism so that individual will and desires should be compromised for the sake of the society and the church. With Luther and Calvin as their predecessors, the Puritans believed that reconciliation and salvation can happen as heavenly benediction.

For Hawthorne, the Puritan world is not a part of his existence but like a haunted past it casts its shadow in his literary world. *The Scarlet Letter* provides a space that reflects the strictures, religion, community, discipline and punishment of

17th century Puritanical Boston. Religion is the bed rock of life and every action in the life of the individual or of the community is based on it. Any crime followed by severe punishment in the society is subjected to public display in order to discourage the community for further repetition. Relationships between opposite sexes must be restricted by religious parameters so that rape and adultery are not only considered sinful but also subjected to death penalty. Any social deviation is considered as an act against God and it is viewed as violence against divinity. The image of the God presented in the society is that of a stern and strict Almighty and the Divine authority is the supreme power in the universe. It is believed that the fate of the individual is determined by God and humanity can strive hard to obey God's verdict. The community is always reminded that human life is full of sins and therefore excess of mirth, joy and celebration are prohibited in the society. Hawthorne's description of the Puritan crowd seems to be merciless and harsh because of their religious and cultural orientation. Clandestine meetings, rendezvous or even 'unjust' admiration resulted in fornication, lashes and even persecution. Segregation from the community and social ostracisation is another way of moral death of the sinner. The sinner is always exemplified as the living sermon against sin. Communal depravity is worst among all that resulted in self-denial and self-hatred.

Like the society, the family is seen in hierarchical order. Great authoritative power is invested in husbands, fathers, and masters. Women do not have rights to decide independently but all members of the household have certain rights as well as duties. To maintain the sanctity run in the families, women and children are always seen under the control of the authorial father figure. Relationships between men and women are seen as something sacred and divinely oriented and any deviation to it is violation against divinely ordained principles. Loyalty and faithfulness in relationships are must. The microcosmic relationship between man and woman is not an individual aspect of life but is seen in the greater perspective of religion, community, discipline and punishment. The Puritans believed in predestination and at the same time the fear of the Devil and agonising hell are gruelling aspects that haunted them in their day-to-day life. Women are commanded to internalise the messages of the ministers because they are vulnerable, depraved and susceptible to evil. Hawthorne never embraced completely the Puritanical ideals in the novel but reflected on the psychological tension in the lives of the people. Though himself a supporter of Emersonian principles, yet Hawthorne is aware of Jonathan Edward's preaching that formed the vital part of Puritanical life. Hawthorne's reflection on Puritan ancestry in colonial Boston and American selfhood corroborates Sacvan Bercovitch's contention on "the myth of the Puritan origins of the American self". Bercovitch focuses on the plethora of interpretations of the scarlet A, and comments that at the end it relates to "a single, coherent moral-political-aesthetic design" that converge into one single meaning that is "American" self. *The Scarlet Letter* primarily reflects on the second generation settlers in New England. Public scrutiny and judgment are essential because the individuals are to be gauged in terms of his/her right to citizenship assessed. It is an attempt to internalise law within the community. Public spectacle is a crucial thing because it affects the individual more psychologically than physically and in the process becomes accustomed to social needs. But Hawthorne perhaps suggests self-scrutiny and conscience as the best process of self-development rather than social laws. It contains the seeds of antinomianism. The conscience of selfhood cannot be developed by public branding. This is exemplified by the character of Mistress Hibbins, the distorted anatomies of Chillingworth and Dimmesdale. Hawthorne here is trying to diagnose the Puritanical American psychosis from the Boston crowd of seventeenth century.

The character of Mistress Hibbins exposes another most harrowing and shameful history of Salem and how Hawthorne's Puritanical synergist forefathers ignited the fearful incident. The overwhelming fanatic credulity regarding witchcraft in Salem reflected how religion can create delusion in the entire community. Repressive Puritanism has given birth to history of the occult, psychopathology and hysteria. The women gathered in the crowd during Hester's public display are more vulgar in terms of their abusive words that reflect the frustration and anger towards Hester's transgression which they dared not.

Mistress Hibbins evokes the famous history of the mass killing of Salem witches and alludes to the real story of Ann Hibbins, who has been accused of being a witch, condemned and hanged in 1656. Throughout the novel, Mistress Hibbins is shrouded in mystery associated with supernatural evil power like "fiends and night-hags, with whom she was well-known to make excursions into the forest". She has often beckoned Hester to join in her adventurous journey into the world of darkness. Hawthorne suggests Hester Prynne cannot be forced into such social abuse because of her exceptional individuality although many of them suspected Hester as a witch. In Puritanical world, women have been broadly categorised as either docile, submissive, weaker vessel or the robust, violating spirit who are in reality women of rational mind and of high intelligence. When women are seen in the light of demons or witches, they are stigmatised as evil spirit. The existing sexism always finds it difficult to acknowledge that women can be intellectually and emotionally strong and powerful. The Puritanical society privileged men in philosophical, scientific, and religious systems which reinforced their dominant position and presented women as sub-human species. Women have been always presented as dependents on fathers, husbands, and in case of widowhood on sons or surviving male relatives. Hester's independence is seen therefore in the light of witchcraft and evil spirit. Nothing is more common in those days, than to interpret all meteoric appearances, and other natural phenomena, that occurred with less regularity than the rise and set of sun and moon from a supernatural source. Thus, a blazing spear, a sword of flame, a bow, or a sheaf of arrows, seen in the midnight sky, prefigured Indian warfare. Pestilence is known to have been foreboded by a shower of crimson light.

Superstition, black magic and fear of the Devil perhaps affected the lives of women, children and the slaves. Any deviation from the traditional path is seen in the light of scepticism as if the evil spirit is allying to corrupt humanity. Hence, Hester's breaching of the social, religious and moral codes reminds one of the historical literary figures of Margaret Fuller, the much admired yet abhorrent woman that Hawthorne has met in his life. Margaret Fuller's name is significant in relation to American Renaissance and Transcendentalist Movement. A woman of such critical perspectives and high intellectual flair is rare in the contemporary patriarchal America. She has been one of the greatest challengers to Ralph Waldo Emerson while her strong intellectual and emotional power enthralled women and influenced their lives strongly. *Woman in the Nineteenth Century* is one of her most popular books that made a profound impact on women's rights movement. Hester's spirit to liberate one's emotions, sensibilities and the attempt to transcend the Puritanical shackles of repression reflect the shadow of Fuller in her character. She is the living embodiment of human spokesperson who, through her life has preached the community the lesson of endurance, existentialism, patience and suffering. Hester and Fuller both embody that in the name of religious institution, natural instincts and emotions of humanity cannot be repressed and if one attempts, it leads to decay. The various religious, social and political structures in the name of civilizations are hindrance for human development. In *An American Romantic Life,* Charles Capper writes about Fuller as:

> A seemingly ubiquitous, modern American intellectual figure...a conflicted, alienated, avant-garde thinker who, despite or because of her alienation, looked hopefully to popular, world-historical transformations.[11]

Just as women who attended Margaret Fuller's "conversations" discovered her clairvoyant elocution stimulating, the women of Hester Prynne's community gathered at her home for advice and comfort in times of hardship and frustration in their lives. Fuller's leadership and initiative act seemed to the chauvinists as a threat but when Hester silently performed the same role, she became angelic. Anne Hutchinson is another historical shadow which is reflected in the novel. When at the beginning of the novel Hawthorne mentions that her fictional heroine Hester is walking in the footstep of historical heroine Ann Hutchinson who has been imprisoned in Boston Prison house and then banished, he suggests at the "Antinomian" spirits of Hutchinson and her followers who disobeyed Puritanical laws. Hutchinson's struggle for women's empowerment and exposure of Puritanical corruptions and machinations of religion is a carcinogenic which they need to amputate as early as possible. Though the Puritanical authority can forcibly banish Hutchinson, yet that her defiant spirit is unyielding is evident in several fictional characters like Hester Prynne. All these dark negative cynicism of the Puritan society are never supported by Hawthorne and so he could not embrace the encoded worldviews of the Puritans. The novel definitely mocks rigid Puritanical backlash mimicking the Biblical Fall from Paradise. Unlike Hester, the other Puritanical repressive women are in perpetual loss, and this loss entails the loss of their body, mind and identity. They all have lost their sexuality in their 'goodness' and religion acted as the medium for capitulation to this 'goodness' and 'virtue'. Puritanism in New England stifled sexuality of men and women and when Hester Prynne in her crisis and obligation to restrict her erotic selves, finally attempted to reclaim, it appeared she is the passionate witch cataclysmic in her action. But Hawthorne, like his mixed admiration and abhorrence for Fuller or his sister-in-law Elizabeth, recognised the vibrant hues of Hester Prynne that cannot be faded from the Puritanical history.

However, one aspect which Hawthorne never mentioned explicitly is the discourse of racism and slavery. Even though the Indians are not predominantly present in the narrative scene, yet their bewildered presence at the fringe of European settlement disturbs and inflames the ruthless silent history of unlawful encroachment and brutality of the American settlers. Chillingworth's prolonged years of captive among the natives, his accompaniment with Native American, the reference of Apostle Eliot and his life in the midst of primitive Native Americans and the mute presence of the community observing the ceremony of the Election Day reveal that the bloody history of forcible plundering and barbarous annihilation subside in the conscience of Nathaniel Hawthorne. Hawthorn unlike his other contemporary writers avoided the abolition debate. His awareness of slavery is evident in his *Passages from the American Notebooks*. He has also been aware that slavery is not merely physical but also mental and yet remained silent due to his political ideology. Although the Native American characters are phantoms from the past, yet Chillingworth testifies their influence. The reference to American expansion and removal of Indians is implicit in the text. Due to his avoidance to comment directly on this matter critics like Jonathan Arac have labelled him as "master of compromise" while Sacvan used one single critical world to define the first American 'classic' which is "ambiguity". The issue of Indian captivity has been one of the conflagrant parts of settler Americans because any contamination with the Natives, is considered to be regressive. Chillingworth's "savage constume", devilish eyes that appeared like burning hell and his knowledge of native herbs and roots are antithetical in the 'civilised' Puritanical world. His captivity is seen as loss of salvation and civilisation. The physician's shipwreck followed by Indian captivity is a common scenario in colonial America where many explorers and settlers living on the edge of American frontier are scared by the idea of Indian captivity. Even the reference to the Black Man relating to Devil is actually the seventeenth-century belief in the diabolical figure of Indian phantoms and apparitions. Hawthorne has been suggesting this Black Man as the symbol of internal darkness and irrationality which the Indians are supposed to be. Dimmesdale's psychic trouble is equated with this devilish manifestation especially after his visit to the wild forest. Chillingworth's mysterious appearance and disappearance and his doomed future are reflections of the conventional reflections of Native Americans in American colonial literature which Eric Cheyfitz described it as the process of colonial translation in his book *The Poetics of Imperialism.* The divergent meanings of Indian ghosts, apparitions, and their lingering cultural remnants haunting the conscience of the settlers are sometimes unconsciously reflected by Hawthorne. Thus, the absent-present melancholic figures of vagabond Native Americans in Hawthorne's text correlate to the actual removal of them at the margin of the world.

Hawthorne's scepticism regarding science and its control over humanity is reflective of the history of Puritanical pseudoscience and its utility. Jonathan Edward's empirical investigations into natural phenomena and experimentation with the smallpox vaccine already created uproar and raised question about the divine power. During Hawthorne's time, the practice of medicine is primarily concerned with therapeutics that involves processes like emetics, cathartics, diuretics, and bleedings. This new development in medical science is primarily based on the work of Paris clinicians like Laennec, Gaspard Bayle, Pierre Louis, and Auguste Chomel who emphasised on empirical observation and physical diagnosis. In the *The Scarlet Letter*, the author comments that the physician is aware of the most modern development in medical science as well as of the ancient elixir of the Native Americans. Chillignworth practiced both empirical observation and physical diagnosis. At the beginning of his association with Arthur Dimmesdale when the seed of doubt is just planted, he tried various empirical observations. The physician purposely tried to altercate with Dimmesdale such issues like sin, confession and repression. With watchful eye he has construed how Dimmesdale has become nervous at Pearl's shriek that pervaded the window. He observed this vulnerable man's strange behaviour like secret crime and sins. Like a modern physician he has observed the signs of the minister's disease, its symptoms and then found the root of its evolution. With this new 'clinical gaze'[12] as Michel Foucault has termed it, Chillingworth enjoined to scrutinize his patient. With his silent vigil, he has heard the ausculation of Dimmesdale. Ausculation is the newly devised method of treating a patient during Hawthorne's time. In the year 1850, great physician Jacob Bigelow warned the Harvard medical faculty that physical exploration, experiments, autopsies, and auscultation are the modern ways of treatment than therapeutics. The essential and primary aspect of such treatment is observation. This method of observation is synonymous with what Foucault has termed as 'clinical gaze' when he started reflecting upon French clinical methods. Foucault has viewed such requirements as the outcome of political ideology channelled through medical technology. For Foucault, the purpose of medical gaze is to speculate not only the body of the patient but also keeping in mind the socio-political history in the background. And then such method of supervision and observation is nothing but a powerful surveillance. Once Chillingworth arrives, we find this act of surveillance is in process. With his medical gaze, he attempts to appropriate Dimmesdale's and Pearl's bodies under the shadow of his doubt. Hester is haunted at the first sight of the cruel demonised invasive gaze of Chillingworth penetrating the heart of the transgressed woman. In her husband's gaze, Hester feels "a strange, penetrating power, when it was their owner's purpose to read the human soul". Hester is aware of the "intense consciousness of being the object of severe and universal observation," but her husband's gaze makes her feel "all other objects in the visible world seemed to vanish" (*SL* 96). What Chillingworth emits in his voyeuristic gaze is a sense of betrayal, wrath, anger and revenge. Hawthorne's fear of clinical gaze is emphasized once more when seven years later Hester Prynne confronts her fiendish physician-husband and observed the glowing flame of revenge in his eyes. Apart from gaze, tactile methods of treatment are also in vogue during Hawthorne's time. The newly emergent Paris-trained physicians learned how to touch the patient and probe into physical examination and diagnosis. Hester is afraid at the touch of Chillingworth on her baby inside the prison. In the middle of the night, the physician dares to remove the minister's garment "delving...prying...and probing everything" to find out the most private mark on his body. With the license of a physician, Master Prynne gazes upon the most protective surface of the body and diagnoses his disease. His intense desire to venture into the secrets of the patient is an act of violation and hence his ethics is destroyed when he transforms from physician to a miner searching for jewel. Hawthorne describes this how—

> Chillingworth had begun an investigation, as he imagined, with the severe and equal integrity of a judge, desirous only of truth, even as if the question involved no more than the air-drawn lines and figures of a geometrical problem, instead of human passions.... But, as he proceeded, a terrible fascination...seized the old man.... He now dug into the poor clergyman's heart, like a miner...or, rather, like a sexton delving into a grave.... (*SL* 193)

Hawthorne suggests that literature and art can envision body as a natural object. The contradictory and ambiguous marks of human body can be read by an artist and not by a physician. The most vulnerable diseases of mind can be treated better in literature than chemically or clinically. *The Scarlet Letter* condemns the clinical gaze championed by American physicians who celebrated medical power over bodies. Further, Hawthorne attempts to see the discourse of mind and body as political, historical and social attempt to control the body and the spirit and medicine or clinical treatment sometimes involve political hegemony over mind and body.

However, Nathaniel Hawthorne has been critical and to some extent satirical at the Puritans, but could not completely abandon it. Hester Prynne is an attempt to etch an Emersonian Transcendental heroine yet she is not completely successful as she retains some of the Puritanical lingering. Zest for life is against Puritanical principle and Hester's oozing passion is outrageous reminding humanity of their first parents who have been expelled from heaven. The Puritanical world of asceticism has no place for mercy for men and women like Hester and Dimmesdale. Hester underwent purgation because her sin is confessed while Dimmesdale died as he failed to confess. Both Dimmesdale's and Hester's sufferings reveal that Hawthorne could not dare to present the hero and the heroine of his novel as victorious. Whether as a tribute paid to the sanctity of the Puritanical society or as lack of confidence to disavow his ancestral lineage, Hawthorne dared not to transcend and deviate. What can be more painful than psychological turmoil and emotional torture that remain unrecognised in the Puritanical world? Hawthorne focused on such psychological ruin but could not shatter the superficiality of Puritanical restrictions. Dimmesdale's loss of sanity arrived at the cost of conforming to Puritanical repression but does the novel promise a better world of freedom and happiness at the cost of the sacrifice of human passion? Hester therefore remained in the no man's land where she attempted to bridge the antinomies—memory and hope, self and society, nature and institutions; past, present and future.

NOTES

1. A Jacobite referred to the supporter of the royal house of the Stuart and they chose the name Jacobite because it is the Latin form of James II, who is being deprived of the throne in 1688. Between 1688 and 1746, series of revolts happened in Great Britain and Ireland.

The series of conflicts takes its name from Jacobitism. In the war between England and France, the French supported Stuarts' claim to the English throne because France has always been Catholic nation. All these revolts and upraises are aimed at returning James VII of Scotland and II of England. These several revolts are called Jacobite Rebellions by the ruling governments. After the House of Hanover succeeded to the British throne in 1714, the risings continued, and intensified. They continued until the last Jacobite Rebellion ("the Forty-Five"), led by Charles Edward Stuart (the Young Pretender), who was soundly defeated at the Battle of Culloden in 1746. For details see Fremont-Barnes, Gregory. *The Jacobite Rebellion 1745-46*. U.K: Osprey Publishing, 2011.

2. Indian Removal Act—In 1830 the Senate and House of Representatives of the United States of America decided and passed the Act that it will be lawful if the President of the United States of America take away the lands on the west of the river Mississippi, and remove the Native Americans from there. This law was signed by the then president Andrew Jackson on May 28, 1830. The Native Americans are removed to federal territories and they consisted of primarily five tribes namely Cherokee, Chickasaw, Choctaw, Muscogee-Creek, and Seminole.
3. Fugitive Slave Law—This law was passed by the United States Congress on September 18, 1850, as part of the Compromise of 1850 between Southern slave-holding interests and Northern Free-Soilers. The Northern law enforcement officers are ordered to aid in the recapture of more than ten thousand fugitive slaves who have fled to Canada. Anthony Burns, who was one of those popular fugitive slaves, was arrested and his trial in Boston under the provisions of the Fugitive Slave Act of 1850 incited riots.
4. 1848 Women's Convention in Seneca Falls—This was one of those earliest women right's convention in the western world. The event took place for two days when New York women organised it on the occasion of the visit of a female Quaker who was famous for her oratorical skill. The location was the Wesleyan Chapel in Seneca Falls where Lucretia Mott and Elizabeth Cady Stanton, two abolitionists who met at the 1840 World Anti-Slavery Convention in London arrived. This conference for women mainly focused on women's sacred right to the elective franchise.
5. Married Women's Property Acts—Prior to marriage if a woman has got property, then she did not have any right on it. A married woman could not make contracts, keep or control her own wages or any rents, transfer property, sell property or bring any lawsuit. Paulina Wright Davis, Ernestine Rose and Elizabeth Cady Stanton mainly

worked hard to make this law applicable for women. The text of the 1848 New York Statute known as the Married Women's Property Act, as amended in 1849, states that properties belonging to women before marriage should not automatically pass to their husbands. The husband has no right to her wife's property and even after marriage, the property will remain as the wife's property.

6. European revolutions of 1848—This is one of the widespread revolutions of Europe that affected France, Germany, Prussia, the Austrian empire, Denmark, England, Switzerland, Spain and Belgium. Severe famine, reduction in the consumer demand, lack of employment and various other calamities led the emperor fled and as a result the overthrow of the monarchy set off a wave of protest throughout east and central Europe, led by radical liberals and workers who demanded constitutional reform or complete government change.
7. Cresswell, Tim. *In Place/Out of Place: Geography, Ideology and Transgression*. Minneapolis: University of Minnesota Press, 1996.
8. Reynolds S., David. *Waking Giant: America in the Age of Jackson*. New York: Harper Collins Publishers, 2008 p. 269.
9. In William Sewel's *The History of the People Called Quaker*, Hawthorne has read about the persecution of the Quakers in Massachusetts. In 1692, three Quaker women, Ann Coleman, Mary Tompkins and Alice Ambrose are captured by Captain Richard Waldron, a prominent Puritan and a local magistrate. Though the last two women are saved, it is believed that Ann Coleman was punished and lashed dragging her all around the town. His ancestor William Hathorne commanded to lash a woman Quaker called Ann Coleman. The upper part of her body is naked and she is being roped to the tail of a cart. The ignominy in relation to his ancestral crime and violence haunted Hawthorne throughout his life.
10. Hendrickson, Robert. *The Facts on File Dictionary of American Regionalisms*. New York: Facts on File, 2000, p. 172.
11. Capper, Charles. *Margaret Fuller: An American Romantic Life Volume I: The Private Years: An American Romantic Life*. New York: Oxford University Press, 1992, p. xi.
12. Foucault, Michel. *The Birth of The Clinic*. Abingdon: Routledge, 2003.

Chapter 5

THE SCARLET LETTER IN THE LIGHT OF PSYCHOLOGICAL INTERPLAY

> "The heart, the heart, there was the little yet boundless sphere wherein existed the original wrong of which the crime and misery of this outward world were merely types. Purify that inward sphere, and the many shapes of evil that haunt the outward, and which now seem almost our only realities, will turn to shadowy phantoms and vanish of their own accord; but if we go no deeper than the intellect, and strive, with merely that feeble instrument, to discern and rectify what is wrong, our whole accomplishment will be a dream."[1]

Nathaniel Hawthorne's psychological essence in his writings is oriented from historical, cultural and ideological facets of emerging America. Hawthorne's psychological speculation has been unrecognised initially by his biographers and critics because of his advanced study of humanity as reflected in the comment of Van Wyck Brooks who thinks how Hawthorne "had lived too long in these border-regions, these polar solitudes where the spirit shivered, so that the substance of the world about him hung before his eyes like a thing of vapour."[2] The 'border region' that Brooks is referring to as illusionary is the human psyche that Hawthorne attempted to venture in order to explore rampant human desires, repressed primitivism, archaism, neuroses and fantasies. The above extract from *The Moses from Old Manse* reflects that Hawthorne has identified what Sigmund Freud has claimed as the "royal road to the unconscious' which is the most intriguing and yet challenging voyage to know the real self. Ahead of his time, he has revealed that human relationships are primarily based on power dynamics. The emotional tumult is sometimes unbounded and beyond our grasp like Nature. Hawthorne has reflected upon various psychological states of humanity ranging from alienation, ostracisation, repression, sadism, masochism, rebellion and defiance. His work of art enmeshes introspection into the interior selves emboldened by the desire to search for the lost origin of humanity. *The Scarlet Letter* is considered to be the first American psychological romance when for the first time in American literary discourses, the author has dared to lift the veil of human mind in order to know the instinctive primal impulse, the human will that fulfills desires. What Arthur Schopenhauer termed as 'der Wille' in his seminal work *Die Welt als Wille and Vorstellung* (1819) can be co-related to his contemporary American writer Nathaniel Hawthorne's delineation of indomitable will of the mind. Schopenhauer's 'der Wille' is the omnipotent motivation for the entire fundamental physical forces in the universe as well as of human action. This 'der Wille' is so enforcing that it can defy time and space. Hawthorne's Hester Prynne exhibits the same 'der Wille' that creates desire to live, to fight, to protest, to deviate, and to struggle unyieldingly.

With the Puritanical setting where purgation, redemption, sin and divinity are the only instructive doctrinaire for living in this world, Hawthorne is bold enough to mirror the inner turmoil of humanity and the oscillation of the mind between the socially defined parameters of 'moral' and 'immoral'. Through psychological study, Hawthorne reveals the various layers of human mind: innocence, purity, beauty, hopes, triumphs, temptations, sinful tendency, desperate struggles, malignity, desire for revenge, depravation and self-destructive tendencies, hysteria and neurosis. Often called a mystic psychological dreamer, like her heroine of the novel Hester Prynne, he is claimed to be the ghost of New England, half embodied, half endowed with a painful whirlpool between his ancestors and himself. Hawthorne's art of psychological delineation involves symbolisms, secret springs, external manifestations, play of words and metaphysical insight." In order to penetrate the darkest psychological chambers of human mind, Hawthorne has entailed that attention to cultural, historical and subjectivity of the self are essential. His psychologically impinging characters in *The Scarlet Letter* mainly Hester Prynne, Pearl, Arthur Dimmesdale, Master Prynne and Mistress Hibbins must be studied in the socio-political, cultural and religious context of seventeenth-century America.

Hawthorne's writings seem to be like the lenses of telescope and microscope that endeavour to unmask the private self behind the public self. This antebellum novel reflects on the emotional revolution in the mind of characters like Hester Prynne. He chooses to confront the unedited psychology of most admired personalities in order to deconstruct the categorical and cultural understanding of humanity. This does not mean he is avoiding contextless representation but trying to see the psychology removed from conscious social constructions. The challenge of meditating the elusive psychology of Hester Prynne is buried in her silence. Hester is represented as a marginalised character who not only resides at the outskirt of Puritanical society but psychologically she is also secluded as a rebellious individual who is to be abhorred at. With less speeches but more significant utterances in moment of crises, Hawthorne has delved deep inside her mind to co-relate her ostensible silence and invisible effusive flare. On the other hand, Arthur Dimmesdale's mental agony and repression of desires and guilt conscience makes him a forlorn character even in the midst of the Salem crowd. In Hester's disobeying of Puritanical regulations and stern determination to be firm and unyielding, we get a glimpse of this extra-ordinary woman's uniqueness and her rare mental agility all of which are absent in all the male characters of the novel. Hawthorne as psychological novelist excels in the art of analysis of the agony, alienation and seclusion of the characters. Neither Hawthorne employs 'stream of consciousness' technique nor he has used internal monologue yet his careful dictions and his ability to explore the finite microscopic human expressions reveal his magical art of capturing such mysterious glimpses of human mind. The revenge psychology of Chillingworth with calm and poised nature is equally perturbing. Chillingworth's mistake lies in his attempt to see life from utilitarian perspective. His complacency about his scholarly self has naturally led him to withdrawal from mankind. Through him, Hawthorne caricatures science because he is a scientist without bioethics. If Chillingworth represents the scientific movement of materialism, then Dimmesdale represents the nineteenth century movements of Sentimentality, Romanticism, and Transcendentalism. Dimmesdale's penance is gradually represented in his sense of decay and self-destruction.

When Hester is introduced in the novel, Hawthorne has not endowed her with any word but even in her silence, she expresses her resolute mind. Her 'haughty smile' and 'burning blush' are provocative enough to analyse the psychological crisis. Hawthorne here scrutinizes both Hester's individual cognitive self and the social psychology of seventeenth-century New England. The social psychology that Hawthorne mirrors is related to 'attribution theory' of psychology. Attribution theory refers to the process of ascribing some phenomenon or events relating to its origin. The attributional judgements from the public who have gathered to watch Hester Prynne's shameful chastisement also reflect an interpersonal relationship where the audience try to correlate between himself/herself and the victim. The women in the crowd unconsciously reflect in their individual judgement how, in order to fit themselves in the social roles and in abiding religious strictures, they have denied their biological necessity through repression and subjection. The prevalence of sexual perversion, neurosis and hysteria is connoted by the community as witchcraft exemplified by Mistress Hibbins. The discontent in the words of the elder women in the crowd is reflective of stifled sexuality throughout their lives and the anxiety for the woman on the scaffold who has defeated them and subverted all social barriers. Hester has embraced her personal desires by sacrificing morality and invading fear of punishment. She has abandoned cultural process by prioritising individual desire. The blushful glow that the narrator refers to on Hester's face is an intense depiction of the shame of exposition of her inner self which the society claimed to be a nature of the 'fallen woman'. Contrarilly Hawthorne's carefully chosen expression of 'haughty smile' reveals her psychological fortitude to defy society and wade through a crowd of 'ignorant' humanity. Hester's silence is most disturbing and unnerving but we have never come across some moments in Hester's life when she suffered from depression out of humiliation and shame. Her silence is not out of shame that bereft her off any power of articulation, but it is a kind of resistance and defiance to comply with the system.

Hester's dexterity to withstand vituperation to herself and to her child instead of escaping from the place is also noteworthy. Hester's love for Dimmesdale is true and pure; it cannot be tainted by public scandal. If the child is the product of a fit of momentary passion, then Hester would have easily escaped the Puritanical indignation that the society has inflicted upon her and she also would not have hesitated in proclaiming publicly the name of Dimmesdale. Her suffering is a way of purification but to grasp her mind is difficult and challenging. Hester's power is in her silence and the study of her psychology is a mode of self-defence against further incrimination. The readers must understand that Hester is dynamic enough to choose the best weapon and her political strategy is apt not only for the child and herself, but also for Dimmesdale. Yet her mind seems to be conquered and divided—conquered because of her refusal to answer and thereby obey the Puritanical authority; and divided because she is also undergoing the tortuous tribulations.

In comparison to Hester Prynne, Arthur Dimmesdale's psychological dilemma is transparent and easily accessible to Hester, Chillingworth and the narrator. His psychological pandemonium that erodes him day by day is evident in his physiognomy. His remorse is more out of his incapability to destroy his noble image of "miracle of holiness". Dimmesdale's hallucination and bleeding is like Dr. Faustus's damnation and suffering but in case of Dimmesdale it is self-inflicted. Arthur almost reaches the edge of lunacy because of his inability to confess his sin, his incapability to conquer social defamation and thus love Hester without any inhibition, and finally due to sudden shock when Hester declares that the physician is her husband. Arthur's secret "A" near his chest also symbolises his diffident soul to revolt against the Puritanical world. Unlike him, Hester's mind" is the exemplification of a Romantic individualistic spirit that demonstrates the right of the individual to make a choice in this world. Dimmesdale's death is a respite for him because after his confession, he would not have been able to survive unlike Hester who has learnt the art of surviving with courage and determination:

> The heart, making itself guilty of such secrets, must perforce hold them, until the day when all hidden things shall be revealed.... So, to their own unutterable torment, they go about among their fellow-creatures, looking pure as new-fallen snow; while their hearts are all speckled and spotted with iniquity of which they cannot rid themselves. (*SL* 152-53)

Although Dimmesdale's tautology and deceptive words are impressive to the community, yet the narrator shows there is more strength and truth in Hester's words. Her convincing speech in her desperate attempt to retain Pearl under her guardianship shows her explosive emotional psychology and also her power of mind. Her aggressive spirit at that point reveals that she may come up with the ineffable revelation that Dimmesdale is Pearl's father but even in such abysmal experience, Hester never let her unconscious mind reflect any such weakness. But Dimmesdale sees hallucinations, diabolic shapes or group of shining angels. The evils from the supernatural world are nothing but the diffused repressed 'other' hidden in the depth of the unconsciousness of Dimmesdale. This can be best explained in the words of the anonymous author of *The Mysteries of Bedlam*:

> Were the deep oceans dried, and all its secrets opened to one's scrutiny, less varied, less monstrous would its discoveries probably be, than those which would be obtained from the unveiling of one distempered spirit.[3]

He keeps vigils at night out of fear of being caught and fasts nights after nights which reflect that his body has stopped functioning because of his psychic imbalance. He even flogs and scourges himself till blood flows out of his body. Hawthorne, like a true psychologist in depicting the mind of a conscience stricken, hypocritical, and cowardly individual, studies the minister's gesture, speech and behavioural pattern. Hawthorne tries to investigate about sin and what it stands for in case of Dimmesdale's psychic turmoil. For Dimmesdale, sin can refer to repressive need, weakness, failure or even evil but his original sin is self-deceit. He is conscious of his hypocrisy with the Salem community and his mask which he wears to hide his real self but the root of the pang of his survival is self-deception. Hawthorne brilliantly captures the complex psychology of this act of self-deception where the minister simultaneously and yet paradoxically holds a belief and a negation to that belief. Dimmesdale is paradoxically aware, as well as unaware of his repressed belief that his sexual desire is a natural outcome of biological need if not love. Hawthorne is trying to show that desire and shame are parallel feelings which are inter-related. Dimmesdale's shame is the enduring legacy deep inside him because of his attempt and fear of maintaining narcissistic equilibrium and self-dignity.

Dimmesdale's fear of shame saps the foundation of his identity and security and hence he gradually becomes alienated from the community. The fear of shame is inescapably present everywhere around Dimmesdale. The duality of mind-body is a significant element in Hawthorne's writings and shame therefore colonised not only Dimmesdale's mind but also his body. Hawthorne's "moonlight of romance" is often haunted by an unbounded spirit that cannot be controlled by social regulations. Dimmesdale cannot withdraw his libidinal force nor can he rule over his bloated ego. This unresolved antagonism is best highlighted in the forest scene where Dimmesdale cannot resist Hester's temptation nor can he commit to sacrifice his over-estimated identity among the Puritans. Hawthorne is trying to dangerously dig the unconscious root in order to show the political economy of Dimmesdale's mind. His self-preservative instinct is so tremendous that he also denies Pearl's proximity because of the fear of being recognised. Dimmesdale's self-love is greater than anything in the world so that he never expressed his feelings for Hester Prynne nor Pearl. Pearl's shriek from the other side of the river is unbearable to Dimmesdale because Hawthorne shows how the ego only loves itself and finds satisfaction in its own existence. So when Hester secretly meets Dimmesdale in the forest, his instinctual pleasure is not because of any affection for Hester Prynne but out of a satisfaction to release and discharge his upheavaled motions.

Chillingworth's complex psychology is perhaps most intriguing because the psychology of sexual jealousy is an inherent debate and of immense attention from the Biblical world to classical and modern literature. To name a few, whether it is the green-eyed monster, Satan and his intervention into the lives of Adam and Eve, the Aristotelian theory of 'phthonos',[4] the Shakespearean dark tragic Moor Othello, Tolstoy's Kreutzer Sonata, Browning's Duke and his Last Duchess, or Mary Shelley's unfulfilled monster—sexual jealousy has been the fundamental key of unrestrained flow of adrenalin in literature. Harold Bloom suggests in his introduction to Proust that sexual jealousy "is the most novelistic of circumstances, just as incest; according to Shelley, is the most poetic of circumstances."[5] Chillingworth stands for the most powerful human passion, which is jealousy and envy and the reason for this strong passion is not like that of Othello's mindless jealousy but sexual and narcissistic insecurity. To acknowledge envy and jealousy as a personal trait is most disgraceful in humanity and one is more ashamed to acknowledge it consciously than any other vices. Unlike love which is blind, envy is sharp sighted. Even the most subtle observation cannot escape the envious mind. Chillingworth's desire for vengeance against Dimmesdale is a natural outcome of his sense of self-defeat, covetousness and possessiveness of Hester as his wife. The virulent bacillus in his mind already started infecting from the first moment when he has witnessed his wife on the scaffold with an illegitimate child. The unconscious hostility started from that moment even before he recognised the lover of his wife. Chillingworth could have easily reacted with an outbreak of rage but Chillingworth is a psychologist who knows the vindictive way to torture and avenge. In this case, Master Prynne's ego ideal decides upon sadistic fantasies as an outlet of his archaic rage and hence his 'unholy' act is the only therapeutic way to pacify his soul. Roger Chillingworth is a perfect example of double personality whose art of disguise and pretension reflects how scrupulously this man is hiding his deep malice. In his own self-analysis in the prison house when he visits Hester, he acknowledges the gulf of age difference between himself and Hester but at the same time he elevates himself because of his scholarship while Hester is demeaned because of her physical beauty. He is emotionless, calm and determined in his ruthless methods of avenging. The devilish desire for revenge is expressed when Hester identifies how his eyes reflect his mind:

> "There came a glare of red light out of his eyes, as if his soul were on fire" (*SL* 163). He declares this transmogrification as a metamorphosis from a scholar to a fiend:
>
> In a word, old Roger Chillingworth was a striking evidence of man's faculty of transforming himself into a devil, if he will only, for a reasonable space of time, undertake a devil's office. (*SL* 254)

In his psychological game, Arthur is his bait and he wants to relish the delayed pleasure of punishing him instead of vanquishing the culprit at once. Master Prynne has always been enmeshed in his vision of paramount self-importance as a scholar but all of a sudden when that image is shattered just because of Hester's thrusting aside of the authoritative figure of himself as a husband, it is too difficult to accept such devalued self-esteem. This surge of fear threatens him to find out his rival. This psycho-sexual anxiety if not recognised by anyone else is detected by Hester Prynne from the scaffold. The sudden appearance of her supposed dead husband, at that moment, wiped away all the public ignominy that she is being subjected to. On the other hand, her psychological tumult is reflected in the sudden paleness and tremor on her face. Chillingworth, every moment, realises that physically, emotionally, psychologically and even intellectually he is an outsider in Hester Prynne and Dimmesdale's love story and hence his attempt is to make them realise the significance of his position in their lives. Therefore, Hester realises lately that her great mistake in life is in hiding from Dimmesdale the truth of the physician's identity who accompanies him like a leech everywhere. Through Chillingworth's complex psychology, Hawthorne is trying to show the jealous male voyeur and how jealousy is a male prerogative reflecting the right of ownership over the woman, he possessed once. His obsession in digging the heart of the minister is so intense that it seems like a phantom, who is invisibly pursuing Hester and Dimmesdale everywhere. In the midst of the dark night when Hester, Dimmesdale and Pearl are standing on the scaffold, the physician arrives with a predatory gaze. When Hester and Dimmesdale plan to escape from the town along with Pearl, Hester discovers that her husband is the fourth passenger apart from three of them. This voyeuristic quest is out of a sado-masochist purpose where he knows that the end is futile and hence at the end, he effectively witnesses his own destruction as well as Dimmesdale's tragic denouement.

In contrast to these adult psychologies of the fictional characters, the depiction of incomprehensible behaviour of child Pearl is another attempt by Hawthorne to bring in the child's psychological abnormality. Pearl's fluctuation of moods and aberrant nature even perplexed her mother who questions God about such bizarre nature of the child. The narrator calls her 'an imp of evil', emblem and product of sin, because of her strange intuitions and aberrant behaviour. Her bespattering the Governor with water, screaming and making frantic gestures when Hester throws away the scarlet letter and her wild frantic joy in the midst of nature make her unique from the rest of the Puritanical children. Child rearing has been an essential aspect in the Puritanical New England; especially when it focuses on stern dictatorial methods. By the time Hawthorne has turned into a father, the concept of child rearing changed where the focus is more on love, affection, care and gentle authority. Hester's art in rearing Pearl is like her needlework that reflects her passion, patience and her intellectual musings. She has always draped and adorned Pearl in bright gorgeous colour, as a result, Pearl's audacity to adorn herself with wildflowers and seaweed in her fanciful solitary play is nothing unnatural. Pearl's psychology is an extension of Hester's psychology or rather she is the reflection of Hester's childhood because she inherited her mother's passionate, rebellious nature. One is amazed at Hester's immesurable self-control in confronting her ordeal on the scaffold and how after the day's commotion, her motherly self bears patiently the painful tortuous cry of baby Pearl inside the prison.

Unlike her mother, Pearl does not have "the principle of being". She has developed fluctuating moods and vulnerable feelings. She is so aberrant that even her mother fails to forecast Pearl's anomalies. But if one penetrates into Pearl's psychology, one must realise that Pearl's experiences in life have taught her that the world around her is hostile, apart from nature and her mother, the entire world seems to be in animosity with her. The abuse inflicted at Pearl by the society including children, ministers and commoners definitely result in neurological deviation. Hawthorne has analysed the complex interplay of psychological and physiological forces in Pearl. Unlike other babies, when little Pearl is born in this world, Pearl in her unconscious level of mind has archived irrational, perplexing, abusive faces of hatred and anger instead of adorable gaze. One cannot deny the impact of Hester's internal turmoil and strife that affected Pearl in her mother's womb. Both the genetic influence and environmental influences have been the root cause of Pearl's defiant spirit. Apart from Pearl's wild mind, her hostile aggression is aimed at hurting others which reflects her adopted father Master Prynne. Psychologists have concluded that aggressive hostility in children is developed when they are rejected or denied. Though Hawthorne has tried to trace Dimmesdale and Hester's origin, there is no reminiscence or reference to Chillingworth's childhood and there is an apprehension that Chillingworth can be an orphan, denied of parental love and care. Initially both Master Prynne and Pearl are first rejected or ignored by the world but later they rejected and ignored it. For Chillingworth, isolation arrived by his self-chosen world of knowledge while for Pearl it arrived because of her sinful birth but later both of them embraced isolation with full force.

> D.H. Lawrence, while commenting on Pearl's unique psyche explains, "We cannot help regarding the phenomenon of Pearl with wonder, and fear, and amazement, and respect.... Nowhere in literature is the spirit of much of modern childhood so profoundly, almost

> magically revealed..." and he further adds "she has a sort of reckless gallantry, the pride of her own deadly being."[6]

In *Studies in Classic American Literature*, Lawrence explains the danger and pleasure of characters like Pearl:

> ...poor, brave, tormented little soul, always in a state of recoil, she'll be a devil to men when she grows up. But the men deserve it.... Poor little phenomenon of a modern world, she grows up into the devil of a modern woman. The nemesis weak-kneed modern men.[7]

Why does Lawrence claim that Pearl is modern emanating rebellious soul dangerous to men? Lawrence's warning hints at the alternate impulsive self that exists in every child which when the surrounding environment provokes, comes out as behavioural abnormality. When the child easily accepts and accords with the surrounding atmosphere, it is termed by Lawrence as 'sympathetic impulse', and the 'voluntary impulse' occurs from the child's inner self which reacts with violence to the surrounding environment. Lawrence exemplifies this with the simplest example of the baby, feeding milk from the mother's breast. When a child draws milk silently, it is the 'sympathetic impulse', as if drawing away all love and happiness of the mother's soul but when the same baby savagely grabs and claws the breast kicking and howling, Lawrence explains that the 'voluntary impulse' is at work because of the 'violent little pride'. When Pearl is bouncing in the midst of the nature or speaking spontaneously with the river, her 'sympathetic impulse' is at work but her sadistic laughter, shriek and obstinacy that scared Hester is due to her 'voluntary impulse', as if mocking the world that betrayed her.

Hawthorne's attempt to split the diabolical and spiritual aspects of Pearl's psychic growth is because of his own experience in his childhood of the conscious and the unconscious as well as of his daughter Una's strange psychology. Hawthorne may not use the modern technique of stream of consciousness which Lawrence, James Joyce, Virginia Woolf and May Sinclair have used but it is no doubt that being the first American psychological novelist, he has paved the way for his successors. Hawthorne's autobiographical elements in his writings have reflected nadir of psychological turmoil and that the actual action is the mind than in the external world. The source of psychological mystery in Hawthorne's dark romances primarily *The Scarlet Letter* is his own philosophy of mesmerism in viewing the world as well as his own life. It is the law of mesmerism in his writings that unleashes his technique of discovering new insights, wisdom, revelations, repression and psychological journey of the self. In the "Custom House," chapter, Hawthorne secretively repents the crime of his forefathers. Though Hawthorne believed in the principle of detachment between the artist and his creation, yet consciously and unconsciously he has sometimes availed himself and his mystic psychology as a means to wonder into the interplay of light and darkness of the minds of his fictional characters. In *Graham's Magazine*, Edward Percy Whipple recognises in *The Scarlet Letter* the "movements of morbid hearts when stirred by strange experiences...."[8] What Hawthorne aimed to reveal in the novel is that the mysterious shadow of the past in the present, the 'uncanny' fear of the witchcraft, the winding dark forest are all reflections of the light and darkness of human soul. Hawthorne's art of anatomy of human mind is exceptionally postmodern and the way he attempts to unravel the profound intricacies reveals that a novelist is not merely an artist but also a psychologist, a philosopher and can also possess preternatural divinely or monstrous power to read the mind of god's most complicated creation:

> In the depths of every heart, there is a tomb and a dungeon, though the lights, the music, and revelry above may cause us to forget their existence, and the buried ones, or prisoners whom they hide.[9]

NOTES

1. Hawthorne, Nathaniel. *Earth's Holocaust* (*From "Moses from an Old Manse"*), BompaCrazy.com, 2005, p. 189.
2. Brooks, Van Wyck. *The Flowering of New England, 1815-1865*. New York: E.P. Dutton and Company, 1936, p. 224-25.
3. Anonymous. *Mysteries of Bedlam Or Annals of the Madhouse*. London: T.B. Peterson, 1850, p. 92.
4. Aristotelian *The Art of Rhetoric* defines 'phthonos' as the pain felt towards another's prosperity. It is purely an Aristotelian term for envy.

For Aristotle, the emotion phthonos is related to moral badness and happens between two equal persons.

5. Bloom, Harold. *Marcel Proust*. Infobase Publishing, 2009, p. 20.
6. Lawrence, D.H. *Symbolic Meaning*. Viking Adult, 1964, p. 137.
7. Lawrence, D.H. *Studies in Classical American Literature*. U.K: Cambridge University Press, 1979, p. 105.
8. Allan Poe, Edgar. Graham, Graham, George R. Ed. *Graham's Magazine*. U.S.A: Indiana University, 2009, p. 145.
9. Hawthorne, Nathaniel. "The Haunted Mind" in *Best Known Works of Nathaniel Hawthorne*. U.S.A: Kessinger Publishing, 2003, p. 423.

Chapter 6

THE NEW EVE HESTER PRYNNE AND SEXUAL POLITICS

In one of his letters in the *Salem Gazette,* Nathaniel Hawthorne wrote a biographical essay on Anne Hutchinson, the American feminist. In that letter he claims that the Puritanical society's marginalisation of Hutchinson as a disruption is unexpected but at the same time, the inequality between man and woman is an inherent fact:

> Woman's intellect should never give the tone to that of man; and even her morality is not exactly the material for masculine virtue. A false liberality which mistakes the strong division-lines of Nature for arbitrary distinctions, and a courtesy, which might polish criticism, but should never soften it, have done their best to add a girlish feebleness to the tottering infancy of our literature. The evil is likely to be a growing one.

This comment is unbelievable from a man like Nathaniel Hawthorne in whose life women have made more impact than men. The company of various women in his life, like his intellectual wife, stimulating sister-in-law, his two devoting sisters, his outspoken daughters and widowed mother have made him strongly realize that women are not meant for domination or subjugation but they are spiritual, emotional and intellectual partners without whom a man's life is incomplete. Irrespective of such women in his life, in the same letter Hawthorne further adds:

> Differences between the sexes were total and innate. Women were inherently more religious, modest, passive,

> submissive and domestic than men, and were happier doing tasks, learning lessons and playing games that harmonized with their nature.[1]

Hawthorne is considered to be the first American male writer to create a novel based on a female protagonist endowed with stunning beauty, sexuality, artistry, and intelligence in the superficial, oppressive and judgemental Puritanical society. Even in his short stories and romances, Hawthorne has penned variety of female characters ranging from strong, independent-minded, and self-confident, to women who are sacrificed and destroyed because of patriarchal dominance. Apart from such brilliant strong characterisations like Zenobia or Hester, Hawthorne has also beautifully sketched Old Esther Dudley in his short story "Old Esther Dudley" who represented a legacy of an ancient world and also served as the relic of the past. Aristocratic in her ancient lineage, eccentric in her behaviour, she is abundant with effervescent magical power and affection for her children. Similarly the proud character of Hepzibah Pyncheon from his novel *The House of the Seven Gables* also represents the brave spirit in woman while Phoebe Pyncheon from the same novel representing the simplicity of country life and tender love. In "Rappaccini's Daughter", Beatrice, the daughter of the infamous scientist Signor Giacomo Rappaccini in 16th century Padua, is a beautiful, kind and innocent young woman who is isolated from society because of her father's diabolical knowledge of botanical poisons and his experiment upon her. Randall Stewart in the essay "Hawthorne's Female Characters"[2] has categorised Hawthorne's female characters into three types: "the wholesome New England girl, bright, sensible, and self-reliant", "the frail, sylph-like creature, easily swayed by a stronger personality" and "the woman with an exotic richness in her nature". It is difficult to categorise Hester Prynne in any of these categories because her 'exotic richness' is equally mesmerising like her 'self-reliance.'

As a revolutionary character born from the womb of the prison, Hester emerges with the mark of original sin. Hawthorne never imagined that her occult heroine will reborn again and again in American popular culture and historical imagination haunting and questioning about women's emancipation. Though a marginalised figure, who stands at the limbo of history, yet Hester is the gateway for Mr Prue, Hawthorne and the readers to realise that all history is contemporary. She is not a mythical cultural icon but a living memory pricking the American consciousness and reminding the struggle of first settler women. Hester is saturated in Puritanical codes of living for she evokes in Hawthorne the story of the barbarity of his first ancestor William Hathorne who gave heinous punishment to Ann Cole. Ann Cole is being whipped and dragged behind a horse-cart and finally banished from the community into the dark ominous woods. She reminds him of John Hathorne who "inherited the persecuting spirit and made himself so conspicuous in the martyrdom of the witches, that their blood may fairly be said to have left a stain upon him" (*SL* 16). Hester therefore reflects the repressed guilt about the ancestral legacy of cruelty and inhumanity in Hawthorne. Her creation is the outcome of Hawthorne's frustration and psychic condemnation that tortured Hawthorne throughout his life. Hester Prynne personifies Hawthorne's consciousness of a primitive, unreasonable mind that is waiting for a revolution. Like Hester, he is also imprisoned in the Hathorne family legacy and striving against it. This evergreen heroine of American literary repertoire also reflects the American unconsciousness of the 'other', hinting at its repressions and fears. Hester stands on the scaffold of history, gazing and gazed upon, wrestled with and abused, but cannot be easily exhausted or erased.

The origin of Hester's name is intriguingly intertextual because she echoes the Greek goddess Hestia, or the Roman equivalent Vesta. The divine quality is never ignored by Hawthorne reminding us of the very first emergence of the heroine out of the prison door with her illegitimate three months baby near her bosom as if she reminds us of Virgin Madonna. Locating his heroine in a rigid Puritanical society, Hawthorne has no other choice but to punish Hester for her adulterous union with her pastor, though his sympathy with Hester betrays itself occasionally throughout the narrative. This tacit support of Hawthorne with Hester as a subtext also sometimes gives this impression that Hester might emerge as the victorious woman. Apart from her Greek epistemology of her name, one cannot deny the biblical Queen Esther whose relation to sorrow, duty and love are seen to be reflected in Hester Prynne. After all, one cannot deny that *The Book of Esther*[3] which has been demonstrably part of the Puritanical canon. Hawthorne has been an avid reader of Bible and hence Queen Esther must be there in his mind.

It is believed that Hawthorne has attempted to represent the modern Eve in Hester Prynne. This archetypal figure with new dimensions is inspired from Hawthorne's own wife but deep down he desired to deconstruct the antebellum ideal of 'True Womanhood/Angel' in the house. In his letter to his would be wife Sophia Peabody, Hawthorne addresses "Whether in bliss or agony, still you are mine own Dove—still my blessing—still my peace"[4] Hawthorne refers to the unalterable love for his wife and though she is his dove yet in his short story, "The New Adam and Eve" (1843) we find Eve is rejecting the age old stigmatisation that she is a 'temptress'. Unlike the Biblical Eve who is persecuted as the cause of the Fall, Hawthorne's Eve is the harbinger of salvation and not a blind follower of Adam. On the contrary Hawthorn's men of spiritual weakness like Dimmesdale require the spiritual guidance of this Modern Eve. Gilbert and Guber in *The Madwoman in the Attic* explain how the virtue of a 'good woman' remains in her virtue "making her man great". The Angel is meant to please the man, to lift him up and to give him the appearance of greatness. In Gilbert and Gubar's discussion, the "Victorian angel-woman should become her husband's holy refuge from the blood and sweat that inevitably accompanies a life of significant action," as if her purity, is like a living *memento* of the otherness of the divine". Gilbert and Gubar also suggest how in the patriarchal society men should decipher a realistic image of woman: "For the more secular nineteenth century…the eternal type of female purity was represented not by a Madonna in heaven but by an angel in the house".[5]

Through Hester Prynne's depiction, Hawthorne has captured the entire gamut of the Puritanical world and the position of women in the society. His psychological intervention through depiction of the gathered women's conversation in the 'display' of Hester Prynne as a sinner, reveals their lack of power and authority in life. The women's individual augment of opinion regarding Hester reflects momentary thrill of authority which they never possess otherwise. Their opinions reflect repression of their own desires which Hester Prynne dared to flaunt and therefore Hester has intensified their frustration. Their disgust and shame for Hester are indicative of their hapless powerless inferiority and envy. Hawthorne speculates this most terrible point of crisis where Hester is compelled to swallow unbearable public humiliation and bitter criticism. In the essay "The Obliquity of Signs", Millicent Bell explains this moment as "Hawthorne's antithesis between the solitary soul and society"[6] and this conflict of individual's stark isolation to their community is also autobiographical as Hawthorne has remained a secluded character throughout his life.

The sado-masochist crowd enjoy seeing the adulteress being punished as if satisfying their vaulted anger and disgust. Hester's punishment is seen as a necessary requirement for the purgation of the society and also to teach a lesson to those who dare to transgress. Walking down the memory lane, the readers are informed that at premature age, she is being married to a learned scholar older in age, whom she never loved but with great approbation admired his immense scholarship and knowledge. Hester is born of noble lineage in a "genteel but impoverished English family" in England, and like a true Christian has received all the virtuous preaching and lessons from her parents. Her marriage with Master Prynne is of necessity without any compatibility, passion and love. After a brief season in Amsterdam, it is decided that they should join the Puritans in Boston and while Hester ventured across the Atlantic first, her husband planned to join later. Soon the unfortunate news arrived that Master Prynne is presumed to be dead because of shipwreck while Hester in her full blooming youth, fell passionately in love with the most adorable minister of Boston, Arthur Dimmesdale. The illegitimate baby girl born out of this reprehensible relationship is named as Pearl. Being biologically privileged as a man, without any physical evidence in this 'adultery', Arthur Dimmesdale has remained in oblivion in the entire abomination while Hester Prynne remained at the receiving end of the scandalous diatribes. However, the real story begins when pilloried Hester spots her elderly husband in the crowd whose wrathful gaze of vengeance and sense of defeat silently ruminated the tempest of catastrophe in Hester's mind. From the Biblical perspective, marriage is covenant love ordained in heaven by God as suggested in the Genesis (2:23): "This at last is bone of my bones and flesh of my flesh; she shall be called woman, because she was taken out of man." Hence in this solemn obligation, any violation is seen as violation against God. Hester is therefore a violator against God as is therefore invested with Satanic spirit. Altering his name from Roger Prynne to Roger Chillingworth, the physician pledges to avenge the lover of his adulteress wife while Hawthorne's triangular plot of passionate relationship locates the revolutionary New Woman, Hester Prynne at the fulcrum of strife and turmoil.

Hawthorne lavishes the opulence of physical beauty of her heroine who is a tall young woman with a "figure of perfect elegance on a large scale." Her "dark and abundant hair" that reflect the shimmering "sunshine with a gleam" is reminiscent of the Babylonian seductress Lilith whose sinister power is considered to be demonic. Michelangelo has portrayed Lilith as a half-woman, half-serpent, coiled around the Tree of Knowledge while English poet, Dante Gabriel Rossetti, is captivated by her enchanting long hair. James Joyce reinterpreted the mythical image of Lilith as "patron of abortions." Lilith is considered to be the first wife of Adam and hence many feminists represent her image as emancipatory woman trying to seek independence from Adam. Hester's rich and dark deep eyes are expressive of some abysmal passion and power and the narrator explains how "her beauty shone out, and made a halo of the misfortune and ignominy in which she was enveloped." There is immense nobleness, dignity and gracefulness in her stature combined with a haughty smile. Hawthorne further adds that—

> ...never had Hester Prynne appeared more lady-like, in the antique interpretation of the term, than as she issued from the prison. Those who had before known her, and had expected to behold her dimmed and obscured by a disastrous cloud, were astonished, and even startled, to perceive how her beauty shone out, and made a halo of

> the misfortune and ignominy in which she was enveloped. (*SL* 81)

She is the allegorical untamed American land of rebellion and protest. The chiaroscuro of her black hair and mysterious eyes reflect the wilderness of nature, her celebratory libidinal excess and also a discursive manifestation of the repressed desires which remained latent in her conjugal life with Master Prynne. The narrator's detail anatomy of Hester's discursive body on the scaffold involves the politics of investigation, objectivity and public gaze especially in places like the marketplace, or outside the prison. The body must be distilled into discipline, punishment and surveillance. The blood-thirsty matrons in the crowd want to strip Hester, brand her on the forehead, or kill her. The scarlet alphabet 'A' on her bosom deflects, suppresses, and compresses within itself various radical solutions. Her fecundity which is the object of disgust and disdain will outstrip her punisher and her punishment. Patricia Crain in her essay "Allegory, Adultery and Alphabetization" observes on this physicality of Hester:

> Hester is large as a reminder of her recent pregnancy, and she is large to distinguish her from woman in the nineteenth century. She is large to provide a canvas for the A; she is a sculpture, a painting by Raphael, a picture in an emblem book: *Grammatica*, for example.
>
> She is large, like a monument, to hold the gaze of the audience; she is large because she has to remain visible from afar.[7]

In Hester Prynne, Hawthorne has invested the unprecedented mental strength and fortitude, the transcendentalist qualities, which Emerson extolled in his famous essay, "Self-Reliance" (1841), and which Margaret Fuller apparently rewrites for a female audience in her equally famous but longer work, *Woman in the Nineteenth Century* (1845). Hester's sexual charm is stimulated because she is invested with tremendous power of individual will, a post-Emersonian nineteenth-century version of the Protestant will Puritan spirit. Hester survives freedom in solitude, even when that solitude is a punishment but Dimmesdale with his Puritanical spirit perished because of his lack of individualism. Hester exemplifies that she is strong yet kind, brave yet humanitarian and industrious yet not greedy after wealth and power. Hence, she does not fit into the traditionally constructed patriarchal images of women.

She has withstood the test of time again and again and her defiance is heightened when interviewed by Chillingworth or the Puritanical ministers and governor; Hester remained unalterable. Without any one to defend for her, she alone has fought in Governor Bellingham's palace over the issue of Pearl's guardianship. Her immense self-reliance stands in opposition to Dimmesdale and Chillingworth. She has not only defied law but her words gushing with emotion have the intense power to convince the listener. She becomes her own designer label, advertised in the luxuriant embroidery of her 'A' and in that way she has transfigured. This process of transfiguring of Hester is best eulogised by Harold Bloom in his introductory essay on Hawthorne, transforming the fictive character into living flesh and blood:

> If the mythic being, "Walt Whitman," is our closest representation of the American "Adam early in the morning," then Hawthorne's Hester Prynne, besieged heroine of *The Scarlet Letter*, is still more the fictive American Eve, a worthy rival to Milton's rather English Eve in *Paradise Lost*. Hester luminously stands out against the darkening backgrounds of Hawthorne's vision of Puritan repression. Critics have remarked that Hester's tragedy was to have existed too early in American social history, a judgment I reject. Feminism and our enlightened sexual politics might not have saved the vitalistic, high-spirited Hester from the dilemma of never finding a man worthy of her sexual power and her self-reliance. The Satanic Chillingworth and the pathetic Dimmesdale would have been archaic objects for Henry James's Isabel Archer in *The Portrait of a Lady*, but the sublime Isabel, heiress of all the ages, marries the dreadful Osmond, fortune-hunter, snob, and parody of a Paterian aesthete. At seventy-seven, I meditate upon the thousands of young women I have taught. How many of them—brilliant, beautiful, absolutely free to choose—have emulated Hester Prynne

> and Isabel! Shakespeare teaches us that most remarkable women have to marry down: Rosalind, Portia, Beatrice, Imogen, quite aside from Lady Macbeth in what I fear is the happiest marriage in all the plays. Both Hawthorne, and his reluctant disciple, Henry James, emulate the Shakespearean model.[8]

Although Hester Prynne belongs to seventeenth century, she has all the germ of a radical American modern woman who exemplifies that successful single motherhood is possible. She has been victorious in her own ways to the dismal variety of Puritanical code of law. Through her relationships with two men, Hester metamorphoses from an impetuous woman into a strong willed compassionate woman. She destroyed the bloated ego and such illusionary idea of her aged husband, Chillingworth who believed that "intellectual gifts might veil physical deformity in a young girl's fantasy". Hester's lawful marriage with Master Prynne seems "ugliest remembrance", while she still hopes to reunite with her "illegitimate" lover Dimmesdale. It reflects her independent thought and spirit of rebellion and by the end of the novel, Hester becomes a proto-feminist mother figure.

The Puritans viewed motherhood as a glorious gift without which womanhood is incomplete. Hester Prynne however deconstructed the phallic signifier in proving that she is more capable to rear baby Pearl than Dimmesdale who denied his fatherhood till he died. The Puritanical code demands from Hester some way of relinquishing of her sexuality at the price of her survival and motherhood. The Puritans failed to understand that Hester's apparently "lost" sexual nature which is transferred to her daughter, whose passionate temperament apparently knows no repression. Hawthorne has invoked the most powerful myth of the Virgin and the child rooted in Pagan culture. The image of virgin mother and holy child as a religious iconography is transformed into the social context so that the narrator observes that a Papist might see in the spectacle of Hester and her baby on the scaffold "the image of Divine Maternity."

The iconic image of the Virgin Mother is always in blue and white hues of holiness and purity but Hester is draped in sombregrey symbolising her sin. Julia Kristeva suggests that the symbolic representation of the virgin body of Mary reduces female sexuality to "a mere implication," exposing only "the ear, the tears, and the breasts".[9] Hester's physicality is also shrouded in grey and hardly any part of her body is visible. Her hair is hidden under the tight-fitting cap while her breasts are shielded by the scarlet letter. But the irony is that Hester Prynne stands before the million gaze as if "fully revealed" yet fully concealed. What Hawthorne wants to suggest is that mere physicality has no significance, not even sexuality unless cultural value is inscribed on it. The scarlet letter is the cultural inscription on her body that provokes the Puritans to strip her off.

When Hester removed the scarlet letter in the forest, Pearl fails to recognise her biological mother. For Pearl, her mother's body inscribes her own identity. The absence of the scarlet letter from Hester's bosom makes her body as the space of the 'other'. Hawthorne captures the hyper sexualised power evoked when she unclasped the scarlet letter from her bosom and removed the cap that confines her hair. Pearl's fear reminds how the female body is the locus of patriarchal fear and sexual longing. Pearl is the extension of the same space of unscathed passion and hence she appears too captivating not only to the wild sea captain but also to the Puritanical authoritative figure like Wilson and Bellingham.

Single mothers, widowed mothers, abandoned mothers, impoverished mothers, and criminal mothers are some of the deviant form of motherhood that the Puritans never considered to be normative societal standards. These unregulated mothers always contested for a space of survival as their space is always intervened by politics and religion. Hawthorne contrarily reflected that for Hester Prynne, maternity is her weapon. It is a stigma and also a weapon against patriarchy. Anne Hutchinson is banished from her community and ultimately killed in an Indian attack. Hester survived because of Pearl. This unregulated space of motherhood in Hester's life is both reclusive and a space of freedom. She lived at the outskirt of the society but she has greater freedom than other mother in the society. Hawthorne showed throughout the novel that Pearl remained untouched by Puritanism and Hester is the only decision maker in Pearl's life. Hester's motherhood is against convention, she is a misfit and an outcast yet she enjoyed greater power in her motherhood than any other woman of New England. Her confidence and pride in single motherhood suggests antebellum rhetoric of republican motherhood. Hawthorne's description of Hester's first appearance with the baby is similar to her descriptive character sketch of Anne Hutchinson:

> In the midst, and in the centre of all eyes, we see the Woman. She stands loftily before her judges, with a determined brow, and, unknown to herself, there is a flash of carnal pride half hidden in her eyes, as she surveys the many learned and famous men whom her doctrines have put in fear.[10]

In her motherhood we come across the ignited spirit of female leadership, independent decision maker and above all her individual spirit to act both as the father and the mother. Hester became mother at her own will and she made a choice for the father of the child. In the process, she continues her day-to-day existence with dignity, raises her daughter Pearl in such a way so as to develop a mind of her own, acknowledges her own free will, and convinces both the fictional towns people and the readers that the alphabet A is not a sign of shame but also suggests her unyielding spirit and her autonomous strength untouched by masculinity.

If Dimmesdale is gifted with some spiritual power to utter spontaneously those golden words that compel his audience to be surcharged with emotions, then Hester Prynne's prayer echoes her honest anguish and afflictions. When the governor determines to take Pearl away from her, Hester frantically exclaims: "God gave me the child! He gave her in requital of all things else, which he had taken from me.... Ye shall not take her! I will die first!" (*SL* 168) Hester's strength lies in her honesty in contrast to Chillignworth or Dimmesdale.She acknowledges to Dimmesdale that by hiding her pregnancy from the minister, she has done a mistake: "A lie is never good, even though death threatens on the other side!" (*SL* 291) She is also transparent to Chillingworth regarding their conjugal life: "thou knowest that I was frank with thee. I felt no love, nor feigned any" (*SL* 112). She has kept her promise in carrying her husband's secret identity, and she tells the truth to Dimmesdale only after she is released from her pledge. Even with Pearl she never lied but represented everything with such simplicity so that the child can easily understand.

In the saga of the fallen woman, Hester Prynne exemplifies moral dereliction and moral inadequacy but the modern-day feminists have demonstrated that "Hester Prynism" is the inspiration of American woman military. Interestingly, the first woman bomber pilot, Lt. Kelly Flinn is being fired from her position in 1997 by the Air Force under the charge of adultery. As a radical model of a rebellious woman, Hester is the subject of indefinite interrogation and self-reflection. Conventionally, the fallen woman must die at the end of her story, perhaps because death is seen as the only honourable symbol of transforming the fall. Hester has used her silence as an act of resistance and like a modern Eve whose heel will bruise the serpent's head; she remained victorious at the end, proudly wearing the scarlet alphabet 'A' as the symbol of her love. Hawthorne unlike the English Victorian writers like Browning, Tennyson or Hardy cannot present his fallen woman as the abased figurehead of a fallen culture thereby justifying her crime. Hester is not concerned with virtuous wifehood and is hence seen in the mysterious shadow of witchcraft. Her sexual vibrancy is defined by the community as the malicious dark power of a seductress.

In the web of love, passion, betrayal, sin, guilt and revenge, Hester's heroism lies in facing the trials and tribulations alone and finding the art of survival through her artistic proliferation as a seamstress. From ancient times sewing and stitching are traditional cultural and aesthetic representation of femininity. Hawthorne reveals this fine artistic quality in Hester Prynne not just to present her in the traditional role of a seamstress, but he has a deep psychological introspection behind it. This quintessentially domestic feminine activity becomes an outlet for Hester's nexus to the world at large. We can anticipate a modern woman entrepreneur in Hester who is economically self-dependent and also takes the trouble of assisting the poor and the wretched. One should not misinterpret Hester's silence and her artistic outcome as Penelopian[11] submissiveness and female resistance. In case of Hester, the artistic creativity is the outcome of the repression of her sexual longing and passionate stigmatised by society. Art and sexuality are inextricably interlinked by Hawthorne. He has beautifully tried to philosophise human sexuality through art by reflecting on the Puritanical principle of self-denial and restriction to individual autonomy. Foucault has satirised how sex has been acknowledged even in marriage so long it remained "utilitarian and fertile". Hester's relation with Dimmesdale cannot receive social credence because the concept of sin dominates the matrix of sex. In the novel *The Blithedale Romance*, the character of Miles Coverdale is another example of sexually repressed isolated artist. In "The Artist of the Beautiful," Owen's artistic pursuits give way to creation of an artistic butterfly imbued with spirit. This is the outcome of his lack of self-confidence to express love for Annie, since—

> he had persisted in connecting all his dreams of artistical success with Annie's image; she was the visible shape in which the spiritual power that he worshipped, and on whose altar he hoped to lay a not unworthy offering, was made manifest to him.[12]

In the story "Drowne's Wooden Image," the sculptor, Drowne, erects a vivacious statue of a woman teemed with ardent life force. In *The Marble Faun*, Kenyon and Hilda exasperatedly express their repressed hidden love through sculpture and paintings because of social constrictions. Hester's exquisite embroidery is a testimony to the surging passions within her:

> Women derive a pleasure, incomprehensible to the other sex, from the delicate toil of the needle. To Hester Prynne, it might have been a mode of expressing, and therefore soothing, the passion of her life. (*SL* 125)

Hester is victorious and till the last day of her life, she has taken her own decision. Even when she is martyred almost as an angel, she has no reactions. The same society defamed her as an adulteress as well as Abel. Her decision to confront and withstand echoes words of Milton's Samson: "calm of mind all passion spent" as if prophesising the second coming of Christ. Hawthorne's Coverdale in *The Blithedale Romance* attacks Hollingsworth for "the intensity" of his "masculine egotism" and claims a woman ruler for his Utopia:

> I should love dearly—for the next thousand years at last—to have all government devolve into the hands of women.... Oh, in the better order of things, Heaven grant that the ministry of souls may be left in charge of women![13]

Women like Hester Prynne or Anne Hutchinson have reflected the androgynous tendency to break the patriarchal chains of limitations and what the society claimed as self-restrain is reversely shown as 'submission' by these women. *The Scarlet Letter* published just after the Seneca Falls of 1848 reflects the effect of emerging feminism and spirits of women like Harriet Martineau, Geraldine Jewsbury and Margaret Fuller. In Hester Prynne, Hawthorne has mingled transgression and conformity. Her existential act is a transgression in the Puritanical society because her choices have exceeded the limits and thereby breaching unjust commands. She is free yet imprisoned and though she wears the scarlet letter, yet she wears it in her own way. Though she is stigmatised, she has re-invented the meaning of the alphabet 'A' and re-established new identity. Even in her adherence to the society, Hester is always noted for her individualism. Her return to New England after Pearl's marriage is interpreted by the society as faithful conformity while for Hester it is due to her love for the minister, who died in that land that beckoned her back to New England. In overthrowing submission, exonerating libidinal energy, Hester is the living epitome of continuous transgression. The desire for autonomy in Hester has taken two kinds of form—physical and metaphysical. Hester like Flaubert's Madame Bovary has given a new definition to female desire and this desire includes all her chasm of contradictions in character—holy yet sinful, conventional yet radical. If the German philosopher Friedrich Nietzsche has developed the discourse of 'The Superman' who is the incarnation of human willpower, then Hester Prynne can be definitely claimed as 'Superwoman', who has the extraordinary strength of emerging with feminine Will Power.

NOTES

1. Welter, Barbara. *Dimity Convictions: The American Woman in the Nineteenth Century*. U.S.A: Ohio University Press, 1976, p. 4.

2. Randall Stewart, "Hawthorne's Female Characters" in *Nathaniel Hawthorne*. New Haven: Yale University Press, 1961, p. 279.
3. Dorothy, Charles V. *The Books of Esther: Structure, Genre and Textual Integrity*. Mansion House: Sheffield Academic Press, 1997.
4. Hawthorne, Nathaniel. *Love letters of Nathaniel Hawthorne*, 1839-1863. Vols. 1-2. U.S.A: NCR Microcard Editions, 1972, p. 101.
5. Gilbert and Guber in *The Madwoman in the Attic*. U.S.A: Yale University Press, 2000, p. 112.
6. Bell, Millicent. "The Obliquity of Signs" in *The Massachusetts Review*. Vol. 23, No. 1 (Spring, 1982), pp. 9-26.
7. Crain, Patricia. The Story of A: The Alphabetization of America from the New England Primer. U.S.A: Stanford University Press, 2000, p. 192.
8. Bloom, Harold. Nathaniel Hawthorne. U.S.A Infobase publishing, 2000, p. Xi.
9. Kisteva, Julia. "Stabat Mater," *The Female Body in Western Culture: Contemporary Perspectives*. U.S.A: Harvard University Press, 1986, p. 99.
10. Hawthorne, Nathaniel. *Tales and Sketches: Volume 2 of Library of America*. New York: Literary Classics of the United States, 1982, p. 23.
11. Penelope is the faithful wife of the legendary hero Ulysses from Homer's *Odyssey*. When twenty years have passed after the battle of Troy, the people of Ithaca which is the kingdom of Ulysses have started believing that Ulysses is dead except Penelope. All have already assumed that Penelope is now widow and should marry. As a result Penelope started receiving various proposals from great kings and even sometimes they thronged in the kingdom to woo her. She would have none of them; the hope that her husband would return was faint, but it never died. These men are ruthless, rude and greedy, and are determined not to leave until Penelope consents to marry one of them. Finally she declared that she could marry when until she would finish weaving an exquisitely shroud for Ulysses' father, the aged Laertes. While these men agreed to wait, Penelope used to unweave each night all her weaving she finished in the day.
12. Hawthorne, Nathaniel. *Selected Tales and Sketches (The Best Short Stories of Nathaniel Hawthorne)* Digireads.com Publishing, 2007, p. 224.
13. Hawthorne, Nathaniel. *The Blithedale Romance*. Arc Manor LLC, 2008, p. 95.

Chapter 7

THE CHILD OF NATURE: PEARL

In *An Essay Concerning Human Understanding*, John Locke claims that children are not born with innate ideas and their minds are 'tabula rasa' or empty slate which must be instructed and moulded accordingly. He emphasised on 'Reason' as the fundamental way to guide them and proper education is necessary for fruition and the maturity of the mind. Freedom or liberty for Locke refers to the ability to make a choice and does not suggest exemption from restraint:

> Let a child be but ordered to whip his top at a certain time every day, whether he has or has not a mind to it; let this be required of him as a duty...and see whether he will not soon be weary of any play at this rate? Is it not so with grown men?[1]

Perhaps Locke's theory has the undertone of cultural meanings in relation to child identity. Hawthorne's Pearl cannot be fitted into the Lockian theory but suggests that in the child, the essentialism of identity relates not only to family, parenthood but also to nationhood. No doubt Pearl is the messianic child figure in whom Hawthorne has invested the power to usher in a new paradise, which is democratic United States of America. The mental hygiene movement originating at the Johns Hopkins University focused fundamentally on the child's upbringing in the liberal democratic state. *Uncle Tom's Cabin*, another contemporary text of *The Scarlet Letter* almost raised innumerable sobs because of the character of little Eva.

Though suffering Eva is the product of evils of slavery, yet the child figure happened to be the resonating symbol of political, social and emotional vulnerability. John Winthrop's fascinating example of Anne Hutchinson's stillborn child has always signified in the Puritanical society the demise of evil and colonial upheaval. Thomas Paine used the image of the vulnerable child to segregate mother England's relation to New England. Thomas Paine's argument that "the infant state of the colonies" justifies their "separation from a corrupt parent" almost seems to be so applicable to the Puritanical order of segregating Pearl from her biological 'corrupt' mother Hester Prynne. The child in emerging America always stood as a test case for power dynamics and marginality. Thus the centrality of the figure of the child as the favourite trope and structural element in American literature is a long standing issue in relation to historical, political, religious and cultural discourses. Hawthorne's child character Pearl, daughter of Hester Prynne stands in the rich American venue with the promise of enlightenment, liberalist ideals of freedom, equality, and liberty. Hawthorne's symbolic child character also raises questions in relation to concepts of marginality, social dependency, lost histories, autonomy and independence of America as the 'cradle of liberty.'

The most complex modern child in American literature who has always been seen as the personification of her parental sin and yet endowed with immeasurable innocence and intelligence is Hawthorne's elf-child, Pearl in *The Scarlet Letter*. She illustrates freedom and liberty, Nature and passion and if she owes allegiance to anyone, it is only Nature. She is beyond the reach of Puritanical regulations and divine salvation but like an uncontrollable natural force, Pearl cannot be restricted within the social parameters. Like Hawthorne's daughter Una, she is a dynamic force than a static symbol. Hawthorne's daughter Una is said to be the primary source of Pearl's characterisation. When Una is born, Hawthorne has made several entries on her enigma and weird personality:

> ...here is something that almost frightens me about the child—I know not whether elfish or angelic, but, at all events, supernatural. She steps so boldly into the

> midst of everything, shrinks from nothings, has such a comprehension of everything, seems at times to have but little delicacy, and anon shows that she possesses the finest essence of it; now so hard, now so tender; now so perfectly unreasonable, soon again so wise. In short, I now and then catch aspect of her, in which I cannot believe her to be my child, but a spirit strangely mingled with good and evil, hunting the house where I dwell.[2]

When Una is born, feminity in contemporary America prescribes to code of behaviours which are socially constructed. Una's boldness appeared not only masculine but weird as a girl child and hence she appears almost anomalous, uncanny and supernatural. This reminds us of Spenser's Una seen through the lens of monstrosity and far removed from the traditional feminine doll like passivity. Like Una, Pearl becomes the ravaged battleground for critical discourses on gender perspectives. Pearl's defiance is a subject of horror to the patriarchal society. She creates her own laws, makes imaginary play mates and is happy to live in her own world like Una and her tempestuous nature. Pearl is perhaps such unique creation by Hawthorne who stands as both divinely and egregious. Pearl has the purity of being reared in the midst of nature but then she is not born of a mother of 'chastity' and hence she cannot be enshrined as 'angelic'. No doubt, Pearl's assertiveness and aggressiveness cannot be viewed by patriarchy as the sign of virtuosity and in the light of William Blake's philosophy this can be termed as the "Female Will" or the independent absolute self of a woman.

When we meet Little Pearl for the first time, she is an infant of three months, in a period of gestation, like Blakian "Ohio",[3] and represents the possibility of cohesiveness—a union between nature and society, individual passions and principles. Pearl is the moral self of both Hester and Dimmesdale. She is the Wordsworthian child who can resurrect the decaying spirit with her kiss and hence Dimmesdale gathers strength to confess his sin. In that way Pearl also regains a new identity from her narrow marginalised anonymous half orphanage. Pearl seems to have melted into a natural environment, caressed by the sun, enveloped by the forest and identified with the brook. In the midst of mother forest, wild fauna and flora, Pearl recognizes a kindred wildness. Hawthorne's Pearl is often claimed as a 'hieroglyphic'[4] who stands as a character on flame and therefore she will be difficult to decipher. She is uniquely intelligent, interrogative, fluctuating in her moods reminiscent of the Wordsworthian philosophy that the "child is the philosopher".[5] Hawthorne's philosophy of purity of soul uncontaminated by humanity is revitalised through Pearl. She seems to be more absorbed by nature than attracted by humanity. Her playmates include sun, dark black forest or the flowers. She symbolises the prelapsarian innocence as Hawthorne says of Pearl: "The infant was worthy to have been brought forth in Eden" and records the rumour that even a wolf in the forest, responsive to her primitive innocence, "came up, and smelt of Pearl's robe, and offered his savage head to be patted by her hand" (*SL* 294-295). Pearl is always associated with flower metaphor. When the Reverend Mr. Wilson asked her who has made her, Pearl immediately explains that "she had not been made at all, but had been plucked by her mother off the bush of wild roses, that grew by the prison door" (*SL* 213). Pearl like her mother discards reason and order of human society and embraces wilderness. She is also likened to a "floating sea-bird" (*SL* 322) or "a wild tropical bird, of rich plumage" (*SL* 212).

In the opening chapter of *The Scarlet Letter* Hawthorne refers to "a wild rose-bush" growing at the side of the prison door. Its flowers "might be imagined to offer their fragrance and fragile beauty to the prisoner as he went in, and to the condemned criminal as he came forth to his doom, in token that the deep heart of Nature could pity and be kind to him" (*SL* 73). The rose bush in the wilderness "sprung up under the footsteps of the sainted Anne Hutchinson" has immediately drawn attention to Pearl. It symbolises the natural world before the Puritans settled in New England. When Pearl and Hester visit Governor Bellingham's mansion, Pearl cries for the red rose from the garden. The primitive, mysterious lawlessness is seen in the wild rose blossoming with such passion like Pearl. Hawthorne's selection of the child's name has much to do with her significance in the life of her parents. She is the source of strength in Hester's life and her rarity and preciousness lies in the fact that she is the symbol of natural liberty. She is angelic whose talismanic presence performs an act of chastisement. She embodies the new woman with her freedom of choice and as a "half-fledged angel of judgment". Hawthorne reflects that Pearl has "nothing in common with a bygone and buried generation"; she "had been made afresh" and "must perforce be permitted to live her own life, and be a law unto herself." The Puritanical world may see her as "imp", "perverse", "demon offspring", "elf-child", "witch baby" but like a real pearl, created from irritation and extracted from its living source, Hawthorne's Pearl is the emerging revolutionary spirit of women.

Pearl's appearance and reference in the novel are to be found primarily in four of the twenty-three chapters of the novel (i.e. chaps. I, IX, XI, XVII) and also in the conclusion. However, Pearl's reference implicitly or explicitly occur throughout the novel. As the symbol of her parents' sin, messenger of anguish and joy, moral guardian and rebel against Puritanical order, her presence in the novel is unavoidable. She serves as the connecting link and electric chain for Hawthorne to build the plot. Preconciously intelligent, bewilderingly subtle, frighteningly independent, and penetratingly wise, her perversity is the protesting medium against social and religious authority. Pearl admonishes patriarchal hegemonical ideal of womanhood. Her instinct of truth and unconscious awareness in recognising the good and the evil, or Chillingworth as the Black Man or inherent affection towards Dimmesdale is more prophetic that reflects the purity of her soul uncontaminated by social evils. This is complemented by her physical beauty as if she reflects Wordsworthian Lucy in terms of natural intimacy and osmosis with nature. Like Ruth or Lucy who is "a lovelier flower/ On earth", Pearl is segregated from human companionship of the civil society. What Wordsworth uttered for Ruth can also be expressed for Pearl:

> A slighted child, at her own will
> Went wandering over dale and hill,
> In thoughtless freedom, bold.

When Wordsworth reflects on the solitude of Lucy Gray, it seems that he is reverberating life of Hester Prynne's child:

No mate, no comrade Lucy knew;
She dwelt on a wide moor,
—The sweetest thing that ever grew
Beside a human door![6]

Pearl's beauty corresponds to freedom and passion, the spontaneous wanton energy, her frolicking laughter, the mysterious untamed enchantment, her impetuous conversation with the falcons, her sportive spirit of hide and seek with the sun and the cloud—have contributed the wild beauty of Pearl. Pearl stands for regenerative, reincarnative and talismanic force. She is the hope of a world free from pretensions and repressions. Pearl is nurtured by her human mother Hester and nourished by Mother Nature. Pearl's wilderness is not of savagery but of the Blakian stage of Innocence:

> "rich and luxuriant beauty; a beauty that shone with deep and vivid tints; a bright complexion, eyes possessing intensity both of depth and glow, and hair already of a deep, glossy brown and which, in after years, would be nearly akin to black." (*SL* 151)

Hawthorne here invests Pagan values in Pearl especially in her glossy, brown hair and 'bright complexion' that suggest that Pearl is a mismatch to the dull shabby world of the Puritans. Pearl's exuberant beauty and tyrannical will may be anti-Puritan but there is no repressive secret. She is also the moral guardian for Dimmesdale and an efficient cause of the salvation of Hester and Dimmesdale and particularly provides the motivation for the public confession of Dimmesdale. She enables Hester to face hardships and sufferings but at the same time is the source of her spirit of struggle and pride. She saves Hester from human isolation during the years she has been set apart to infamy. The second scaffold scene provides another example of Pearl's hinting Dimmesdale towards the path of transformation. The forest scene illustrates Pearl's efforts to affect her parents' salvation by pointing out to their error in judgment and action. In the final scene Arthur requested Pearl to kiss him as the sign of reconciliation that she has refused him in their past reunion. The narrator explains that Pearl kissed his lips as she has kissed the lips of her mother when she has restored the scarlet letter to her bosom in the forest but for the first time Pearl's precious tears are seen almost transmogrifying her father from his sin to salvation. She is the redemptive force that allowed the pent up human emotion to be gushed out after years of repression and fear.

Through the introduction of the character of Pearl, Hawthorne is trying to contemplate on the concept of domestic world of children and how significantly it affects their psychology.

The Hawthorne couple is said to have created the paradise of happiness for their three children irrespective of tempestuous strife and poverty in their journey of life. Hawthorne believed that domestic bliss is fulfilled by the presence of both the parents since in his early childhood Hawthorne has felt the emptiness due to the absence of his father. In his short-story "Little Annie's Ramble" published in 1835 in Youth's Keepsake, we see his attempt to capture child psychology in the domestic world. In this story Hawthorne explains to be jovial and happy is more important for a child than to be moralised and sermonized. When Pearl proclaims "I am Mother's child", her statement is a denial of patriarchy. Denial and absence of a fatherly figure have been always perturbing in Hawthorne's life and such paternal deprivation and ambivalence about the fatherly figure has always created some fear of identity crisis in Hawthorne's life. It relates to bigger issues like legitimacy and authenticity of the child. Hawthorne even did not have any memory about his naval-captain father to cherish and cling to as the vestige of fatherly identity. This is aggravated by his mother Elizabeth's bridal pregnancy in the Puritanical era. Written upon the death of his mother, this novel problematizes the question of illegitimacy that always haunted Nathaniel Hawthorne. The image of the ship captain appears also in *The Scarlet Letter* who throws a gold chain towards Pearl to draw her attention. The chain may symbolise wealth but also signifies bondage as the narrator describes how it looks like a hangman's noose or like an iron chain that oppresses a slave or drags a body to the ocean floor. The aporia of emotional ambivalence and physical absence of a father figure is a social improvisation which Hawthorne feels can clinically unnerve someone. The fact that for the first time Pearl's tears humanised the child after the confession of her father shows that as if this paternal validity is essential. The questions of legitimacy and illegitimacy are directly proportional to one's own identity. Interestingly like Pearl, Chillingworth's parental background has remained anonymous and when at the end of the story, it is disclosed that the physician has entailed all his property in the name of Pearl; it seems that Chillingworth has recognised Pearl to be in the same boat of inhibition and identity crisis. Interestingly after Chillingworth invests Pearl with his estate, Pearl is shown to be living happily ever after. Her happy married life is almost legitimated by Chillingworth whose own mysterious orientation is never resolved by the narrator. Both Pearl and Chillingworth are like palimpsest paradoxically unreadable and yet induced with multiple meanings. Both Chillingworth and Pearl undergo transformation and are more symbolic representations. Despite Dimmesdale's ownership of "her father's cheek," Chillingworth transformed wild Pearl into "Pearl Prynne" by giving her social recognition and by becoming himself her social father. His struggle for legitimacy throughout his life ended when he ensures Pearl with legitimate identity. The curse of being a fatherless child ultimately ends with blessedness when Pearl has the choice of a host of fathers ranging from heavenly father, biological father and the surrogated father and yet her resonating words echo the spirit of feminism: "I am Mother's child."

Pearl is another version of the scarlet letter while for the society she is the symbolic representation of Hester's sin. Pearl is adorned in bright colourful attires that mimic the scarlet letter. Hester is proud to reveal that Pearl is the reflection of the same rebellious spirit of her mother. Though Hawthorne has never depicted Hester in her passionate youth yet we can imagine it when we see such jubilant spirit of Pearl. She cannot be confined within any rules and regulations but is the mistress of her own whims. She is Hester's conscience as well as her passion. Pearl is instinctively attracted by the letter on her mother's bosom and for her; the identity of her mother is associated with the letter. When Hester throws the letter away, Pearl cannot reconcile her mother's resurgent youth and until Hester wears it, she remained detached from her mother. Pearl desires for another similar letter on her own chest but this time naturally adorned by grasses and leaves. For Pearl, this new alphabet "A" stands for angel. Like her mother, she is wild and capricious but at the same time a vibrant passionate artist who knows how to play with imagination. In her artistic effusion Pearl stands for freedom. Her frantic outburst of excess of emotion and passion are all channelled when like her seamstress mother, she decors herself with flowers and leaves, neatly and artistically suturing nature and humanity.

In "Little Annie's Ramble," from his 1842 collection, *Twice-Told Tales*, Hawthorne has written,

> As the pure breath of children revives the life of aged men, so is our moral nature revived by their free and simple thoughts, their native feeling, their airy mirth.... Their influence on us is at least reciprocal with ours upon them.[7]

Like a treasure inside the oyster, Pearl is the most precious child character in American Literature who stands for enormity and purity of the sea of life. Like the beautiful pearl that remains hidden inside the sea and is discovered as the nature's transcendental creation, similarly the child Pearl is the harbinger of light, beauty and purity. She is the reincarnation of the best potentialities of humanity, like the Coleridgean incipient beauty endowed with human sensibilities as well as shower of benign spirituality.

NOTES

1. Locke, John. *The Works of John Locke to which is Added the Life of the Author and a Collection of Several of His Pieces*. Oxford University Press, 1823, p. 68.
2. Doren, Carl Van. *The American Novel, 1789-1939*. Library of Alexandria, 1947, pp. 430-31.
3. Ohio is the first stage of the journey of life in Blakian philosophy. It is prior to Innocence.
4. A hieroglyph is a kind of a script which consists of pictures. Its origin is in the ancient Egyptian writing system. In Neoplatonism, especially during the Renaissance, a "hieroglyph" was an artistic representation of an esoteric idea, which Neoplatonists believed actual Egyptian hieroglyphs to be.

5. William Wordsworth in his poem 'Ode on Intimations of Immortality' has explained how a child in its purest form and in the solemn joyous relationship with nature becomes the true philosopher of life. The way the glory of nature affects the child's mind cannot be explained by an adult and the child at that stage can best define what is 'truth.'
6. Wordsworth, William. *The Miscellaneous Poems of William Wordsworth: In Four Volumes*. Vol. 1 Longman, Hurst, Rees, Orme, and Brown, 1820, p. 14.
7. Reynolds, John Larry. (Ed) *A Historical Guide to Nathaniel Hawthorne*. Oxford University Press, 2001, p. 80.

Chapter 8

ARTHUR DIMMESDALE: A BUNDLE OF CONTRADICTIONS

Surrounded by darkening forest, the "City Upon a Hill" of the Puritans of Massachusetts Bay Colony is seen to be the edification of culture and certitude. They believed that religion is the bedrock of this 'new Eden' and hence the emissaries of the new form of Christianity are the most essential luminaries on whom the emergence of the nation is dependent. The ministers are supposed to set the example of the essence of spirituality and any unlawful sexual practice by them is considered to be sinful. Sexual indulgence outside the code of marriage is seen to be evil and therefore John Winthrop often articulated stories about how children born out of illegitimate relationships appear monstrous. The ministers are strongly encouraged to repress their natural desires as a way of fighting against wicked impulses. Dimmesdale's erotogenic masochism is the outcome of debasing his body with a sense of desecration. The body is not a temple but an abhorrent vault for him which he hates consciously but unconsciously admires because it is the same bodily presence that causes adorations among Salem community. Being the Puritanical ministers he is fully aware that holy marriage is the true union with Christ while the union of Adam and Eve is considered to be the forbidden state. The irony lies that Dimmesdale knows deep down in his heart that the bodily need is natural no matter how blatantly obscene and filthy it seems. Adultery or sexual liaison in the lives of the ministers is seen as blasphemy in order to remain at morally high vantage point. Arthur Dimmesdale thus vividly illustrates the conflicting trauma of being eternally in shame and anxiety. D.H. Lawrence in his sarcastic observation on the duality of human mind has selected Hawthorne's most extrusive fictional hero, Arthur Dimmesdale in order to show the bigotry of Puritanical New England:

> You have your pure-pure young parson Dimmesdale.
> You have the beautiful Puritan Hester at his feet.
> And the first thing she does is to seduce him.
> And the first thing he does is to be seduced.
> And the second thing they do is to hug their sin in secret, and gloat over it, and try to understand.
> Which is the myth of New England.[1]

Dimmesdale's commission and omission of the 'sin' are reflection of the duality of his mind and his manipulative personality. Being the Puritan minister of seventeenth-century New England, Dimmesdale is well aware how public exhibitionism of the sinner is essential and yet every action and every word of Arthur Dimmesdale is pretentious and double standard. He is the egoistical Adam in the Eden of New England filled with inherent pride and ambiguity like his creator Nathaniel Hawthorne. Hawthorne's conflict between emerging psychology and traditional theology becomes blatant in this self-divided character who is an embodiment of extreme narcissism and dissembling religion. This cognition of Dimmesdale can be best explained in the words of the German-American political theorist Hannah Arendt:

> But it could be that we...will forever be unable to understand, that is, to think and speak about, the things which we are able to do.[2] Dimmesdale is eternally hesitant to explain why and how he indulged in his relationship with Hester Prynne because never in the text the narrator mentions any such moment that expresses the minister's love for the indomitable Hester Prynne.

Hawthorne's rebellious irony, scepticism in Puritanical order and the anatomy of sin and guilt all converge in the character of Dimmesdale. The story of Adam Blair by John Gibson Lockhart is similar to that of Dimmesdale. Adam Blair, like

Arthur Dimmesdale, is a Calvinistic minister who becomes the lover of a married woman and at the end overwhelmed with remorse, makes a public confession. The real life sources of the fictional character of Dimmesdale are innumerable and varied. Hawthorne's maternal ancestor, Nathaniel Manning who had committed incest with his two sisters left an indelible mark in Hawthorne's memory. The image of the Biblical character of David who committed adultery is also reflected in the character of Dimmesdale. Hawthorne also has been thoroughly aware of the Puritanical poet Michael Wigglesworth and his controversial homosexual relationships with students or John Cotton and his relationship with Anne Hutchinson. Hawthorne satirically chose Arthur Dimmesdale's name reflecting the chivalric romance of the Arthurian legendary world but his last name 'dim' suggests the faint perspective of his character. Even 'dale' suggests hollowness in his religious faith and love for Hester. Dimmesdale is the perfect example of Hawthorne's detestation to repression and the fatal consequence of it. His animalsque self which Chillingworth has rightly diagnosed is in conflict with his egoistical self. This dilemma is termed by E. Michael Jones in the essay "The Dimmesdale Syndrome: Why Confession is a Necessity" as "Dimmesdale syndrome". Dimmesdale syndrome thus relates to duality of mind and the eternal conflict of human mind. This duality is an inherent contradiction of the minister—his words are manipulative yet impressive, plaintive and pleading, emotional but lack sincerity.

Dimmesdale's first appearance eventuates when Hester Prynne with her three months old 'sinful' baby standing on the scaffold is swallowing the venomous abuses of the Salem community. In the words of Mr Wilson, he is the 'godly youth' whose 'tenderness and terror' are admired by all men and women including the ordinary, the powerful and the influential. Hawthorne has aptly captured the irony in the words of Governor Bellingham who requests the youthful minister Dimmesdale to enforce confession of Hester Prynne with his magical power:

> "Good Master Dimmesdale," said he, "the responsibility of this woman's soul lies greatly with you. It behoves you;

> therefore, to exhort her to repentance and to confession, as a proof and consequence thereof." (*SL* 100)

No doubt, the responsibility of Hester's abatement is related to Dimmesdale who most calmly enacted his stagecraft wearing the mask of the most spiritual minister of the world. The plaintiveness of his utterance surcharged the ambience with immaculateness as he sincerely urges Hester to name her lover:

> What can thy silence do for him, except it tempt him—yea, compel him, as it were—to add hypocrisy to sin? Heaven hath granted thee an open ignominy, that thereby thou mayest work out an open triumph over the evil within thee, and the sorrow without. Take heed how thou deniest to him—who, perchance, hath not the courage to grasp it for himself—the bitter, but wholesome, cup that is now presented to thy lips! (*SL* 102)

Such conscious attempt to hide one's own sin requires an alertness and playfulness of mind because the minister knows that Hester will never be able to utter his name. Even in Governor Bellingham's mansion he succeeds in convincing and winning the Puritanical authority by highlighting the essence of bonding between mother and child. In reality it is rooted in self-centredness because he is afraid that any kind of segregation between Pearl and Hester is dangerous because Hester may transcend the line of sanity and reveal Dimmesdale's identity. Being a minister his immediate reaction is that his involvement in adultery with Hester Prynne should be revealed which prompted him to speak so powerfully but his other self is assured that it is beyond his capability to self-declare his own sin. His message to Hester Prynne in the first scaffold scene is to initiate and help him in unleashing his identity but ironically being a minister his purpose in life is to unburden the sins of humanity by making them confess. However, irrespective of his impassioned yearning to be exposed by Hester, one cannot avoid the subtle suggestion that he has made to Hester. His urging is more to lighten Hester's shame by being a companion in their joint sin rather than self-loathing and repentance.

Dimmesdale is in his blind in self-glorified image and it is difficult for him to place himself in the fallen state. He lives in eternal penumbra and suffers perpetually. The tragedy remains in Dimmesdale's denial of his real self and deception to himself. Though Dimmesdale believed that shame is unalterable, inexpressible, and unbearable, yet it is his bloated ego that caused his tragic downfall. Dimmesdale's failure lies in his willing myopia to his pilloried image and incapability to come out of it. His false selfhood is profoundly threatened by emptiness and pretension. The fear of shame has triggered his repressive self-defence and self-loathing. Dimmesdale's mask of a concerned reverend only symbolises despair and death. Dimmesdale's idealization of himself through the eyes of his congregation seals his fate for the final catastrophe.

He is confidently aware of his artistic ability to outpour humanity with captivating words. He knows that the centre of power of his existence emanates from his "eloquence and religious fervor" which "had already given the earnest of high eminence in his profession". During the Sermon on the Election Day, his passionate outpour seemed to have reached the crescendo of eloquence and have erased the line between reality and his illusory world. The more he suffers from the pangs of sin and detachment from Hester, the more blazing are his preaching and his voice "breathed passion and pathos, and emotions high or tender, in a tongue native to the human heart" (*SL* 363). Only Chillingworth and Hester can understand the reason of oozing of such fuming outpour of passion. And no doubt Hester Prynne is equally captivated and drowned in the passionate speech so that she "listened with such intentions, and sympathized so intimately, that the sermon had throughout a meaning for her entirely apart from its indistinguishable words" (*SL* 363). Chillingworth detected the reverberated libidinal energy in the man's speech and can guess how the same 'animalsque' spirit captivated his jilted wife. Dimmesdale's capability to entwine his listeners into tumultuous passion is like sexual arousal concluding in an orgasmic discharge and relief.

Hawthorne is often criticised as a romantic fabulist far removed from realist writings and therefore Melville has held him as transcendental symbolist. However, Hawthorne never accepted history as the Bible of universalism. His scepticism about its influence and manipulation by the ministers and clergies always haunted him. Therefore, it is difficult to see Dimmesdsle in the light of tragic protagonist all though the novel aligns with Greek tragedy due to a single story, few principal characters, largeness, unity of treatment, directness, sternness, relentlessness. It begins with a sense of guilt subjected to Nemesis and justice. Dimmesdale is more an Everyman who is always trapped in the Hamletian dilemma 'to be or not to be'. Hawthorne's romance reflects that Dimmesdale is not malicious or evil and he is the Aristotelian 'good' man who struggles with his sin and his silence. His suffering is therefore an eternal alienation, even though he has remained very much at the centre of Boston crowd. Dimmesdale's dilemma and his failure to confess are complicated by the people with whom he has spent his life. John Wilson and Governor Bellingham, the chief representatives of church and state, are ill-equipped and incapable to understand his situation. Confession in the Puritanical world is not rewarded with mercy but only with hatred and severe punishment. The psychosis of confession for Dimmesdale is due to his awareness of the harsh and inconsiderate population who will never see the world from his point of view. Moreover, Chillingworth's poisonous companionship has already ruined him as he suffers every moment as the physician alerts him conscience that he is a fallen man. Trapped in orthodox Calvinist belief, Dimmesdale's weakness is found in his incapability to overcome them. Though Dimmesdale's character may not be fully tragic in terms of Aristotelian principle, yet the conflict of ego, the fear of shame and the flood of emotions intensify the tragic spirit in *The Scarlet Letter*. Hester is equally a tragic protagonist since her hamartia is her over ambitiousness and excess of passion which is symbolised by the colour scarlet. The scarlet letter is the symbol of passion, blood, death, childbirth and life. Hester and Pearl both symbolise this cornucopia in the Puritanical world of restrain and control. Yet, Pearl and Hester survived while Dimmesdale meets his tragic end followed by Chillingworth's disappearance. Hester in the long run learnt the art of survival and therefore she devised her own way to express her passion which is through her art of needle work. Dimmesdale's hamartia lies in his lack of courage to confront the truth. The fear of shame is the biggest hindrance in his life. Dimmesdale's tragic fate is born out of his shame like his creator, Nathaniel Hawthorne. Hawthorne's appearance after the death of his father has been like a ghostly presence, timid and shy. Dimmesdale's conflict with his dividing selves—the passionate rebellious and the timid conformist became so intense towards the end that at one point he is afraid to unleash his deceptive self. Hester for prolong period has undergone the litmus test of shame yet the narrator has presented her as haughty, unabashed, and confident in her shame, capable of looking back sharply at those who have accused her. She has fascinatingly embroidered the shameful symbol and takes pride in dressing Pearl, the sinful fruit in the same flaming colour. Hester seems to be full of defiance, full of fire, full of wildness, and strength of mind to fight against the world and also defeat Chillingworth's evil spirit. Hester's diplomacy saved her from being the tragic heroine unlike the real life tragic heroine Margaret Fuller.

But in Dimmesdale, we have not seen any such commitment and undying love for Hester or Pearl. At the very introduction of Hester Prynne as a sinner, the narrator ironically reflects the truth when Mr. Wilson tells Dimmesdale that "the responsibility of this woman's soul lies greatly with you". With his brilliant technique of innuendos, Hawthorne sends messages to the readers that Dimmesdale is Hester's partner in the adulterous deed. Dimmesdale, is definitely the personification of "human frailty and sorrow," but the biggest lack in this character is honesty. Hawthorne describes him as young, pale, and physically delicate and the most prominent feature in his body is his large melancholic eyes and a tremulous mouth, suggesting great sensitivity. He has a voice laced with passion that enthrals his audience with pathos and joy. The entire voice like ocean waves brushes and sways the minds of Boston. There is no honesty in love for Hester and their offspring, there is no honesty in his religious ardour and finally he has been dishonest to himself. Hester is perturbed to see Dimmesdale's deterioration but Dimmesdale hardly feels the pain of Pearl's existence without the identity of her father. On the contrary, Pearl disturbs his egoistical self and her presence makes him uncomfortable and also to a certain point embarrasing. Towards the end, Pearl kisses the minister's cheek, not as an acknowledgment of his paternity, but perhaps it is lavished as a reward for a victory greater than the mere acknowledgment of personal sin. This victory is about the breaking the spell.

The ambiguity and the dilemma with which Dimmesdale is presented create both a sense of pity and shame. Though Dimmesdale can be claimed to be the hero of the novel, yet we do not see the heroic grandeur in the man. Dimmesdale's hypocrisy is the narcissistic trend in every human being. He is not a hard core villain without any sense of remorse but his tragedy lies in his lack of mental agility to discern morality and immorality. While Dimmesdale's theoretical intellect indulges in abstract discourses with Chillingworth, the other half of his mind is "darkened and confused by the very remorse which harrowed it". Dimmesdale is never confident in his decision and his lack of confidence is because of his two opposite selves conflicting against each other. He has a vague suspicion that Chillingworth is not to be trusted, but he has equally vague and distrustful intimations about everybody. He is convinced by Hester to participate in the elopement devised by her from the torments of Puritanical world but ultimately fails to keep his promise. He cannot protect himself because he cannot trust his own thoughts. He covers his chest with his hand because he suffers from insecurity that one can see his guilt. He is possessed by the fear of visibility which is symbolized throughout *The Scarlet Letter* by the "too vivid light of day." In his meeting with Hester in the forest, he finds, that no "golden light" was ever as "precious as the gloom of this dark forest", and yet he feels that he cannot be too clearly seen. These are enough indications that Dimmesdale is gradually perishing as he chooses to remain in oblivion. In the second scaffold scene we find Dimmesdale is reduced to a mere shadow. The fear of confession is so terrible in him that he prefers to die silently rather than living death out of shame and insult. Why does the minister suffer when he has the option to easily hide his 'sin'? The answer to this question is best elucidated by Dimmesdale himself: "Were I an atheist—a man devoid of conscience—... I might have found peace, long ere now". It is easy to commit sin when one does not suffer from guilt conscience. For Dimmesdale the guilt conscience arises because he is otherwise a religious learned scholar who has devoted his life to high morals of Puritanism This is further enhanced when he finds that her partner in the act of sinning is undergoing purgation while he cannot. But Hawthorne does not present human mind in such simplistic way of binary oppositions like good and evil, saint and sinner. He tells that there is "no state of society" in which Dimmesdale would "have been what is called a man of liberal views," adding that "it would always be essential to his peace to feel the pressure of a faith about him, supporting, while it confined him within its iron framework". Dimmesdale's egoistical self is aware of his elevated image in the community. Dimmesdale's pleasure is in his hamartia that he commands the world without commanding. His predominant self which he endears most is his public image as the beloved minister. As a result, when he views himself as a sinner confessing to the society, he cannot tolerate his disintegrated image. When he sees the world through moral categories he finds difficult to place him on the same pedestal with Hester. He must inevitably see himself in precisely the same way in which the crowd perceived Hester in the first scaffold scene: an ostracised sinner who has violated the codes of morality. But at the same time he cannot force himself into psychological evasion of his sin. His repression reached that heightened point and therefore he is moving towards the verge of lunacy.

We pity poor Mr. Dimmesdale profoundly, but we are also interested in him as the subject of an experiment in analytical psychology. Our compassion is aroused when he is twitched upon the rack by Chillingworth and yet fails to confess.

Now he has a good time all by himself torturing his body, whipping it, piercing it with thorns and macerating himself. It's a form of masturbation. He wants to get a mental grip on his body. And since he can't quite manage it with the mind, witness his fall—he will give it what for, with whips. His will shall lash his body. And he enjoys his pains.[3]

Dimmesdale's moral enemy is the forbidden impulse while his psychological enemy is his guilt. Dimmesdale is not a stentorian dogmatist loudly condemning sin. If Dimmesdale would have been a typical Puritan minister, perhaps it would have been easier for him to absorb his sense of guilt but being an educated scholarly and spiritual sermonizer, he is more susceptible to anguish for Hester's suffering and his own sin. This suffering is aggravated by Hester's extraordinary capability to bear the burden of sin and by Chillingworth's psychological torture. Ultimately, death is the distillery extracting the valuable spiritual essence. The same body which has been the object of passion, sin and repulsion must lose its significance. Dimmesdale's character echoes the dilemma of every modern individual who cannot be painted in the shades of divinity or Satanic hues but As Emerson has articulated in his 1841 essay "Self-Reliance": "Nothing is at last sacred but the integrity of your own mind. Absolve you to yourself and you shall have the suffrage of the world."[4]

NOTES

1. Bloom, Harold. *Hester Prynne*. Chelsea House Publishers, 1990, p. 85.
2. Arendt, Hannah. *The Human Condition*. University of Chicago Press, 1958, p. 56.
3. Lawrence, D.H. *Studies in Classic American Literature*. Vol 2. Cambridge University Press, 2003, p. 87.
4. Emerson, Waldo Ralph. *The Essential Writings of Ralph Waldo Emerson*. Random House LLC, 2009, p. 135.

Chapter 9

CHILLINGWORTH: THE BLACK MAN AND HIS ALCHEMY

> Leave him alone for a moment or two,
> and you'll see him with his head
> bent down, brooding, brooding,
> eyes fixed on some chip,
> some stone, some common plant,
> the commonest thing,
> as if it were the clew.
> The disturbed eyes rise,
> furtive, foiled, dissatisfied
> from meditation on the true
> and insignificant.[1]

The above description of a 'brooding' man deeply speculating about the metaphysical world with deep introspection seems to be an apt depiction of the most scholarly satanic modern character, Chillingworth or Master Prynne, the fictional character who happens to be the physician and husband of Hester Prynne in *The Scarlet Letter*. However, this poem titled "Hawthorne" written by Robert Lowell is a eulogy to the writer Nathaniel Hawthorne where Lowell has tried to reflect on Hawthorne's personal traits, the philosophical mind behind his unique fictions and romances and how at some point the writer's buried self can cast his shadow over his fictional characters. Chillingworth seems to be the king of incantation, black magic, the antagonistand above all he is an extraordinary character who essentially depicts how Nathaniel Hawthorne anticipated psychoanalysis as the crux of the study of human complexities. Chillingworth's character raises diapason of questions ranging from masculinity, hegemonic manhood, and power of medical science, clinical study to religion and human ethics. Chillingworth appears ghastly, abominable and haunting towards the end but his character is most intriguing and quixotic and adds the most precious spice in the plot of jealousy and betrayal.

He is the Mephistophelean old physician who is trapped by Fate to explore his suspicion about Dimmesdale and gloat over his tortures. His medication seems to be like some concoction or sublimated hell broth that intensified the tragic romance. Chillingworth's character undergoes metamorphosis because of his aggrieved awareness of being a cuckold that injured his intellectual pride. He is the perfect example of Hawthorne's criticism of ideological self-perception in the emerging America. Chillingworth's revenge is psychosexual where his target is to remove the 'tabooed' impulses which he denied in himself. His playful torturing of Dimmesdale is almost a phallic persecution of the hypocritical minister of Salem. Without any masculine sexist attraction, Chillingworth is small, thin, and slightly deformed, with one shoulder higher than the other. Although he "could hardly be termed aged," he has a wrinkled face and appears "well stricken in years." What is striking in this man is a look of calm intelligence, with "strange, penetrating power," in his eyes that are dim and bleared, because of hours of study under lamplight.

Our first impression of this character is reflected through the filtered views of Hester Prynne. Interestingly, Chillingworth always appears to be out of place. As a convict among the natives he is the outsider, as a white man in the Puritanical crowd when Hester Prynne stands on the scaffold, he is still an outsider who hardly knows anything about the present context. The slightly deformed Master Prynne has dedicated his youth to study and desire for knowledge but when in his middle age loneliness haunted him, his eye settled on young Hester. To discover one's own wife being held up to public opprobrium for adultery is not only humiliating but also a sexual insult and a psychological trauma. T. Walter Herbert describes Chillingworth's repulsive reaction to find Hester with an illegitimate child as 'masturbatory,'[2] something which Hawthorne describes as "snake-like writhing." The snake reminds the Biblical snake of Eden, Satan and his jealousy. In the static symmetry of conjugal life of Hester and Master Prynne, the physician remained almost detached from the relationship but in this triangular relationship of adultery and jealousy between Hester, Dimmesdale and Chillingworth, the alliance is inflamed because of the sudden 'unwanted' arrival of jealous Master Prynne. The agony of betrayal and doubt turned the man blind and therefore being though he is aware of his own disregard for Hester in England, he still feels humiliated and forsaken. Hester is seen by the society in the light of immorality and sin but Master Prynne feels himself to be a cuckold because he knows the reason of marital infidelity is due to his inadequacies and follies. Cuckoldry is so shameful in the patriarchal society that it exposes the limits of men's control over their wives' bodies, as well as his fragile selfhood. A cuckold is seen as an incomplete man and hence because of this onus of shame he never disclosed his identity. Now it is time for this failed husband to prove that Hester Prynne has mistaken by relegating him to the category of sexual apathy. Hester has proved to Chillingworth that feminine reproductivity can never be in masculine control but Chillingworth emphasises that Hester is his possession. In order to emphasise his sexual exclusivity, men use violence and Chillingworth's violence is unnerving as it involves violence over the 'soul and body' of Dimmesdale. Being stripped off his proprietorship over Hester Prynne and cuckolded, he undergoes strange metamorphosis. He erased his identity and name and became a fiend. He is always presented as a deformed figure at the outskirt of humanity. Just like Lucifer, the angel of light who is transformed into an ugly repulsive shape after his fall, Chillingworth's deformity is a reflection of his internal transformation and fall. Such deformation in physical representation also relates to his ambiguous parentage which Hawthorne has kept in veil. Chillingworth is a well-established physician and a scholar by profession, but his childhood and his root of identity are anonymous to the narrator. It is suggested that lack of parental identity may refer to Chillingworth's illegitimacy just like Pearl and hence this deformity also relates to his deformity in his orientation and lineage.

When he first steps out of the wilderness, he seems to be an illegitimate figure, standing beside his "Indian attendant" at the edge of the forest. Both psychologically and physically marginalized at the "outskirts" of a crowd, Hester is amazed at this juncture to recognise her husband. He is often described as "a writhing horror," a "convulsion" with physical incapacity. Though asexual or impotent, he considers himself as potent enough to destroy Dimmesdale. The name 'Roger' that Master Prynne has chosen is a colonial epithet for adulterous intercourse or rape. Strangely, Chillingworth could have opted for a second marriage or invoking the colonial laws of coverture, could declare his true identity and decide to punish Hester accordingly. But in the Freudian sense, Chillingworth is unconsciously suffering from 'castration anxiety'[3] and hence he must follow his own book of law in the fanatical pursuit of revenge. Sin is never inherently gendered and hence it is easy for Chillingworth to blame Hester and Dimmesdale in marital fidelity. He chose to overlook that Hester's love for Dimmesdale developed when she knew that Master Prynne is dead. His calculative step, deep seated unnerving revenge, and inhuman desire to punish the culprit justify the pseudo name he has chosen to remain in disguise. The 'chillness' is reflected in his cold detached attitude while simultaneously hibernating the ugliest and cruellest plan to trigger the pain of violating Dimmesdale's sanity. His perverse authority becomes monstrous as he pledges to find the lover of his wife in any parts of the world. This old physician must have cherished for a family life in his old age but at the end, his desire is abandoned when he vanished all of a sudden almost into the bottom of the ocean like Hawthorne's father who died during his voyage into the sea. Both Chillingworth and Dimmesdale die but Hester remains into the fabric of humanity because of Pearl. Chillingworth's green-eyed jealousy is blended with anger, hostility, suspicion and above all a sense of loss. He therefore appears as dark spirit in the prison, the serpent manifest whom Hester cannot trust any more.

Chillingworth's character has been always wrapped in mysterious garb. His dubious origin and sudden arrival is as strange as his impenetrable mind that has several layers of complexities. He holds strange and perverse authority implicitly on many characters in the novel. Although not belonging to the elected members of the Puritanical society, he remains in the company of those men. In seeking revenge, this man assumes the satanic role, aspiring for the divine power to control humanity. His mission is to avenge the father of the illegitimate child. From Chaucer's January to various figures in Shakespeare to Charles Bovary and Leopold Bloom, the cuckold husbands have been treated with varying amounts of humour, pathos, sympathy, and contempt. Few, however, are as villainous as Roger Chillingworth. Chillingworth never followed the Puritanical regulations and his revenge, driven by "new interests" and "a new purpose", suggests the probability for a reign of terror. Being appropriately named as the "Leech" by the narrator, he symbolises the satanic way of infiltrating the poison of revenge into the life of Salem. Like a leech with fiendish desire he sucks the blood of his patient because of probing intimacy. Chillingworth uses the minister like a puppet with homophobic control over his disruptive eroticism. By unearthing and uprooting the secrets of Dimmesdale's mind, the physician violates the law of nature. Hawthorne's depiction of characters like Ethan Brand, Aylmer, Rappaccini, Westervelt and Coverdale, Holgrave, and Chillingworth—are all an attempt to probe beyond human reach and social contract. A weak character like Dimmesdale allowed easily providing the secret route to venture and plunge inside his confused emotional pool. In the tug of war between Chillingworth and Dimmesdale, Hawthorne reflects the suppressed conflict over masculinity. Hawthorne's relationship with Melville has been subjected to much critical analysis. More than simple male friendship, critics and biographers have seen it as a relation that suggests competition, power, or relative sexual and economic potency. However, in his letter to Melville in 1851 Hawthorne explains their relationship as commingling of two souls.

Dimmesdale and Chillingworth are often seen in the queer light of both homophobic and homosexual relationship. In the power relations of the deployment of sexuality, a strange relationship of proximity developed between the two. For

Hawthorne has traced how love and hate, the source of emanation of the two oxymoronic emotions are same:

> It is a curious subject of observation and inquiry, whether hatred and love be not the same thing at bottom. Each, in its utmost development, supposes a high degree of intimacy and heart-knowledge; each renders one individual dependent for the food of his affections and spiritual life upon another; each leaves the passionate lover, or the no less passionate hater, forlorn and desolate by the withdrawal of his object. (*SL* 388)

Robert Penn Warren has claimed that the relationship of 'marriage' between Dimmesdale and Chillingworth is less Freudian or Lacanian but more Girardian.[4] Girard has suggested in his book titled *Deceit, Desire and the Novel: Self and Other in Literary Structure* that how in the triangular relationship the feminine character becomes the objective representation while the masculine characters become the subject and mediator. Both Hester's husband and lover have appeared to be self-centred in one way or the other and while Hester is self-sufficient to live alone; both these men started living together for their individual purposes. In the love-hate dyadic, the minister has unconsciously subjected himself to "a strange kind of intimacy" with the physician, although sometimes consciously he detested his presence. The minister gradually loses his own bodily self-control while Chillingworth being his personal physician becomes the main occupant in keeping an eye on his body and soul. Chillingworth's invitation in their conversation suggests how with an unbridled passion the physician desires to reap the minister's secrets:

> "Thus, a sickness," continued Roger Chillingworth, going on, in an unaltered tone, without heeding the interruption, but standing up and confronting the emaciated and white-cheeked minister, with his low, dark, and misshapen figure,—"a sickness, a sore place, if we may so call it, in your spirit hath immediately its appropriate manifestation in your bodily frame. Would you, therefore, that your physician heal the bodily evil? How may this be unless

you first lay open to him the wound or trouble in your soul?' (*SL* 205)

In the very first conversation between Chillingworth and Hester, the physician's pledge to locate her lover anywhere in this world is an assertion that Dimmesdale will become his sole reason of survival. No doubt his strong possessiveness is revealed when Mistress Hibbins caresses Dimmesdale and he proclaims: "Don't touch him. He belongs to me". No doubt, in the course of the revenge, Chillingworth has associated himself with Dimmesdale more than Hester has done. Regardless of love or hate, Hawthorne has reflected the repressed desires that always try to find some outlet or medium.

Chillingworth also represents Hawthorne's scepticism about medical science and the profession of the physicians. The religious-cultural-historical world of the Puritans is further complicated with medical science and alchemy. Hawthorne has always supported natural science rather than medical science and he has been aware that there are very few skilful physicians who are motivated by religious zeal. More than medicine and alchemy, he seems to believe in the ontological emotions which are quicker in healing than chemicals. Regarding his career choice and medical science as a profession Hawthorne expressed in his letter to his mother: "I have not yet concluded what profession I shall have."[5] He will not be a physician because "it would weigh very heavily on [his] Conscience if...[he] should chance to send any unlucky Patient...to the realms below." During the first half of the century of Hawthorne's time, though physicians are gaining economic and political power yet Hawthorne is sceptical about how far science can cure humanity when there is moral corruption. These two protagonist-antagonist characters, Dimmesdale and Chillignworth also reflect Hawthorne's concern regarding the merits of religion and science in society and how power and authority are inherent in these fields to control mankind. In the letter Hawthorne suggests that medicine with its extreme power can heal or kill, it is a parasitic profession that depends upon "the diseases and Infirmities of [one's] fellow Creatures." Thirty years later, Hawthorne represents how the lifesaving divine profession of medicine can transform into an evil power that empowers

Roger Chillingworth to prey upon the diseased minister Arthur Dimmesdale. In "Rappaccini's Daughter", the character of Dr Rappaccini is presented by Hawthorne as a physician whose alchemy appears to be disastrous not only to the people but also in his own life. Chillingworth is the example of the power of science and transformation that can be dangerous and severe at some points. If religion and art can seek to provide mankind the perfect ideal world, science can equally be magical in its shamanistic transformation.

One cannot deny that the physician at one point has been a high-minded scholar and a philosopher whose purpose in life has been acquiring knowledge and wisdom. Even Hester Prynne has withheld high regards for the man's scholarship. Yet after his arrival in New England he seems to be undergoing some mysterious occult transformation. Though a seventeenth-century philosopher-physician, Hawthorne anticipates in him the mid-nineteenth century American physicians. Like Bigelow, he has profound knowledge in European medicine but also an expertise in American botany as we see him often searching for herbs and flowers. Like the Paris-trained physicians, he is practitioner and scientist but has also become an expert in ancient native medicine. But Hawthorne reveals that all his scientific knowledge is wastage as he fails to control Hester or restrain Dimmesdale from his wilful submission and confession to the society. He has not been able to restrain his wife's fidelity because medication cannot substitute love which he lacked. He cannot prevent the flow of passion between Hester and Dimmesdale even in his presence, and above all he cannot cure his impotency which repelled Hester Prynne. He cannot arrest his gradual deformity nor can induce power to control a powerful passionate beautiful wife like Hester Prynne. No doubt Hawthorne is trying to present an ironic counterpoint to the study and believe that science can remove all the problems in human life.

Chillingworth's treatment of the physician is concomitant to modern clinical medication where the psychological analysis is more important than physical analysis. By eliciting the minister's spasms and winces, he used to observe and diagnose. Dimmesdale offered his body and mind as the case study with evidence, physiological and affective traces of embedded history.

> In their researches into the human frame, it may be that the higher and more subtle faculties of such men were materialized, and that they lost the spiritual view of existence amid the intricacies of that wondrous mechanism, which seemed to involve art enough to comprise all of life within itself. (*SL* 178)

Chillingworth being aware of the advanced form of medical science adopts the most modern form of medication than traditional therapeutics. His main mode of treatment involved operating the psychology than the corporeal substance. He is a perfect physiognomist who gains the knowledge of his patient's secret mind through the delightful study of the body of the patients. He therefore targets to look for corporeal signs in Pearl to detect her biological father. Hawthorne shows his tragic 'anagnorisis' when in the process of discovery of Dimmesdale's secrets, he has undergone transformation from a scholar to a monster. Hawthorne compares him to a metaphorical grave robber who is scavenging the heart of the clergyman in quest of the jewel that may rest in the dead man's body. Thus Hawthorne shows how a man of cold intellectual temperament sacrificed his noble pursuit in the fiendish revenge. The Puritanical society has been extremely superstitious and physician-botanists are often seen as a dark sorcerer. The alchemist's knowledge of herbs and medicine has often seen as magical potion that scared Hester and the towns people. His association with the Black Man that haunts the forest is seen as evil spirit who is in search of polluting and selling the soul to the devil. But this darkness refers to spiritual darkness where he has misdirected his inherent intellectual mind into committing evil and crime. His hubristic self may throw challenge to Hester proclaiming that with his immense scientific power and knowledge he will find out her lover but his Faustian self at the end becomes self-destructive. His boundless desire to control human mind and command human body ends in frustration and devastation. Chillingworth's thirst for science and empiricism made him blind and impotent to the vibrant living beauty of Hester Prynne. He has failed to recognise the living art in his wife. In the "The Birthmark" (1843), the alchemist Aylmer stares compulsively at the mark on his wife's face in order to improve her beauty by removing the mark, but only ends in killing her. In the story "Rappaccini's Daughter" Hawthorne shows how the three physicians gaze upon beautiful Beatrice and finally destroy what nature has bestowed in her.

Chillingworth has committed two sins. His first sin is against nature which he confesses in Chapter Four: "Mine was the first wrong, when I betrayed thy budding youth into a false and unnatural relation with my decay" (*SL* 113). Chillingworth's attempt to seek revenge is the next biggest sin. In The Bible it is said "Judge not, that ye be not judged" but the physician insane in his desire to take revenge, has forgotten that he is violating what god has ordained. Henry James has described Chillingworth's violation of ethics by devising "infernally ingenious plan of conjoining himself with his wronger, living with him, living upon him; and while he pretends to minister to his hidden ailment and to sympathize with his pain, revels in his unsuspected knowledge of these things, and stimulates them by malignant arts".[6] Illegitimate, unredeemed, cuckolded, stripped of his proper name, Chillingworth has, indeed, become a fiend. His eyes glare red. His appearance is monstrous: "a deformed old figure, with a face that haunted men's memories longer than they liked". When he parts from Hester, he goes "stooping away along the earth" more like a devil than a man.

However, Chillingworth's demise is abrupt and Hawthorne never removed the mysterious veil since no one knows why this man bequeathed Pearl as the proprietor of his property. It seems as if what Dimmesdale hesitated to proclaim, Chillingworth has done it by literally usurping the fatherly role of Dimmesdale. The physician has never shown any proximity or interest in the child but in his secret and silent action, he has filled the gap in Pearl's life which perhaps tormented him at one point in his childhood. Apart from sin and guilt, legalism is a great factor in the Puritanical world and when Master Prynne 'legally' transformed Pearl into one of the richest heirs of Salem, Pearl achieves her status quo. Throughout the novel Hawthorne has shown the lack of the father figure as a big dilemma and yet at the end when Chillingworth fills the gap, it is as if he in the process is transformed into humanity from his fiendish self into a fatherly self. Hawthorne ultimately conforms to the patriarchal discourse where fatherhood retains its sovereignty especially keeping in mind the American genealogy and fathering the nation. Thus, Chillingworth's fathering of Pearl is a symbolic and political representation of the allegorical transformation of the savage America into a civilised space of paternalism.

NOTES

1. "Hawthorne" Lowell, Robert in *Hawthorne Centenary Essays*. Roy, Harvey Pearce. Ed. Ohio state University Press, 1964, p. 3.
2. Herbert, T. Walter. *Dearest Beloved: The Hawthornes and the Making of the Middle-Class Family*. University of California Press, 1993, p. 44.
3. Castration anxiety is a term used by Sigmund Freud in his psychoanalytic theory. It refers to the fear in men about masculation. In explaining 'oedipal complex' Freud explains how in the boy child, the 'id' desires to eliminate the father while the 'ego' knows that the father is stronger. This fear of the father as the sexual rival is termed by Freud as 'castration anxiety.'
4. Bradley, L Patricia. *Robert Penn Warren's Circus Aesthetic: And The Southern Renaissance*. University Tennessee Press, 2004.
5. Person, Leland S. Ed. *The Cambridge Introduction to Nathaniel Hawthorne*. Cambridge University Press, 2007, p. 2.
6. James, Henry. *Henry James: Representative Selections*. American Book Co., 1941, p. 48.

Chapter 10

Hawthorne's Narrative Technique in *The Scarlet Letter*

The Scarlet Letter is Hawthorne's supreme artistic masterpiece where his final accomplishment as a writer is fulfilled. Apart from his own career, it is also the turning point in American literature especially because of his innovative narrative method and burgeoning historical romance. By selectively choosing romance as a genre, Hawthorne reflected upon social, economic, religious and political discourses of America. By using the genre of romance, Hawthorne explored the freedom of an artist and the pleasure of mingling real and the ideal.

Historical romance is not the first literary genre to begin with the history of American Literature. Before the Europeans settled in the new found land, the Native American literature was rich in oral tradition. The initial literature in the colonial period is marked by sermons, diaries, slave narratives and poetry. Walter Scott's Waverley novels inspired the American authors like Edith Wharton, Nathaniel Hawthorne, Herman Melville, Mark Twain, Willa Cather, and William Faulkner to re-think about this new genre. Historical Romance is almost an oxymoronic classification because of the inherent contradiction in the name. It suggests delineation of history of American social, political and religious life but romance refers to fiction based on romantic love. Being a fiction, reality is not what is expected and in order to delineate history, reality is the essential requirement. The historical characters are therefore presented in the fiction as anachronistic figures,who create and yet not create the historical verisimilitude.

Such kind of genre is perfect for Hawthorne's subject because of his controversial political position and Puritanical legacy. It also provides the space to unravel history which remained unrecorded or unnoticed and therefore must be re-examined in the light of politics of historicity. The plan to structure *The Scarlet Letter* as a historical romance perhaps germinated in Hawthorne's mind long time back. His Puritanical ancestry, his autobiographical reflections, socio-political history of Salem, the conflict between Whigs and Democrats, shadows of historical figures like Anne Hutchinson, Margaret Fuller, the debate of feminism and position of women in the emerging nation and the contradictions in relation to abolition of slavery and removal of Native Americans —all converge in this historical romance and therefore nothing can be better than this new genre. *The Scarlet Letter* is that magnum opus where Hawthorne has correlated the individual microcosmic world with greater macrocosmic universe. Hester's immoral constitution, interrogation regarding Pearl's paternity, agnostic Chillingworth's healing practice, Dimmesdale's internal conflict all relate to national history about Puritanical doctrine of chosen ones, fatherhood and paternal surrogation of the nation, medical science and its limitations or the corrupt repressed lives of ministers and clergies. Hawthorne is trying to interrogate questions on federal theology, Puritanical doctrines, sanctity, nationality and authenticity. Hawthorne therefore utilizes the most perfect genre to present history outside the subjectivities of the traditional record. He has incorporated specifics like local names, historical characters and incidents and at the same time has kept enough rooms for uncertainties and 'unproved' evidences. The patrilineal genealogy of American history is challenged through the central dilemma of Pearl's paternity. But Hawthorne's ambiguity is reflected in his raising the issue without specific support of enforcement because though Pearl proclaims herself to be the child of her mother, yet at the end she gains social status after inheriting Chillingworth's property. This tonal ambiguity as Hawthorne's idiosyncratic gesture in his personal life as well as in his writings has created an enigma in American literature. It is for this reason Hawthorne has made a clear distinction between romance and novel in his well-known Preface to *The House of the Seven Gables*:

> When a writer calls his work a Romance, it need hardly be observed that he wishes to claim a certain latitude, both as to its fashion and material, which he would not have felt himself entitled to assume, had he professed to be writing a Novel. The latter form of composition is presumed to aim at a very minute fidelity, not merely to the possible, but to the probable and ordinary course of man's experience. The former—while, as a work of art, it must rigidly subject itself to laws, and while it sins unpardonably, so far as it may swerve aside from the truth of the human heart—has fairly a right to present that truth under circumstances, to a great extent, of the writer's own choosing or creation.[1]

Hawthorne has recognised quite early what T.S. Eliot theorised as 'impersonality' by referring to the writer as a catalyst. Eliot has explained that the more perfect is the work of art, the more removed is the artist from that art. To explain the true mind of an artist, Eliot in his essay "Tradition and Individual Talent" compares it to a catalyst that facilitates chemical change but remains unchanged in the reaction. Hawthorne also realised that artistic distance is the crucial element in romance. By using the form of romance, Hawthorne takes the liberty of presenting controversial issues. In the opening chapter, "The Custom House", he may not allegedly be abusive at his political enemies but he is sarcastic enough to criticise and rebuff their ideals. This is well reflected in his satirical description of the inspector of the Custom House:

> I used to watch and study this patriarchal personage with, I think, livelier curiosity than any other form of humanity there presented to my notice. He was, in truth, a rare phenomenon; so perfect, in one point of view; so shallow, so delusive, so impalpable such an absolute nonentity, in every other. My conclusion was that he had no soul, no heart, no mind; nothing, as I have already said, but instincts; and yet, withal, so cunningly had the few materials of his character been put together that there was no painful perception of deficiency, but, on my part, an entire contentment with what I found in him. (*SL* 29)

Hawthorne's addition of the introductory chapter has been disturbing for many critics and publishers since it reflects a bit of personal intonation. The tone of the introduction is almost conversational as if he is conversing and informing his friends and readers. It shows the germ of oral tradition where the narrative voice takes the assertive role of a speaker while readers are more like listeners. The root of this oral tradition can be traced back to his college days when he started maintaining the commonplace book. His notebook has been the storehouse of various discourses, conversations and observations that randomly intrigued him. Oratory is in fact one of the most intriguing aspect of the theme of appearance and reality in the novel. Characters like Chillingworth and Dimmesdale are duplicitous in their play of words, hiding the reality with their oratorical skill. Words are deception and if one knows the art of concealing thoughts with his words, it can become lethal.

The intrusion of the editor of Surveyor Prue's manuscript is actually an attempt to set the fundamental ground of romance. He invites his readers to participate in the artistic journey into the world of romance much like the Coleridgean application of "willing suspension of disbelief."[2] Hawthorne introduces a most complicated narrative element that is a 'double past' including his life at Custom House and Mr Prue's world captured in the manuscript. It seems the narrator is struggling to capture those historical aspects which are vanishing into a limbo, symbolised by the ruptured custom house that suggests the dangerous potentiality of the past being lost into oblivion. The essence of romance is thus set in the mood of eeriness, shadowy figures, the gap between conception and creation, the conflict between public and private life, the power of imagination represented by the haunted upper part of the custom house, or the phantasmagoria of Hester Prynne about her past life in England. The romance convention is well developed when he invites his readers to participate in the discovery of the manuscript from the public world of the Custom House to the private recollections of Mr Prue. He has beautifully enumerated this difficulty of involving his readers into the fictional world of romance:

> "The Custom-House," he observes: "as thoughts are frozen and utterance benumbed, unless the speaker stand in some true relation with his audience—it may be pardonable to imagine that a friend, a kind and apprehensive, though not the closest friend, is listening to our talk." (*SL* 7)

Hawthorne has purposely searched the source of his novel among common men in order to emphasise on the historical aspect as well as to erase the line of distinction between fiction and reality in the mind of his readers. Moreover, the narrator here almost assumes the role of the editor so that any historical discrepancy or violation detected by the reader should be referred to Mr Prue and not to Hawthorne. The function of the introductory chapter is to prepare a proper readership and at the same construct the fundamental structure of romance. At the same time the narratorial voice seems to be apologetic, sympathetic, imaginative and introspective.

Between the narrator and narrate, Hawthorne also introduces the chorus which is fundamentally echoed in the voices of the Salem community. The community at Salem represents the collective audience and readers can at some point identify the collective catharsis with theirs. The response of the audience after Dimmesdale's implausible confession is akin to that of the readers:

> The multitude, silent till then, broke out in a strange, deep voice of awe and wonder, which could not as yet find utterance, save in this murmur that rolled so heavily after the departed spirit. (*SL* 383)

The prompting abuses, violating words and personal opinions regarding Hester Prynne or the informative comment of the man beside Chillingworth in the crowd suggest all choric function. The choric voice reverberates the historical voice of Salem and its history of witchcraft, superstition, supernaturalism and the anticipation of the American Revolution. Hawthorne takes his readers into the ancient world of colonial America when characters like Mistress Hibbins and the Black Man haunted the alleys and by lanes of Salem. No doubt, the flavour of gothic literature is reflected in *The Scarlet Letter* as echoed in the social, cultural, religious and political attitudes of the community.

Hawthorne's evocation of the gothic elements does not entail haunted castle or ghostly figures but it is more associated with a scientific prognosis in relation to human psychology. Though in eighteenth-century England, gothic fiction flourished with Horace Walpole's *The Castle of Otranto* as the popular horror fiction, yet in American context, gothic as a genre did not bloom till mid-nineteenth century. Along with Edgar Allan Poe, Herman Melville, and George Lippard, Nathaniel Hawthorne is considered to the beginner of this new form of literature in American soil.

The Custom House itself is the enervating beginning of the gothic ambience with its spell of ancient legacy where his ancestors have lingered with an "oyster-like tenacity". The history of Quaker-whipping, witch-hanging ancestry, all still linger in the air along with a melancholy terror in the mind of the narrator. The insane and hallucinatory mental condition of Dimmesdale, his imaginary world of weird supernatural creatures, evil spirits, the inversion of the traditional values, his nocturnal journeys, the shadowy passages into the uncanny forest, The Black Man in search of evil soul, the strange groaning at midnight are all gothic elements that reflect the repression of the individual desires of the society and the fear of the 'other'. If not in Dimmesdale, in Hester we anticipate the gothic hero as a rebel who wants to change the American propagandist institutions. Hawthorne has selectively chosen gothic heroism in Hester because of the American root of defiance, of breaking away from Europe's control. With the gothic background, Hawthorne explores the shed of violence like slavery, witchcraft, abolition of Native Americans and the struggle between the wilderness and 'civilisation'. With a plot of betrayal, unfulfilled desire, guilt, retribution and jealousy, Hawthorne has perfectly blended the gothic element. Even the cosmic world seems to be conspiring against humanity as suggested in the symbolical meteor, the dark forest or the primordial wilderness that beckons Pearl. The haunting cemetery at the opening scene suggests that the shadow of death has already stricken 'the new found' land of the Puritans. Above all, characters like ambiguous Pearl, fiend like Chillingworth or Mistress Hibbins are like the shuddering savage unconscious of humanity. Chillingworth's red burning eyes and obtuse figure at the margin of civilisation is blended into the image of Faust who, like Dimmesdale is lonely and isolated. Dimmesdale reminds of the damned soul who has accepted eternal torment from the devil. The character of Mistress Hibbins is not intended merely to invest gothic horror but to show the fearful outcome of repression and squashing of natural orders of the world. The forest is therefore the romantic chasm, the primitive world of freedom where these characters haunt American consciousness.

The Scarlet Letter is therefore invested with gothic elements in order to discover and explore the unconscious of human mind. To enhance the gothic ambience of intense curiosity and fear, Hawthorne has used appropriate symbols and artistic dialogues. He is never affirmative of his opinion but leaves it for reader's innumerable interpretation and analysis. The various natural symbols like birds, flowers, rivers, forest, meteor, darkness, sunlight as well as the man made symbols like scaffold, prison, the alphabet A, Dimmesdale's gloves, prison door or the cemetery—all suggest coherent scientific and philosophical meanings. The primary gothic thrill of Hawthorne's novel is the sense of ambiguity that makes it difficult to distinguish the real and the fictional, fabrication and dreams, imaginations and hallucinations. Apart from fictional characters, it seems as if nature is taking an active part in the drama of humanity.

One of the essential aspects of Hawthorne's narrative technique is avoidance of answering the queries and interrogations that are raised in the novel. Instead of answering questions directly, he seeks ironical approaches. Hence, the disorder created in the course of the plot is solved at the end although at some points readers may anticipate some resolution. In *The Scarlet Letter* when Hester and Dimmesdale secretively hatched the plan of eloping from New England, Pearl's denial to recognise her mother without the scarlet alphabet is also an indication that such happy ending is only a part of the fantasy of mind. This subtle symbolical technique can be realised if one reckons the conscious presence of the omniscient writer irrespective of the narrative voice. As an allegorical witness, he observes and records but provokes the narrative voice to leave it for the reader's interpretation. Here is not only the end of the magic of narrative voice and authorial presence of Hawthorne's style of writing. In *The Scarlet Letter* at certain moments it seems Nature seems to be taking an active part in narration. When Hester and Pearl are wandering deep inside the forest, the forest seems to be Hester's shameful self so that "the trees whispered the dark story among themselves,—had the summer breeze murmured about it,—had the wintry blast shrieked it aloud!" (*SL* 128). Even the brook is an additional narrative voice babbling with Pearl about the mysteries of nature.

Hawthorne's narrative strategies are exclusively unique because of his involvement of contemporary issues like semiotics, ideology and literary structures. His thematic world is supported by narrative art. So when he evokes the emotional or passionate aspects of humanity, Hawthorne's language is more poetic while the language in the introductory chapter on Custom House is more adroit in historical recording. This admixture of the contemporary as well as the historical is the unique art of Hawthorne. As a writer his primary narrative aim is to evoke the artistic mimesis, the world of possibilities rather than affirming the actualities. In his own extraordinary ways, Hawthorne has been able to blend with such perfection the imaginative and the theoretical forces into art. In the dusty attic of the Salem House, Hawthorne may find the origin of this pivotal art of American Literature but it is through the 'Midas touch' of an artist like Nathaniel Hawthorne that the power of art can be recognised. Confronted with the crisis in cultural value and denial of an artist in his own life, Hawthorne has proved to the world the significance of true art and artist. Hawthorne was fascinated by Arabian Night's Aladdin and his magic lantern and it has been his oft repeated references in his writings. In 1858, in his *Italian Notebooks* he mentioned about the white sunlight piercing through the unpainted windows of Saint John Lateran in Rome:

> It is like the one spot in Aladdin's palace which he left for the king, his father-in-law, to finish, after his fairy architects had exhausted their magnificence on the rest; and the sun like the kings, fails in the effort.[3]

Thus, Hawthorne believed that the role of the artist is not creation of an artificial fairy land that segregates life and art but rather he must present the magic casement through which one can think of a better world.

NOTES

1. Hawthorne, Nathaniel. *The House of the Seven Gables*. Mobile Reference, 2008, p. 1.
2. Willing Suspension of disbelief is the phrase used by Samuel Taylor Coleridge in *Biographia Literaria* (1817), chapter fourteen, to explain his theory of the poet's capability to suspend temporarily the disbelief in the reader's mind. Coleridge has theorised the reception process of the reader/audience in art and the role of the artist in it. Coleridge suggests that the poet should hold some extraordinary power to captivate his readers so that the readers willingly suspend their judgement or understanding of reality and dreams. During the moment of artistic representation, the readers'disbelief regarding the incredible or improbable is suspended and through exercise of the imagination they take active participation in the fictional world.
3. Hawthorne, Nathaniel. *The Complete Works of Nathaniel Hawthorne*. Vol. 10, Houghton Mifflin, 1882, p. 74.

Chapter 11

The Art of Symbolism

Symbolism in literature is the philosophical idealism against naturalism. The German poet Johann Wolfgang Von Goethe explains that symbolism "transforms the experience into an idea and an idea into an image, so that the idea expressed through the image remains always active and unattainable and, even though expressed in all languages, remains inexpressible."[1] Goethe's concept of symbolism suggests that the impossibility is not in deciphering the suggested meaning but in its unending implications. On the other hand, for Sigmund Freud symbolism relates to a lost identity 'underneath the sea of life in which we live enisled' reflecting our 'oceanic consciousness.'[2] Freud suggests that through symbols one mind gives to another mind(s) a physical dimension to abstract concepts. The elucidation of symbols drawn from the objective world is however not restricted to any particular meaning. In Puritanical America, the art of symbolism has been in vogue because the theological interpretations are built on symbolic examples in nature. Hawthorne's fascination for symbolism stems from this Puritanical world and this is further intensified because of his romantic spirit. In order to explain God's decree and spirituality, symbolism is considered by the Puritans as the best way to explain the metaphysical world. Sacvan Bercovitch in his introductory essay explains this origin of symbolism in the Puritanical literature:

> American Puritan Literature offers itself as a laboratory for still another, related area of study: the transition from

> medieval and renaissance allegory to modern symbolism.... Allegory originates, as a rule, in an orthodox, absolute design, and proceeds from the abstract to the particular. Symbolism starts in subjective interpretation, and leads from the discrete to the universal.[3]

So Hawthorne's fascination with symbolism has its root in Puritanism but further his enthrallment is reinforced when he started becoming curious about human mind and unveiling it. Besides Hawthorne's writings show that his preoccupation with symbolism is an attempt to identify one with religious, political and social connotations without explicitly referring them. His symbolisms are not merely artistic device but they are profoundly related to American myths, socio-political history, nationality, culture and its origin. Hawthorne strongly believes in the associative power of symbols and hence the way he crafts his symbols in the romance suggests a kind of evocative moral, philosophical and political tone almost taking the readers from the immediate text to the extra-textual territory.

The narrative strategy of *The Scarlet Letter* is full of symbolic epistemology. Hawthorne explains that truth is found not on the surface but in interiors, in the natural symbols and signs that Nature has ordained. The most popular celebrated book that has drawn tremendous attention and debate on American writers is Charles Feidelson's book *Symbolism and American Literature*. In this book Feidelson has discussed how Hawthorne always oscillated between the realistic world of materialism and politics and the mysterious world that can be perceived through the senses and vision. In other words, Hawthorne has been suffering between the allegorical world and symbolical world until Hawthorne decides to end this by "debilitating conflict between the symbolist and the allegorist".[4] *The Scarlet Letter* exemplifies highest art of symbolism ranging from natural to social. The symbols in the novel open like a window of imagination and taunt readers to think about the multi-layered meanings associated with it.

The Custom House in the introductory chapter is a symbolical representation of human sin as well as isolation—the fundamental exegesis on which the entire novel is based on. The detail architectural description suggests that this abandoned ruin has hidden untold history which the world is not aware of. The symbolical representation of public and the private of narrator's self-identity are seen to be reflected in the Custom House. The isolated ruined section is the private place to come across the unconscious of the self, the guilt of the forefathers and the impermissible desires of the mind. It also suggests that as the only concrete surviving object, the Custom House of Salem is the only gateway to unfurl the past. The rotten wharfs, the half-finished buildings, the scattered objects all denote sterility and desolation. The wide spread American eagle at the entrance of the Custom House stands for ferocity suggesting American government and to seek shelter and security under its wings is dangerous. The "wearisome old souls" resemble the monotonous Custom House, as if carrying the same mood of negativity. The old General represents some of the heroic qualities as reflected in his compassion and moral strength which are no more stimulating for these officials. With the eagle's "shield before her breast" and "a bunch of intermingled thunderbolts and barbed arrows in each claw", the bird looks oppressive and militant. Hawthorne suggests that peace and tranquillity are a far cry but indicates the American imperialistic tendency.

Another symbolical element in the novel is the scaffold and the political, religious and social significance of it in the Massachusetts Bay Colony entail the entire gamut of human punishment and civilisation. The scaffold can be called the whipping post meant for public display of punishment of the persecutor. Hawthorne calls it a substitute for penal machine but in the Puritanical interpretation it can be seen as a profane space where all the sins of the world are destroyed. It is a place of the enactment of the sermon and is the holy temple for the ritual of purgation. Made of wood and iron, two hard materials, the scaffold is raised high above the ground for public gaze. Hawthorne has depicted three scaffold scenes—Hester Prynne's first appearance with her illegitimate child when she is subjected to indignation and shame, the second scene relates to Dimmesdale's hallucination and attempted confession in the dark night and finally in the third scene where Dimmesdale confesses on the eve of Election Day Sermon followed by the re-union of Pearl, Hester and Dimmesdale. The scaffold symbolises stability, foundation and backbone of the society and it is the point of transition in the lives of Hester, Pearl, Chillingworth and Dimmesdale. The scaffold seems to have the extraordinary power to invest meaning on the person who stands on it. Hester's presence on the scaffold is immediately denounced with sin, shame and immorality. Little baby Pearl is marked as the child of sin and evilness. Juxtaposed to this scaffold, is another symbol of retribution and trial, the prison house which Hawthorne elucidates at the opening chapter:

> …it may safely be assumed that the forefathers of Boston had built the first prison-house somewhere in the Vicinity of Cornhill, almost as seasonably as they marked out the first burial-ground, on Isaac Johnson's lot, and round about his grave, which subsequently became the nucleus of all the congregated sepulchres in the old churchyard of King's Chapel. (*SL*)

The scaffold, the prison and the graveyard are related to the cycle of trauma, suffering, punishment and death. The prison at the very beginning indicates a society which is rigid, severe and where crime and punishment exist. Both prison and graveyard are associated with the 'fallen' state of man. The prison is described as dark and cold with an "iron clamped oaken door" in order to prevent any daring attempt by prisoners. One is reminded of the political rebellious mythical figure Prometheus for his daring act. The prison and the graveyard are therefore the enduring symbols of human suffering. The ruined spirit finally seeks solace in the graveyard, thus marking the loss of the human form. Thus, if the prison stands for moral evil, the graveyard stands for natural evil, which is Death.

Hawthorne's symbolic view of life is reinforced by phenomenological exploration in the natural world. Apart from historical and constructive study of Hawthorne's art of symbolism, the comprehensive symbols taken from Nature reflect Hawthorne's attempt to revitalise the primordial relationship between man and Nature. For the transcendentalists, Nature is the vehicle of thought and can be related to human spirit. Ralph

Waldo Emerson's philosophical work titled Nature (1836) reflects that in nature, one can recognise one's spirit. It is from nature man can seek beauty, virtue and heroism:

> To speak truly, few adult persons can see nature. Most persons do not see the sun. At least they have a very superficial seeing. The sun illuminates only the eyes of the man, but shines into the eye and the heart of the child. The lover of nature is he whose inward and outward senses are still truly adjusted to each other; who has retained the spirit of infancy even into the era of manhood.[5]

Emerson's *Nature* created tremendous impact in Hawthorne and this is explained by Larry Reynold who writes "When the Hawthornes journeyed to Concord on their wedding day, 9 July 1842, they entered an Emersonian world"[6]. "Tales like the Old Manse", "Buds and Bird Voices", and many others reflect this Emersonian philosophy. However, in later phase, Hawthorne's representation of nature shows a sharp deviation from the Emersonian principle. In *The Scarlet Letter*, Hawthorne reflects the psychic affinity between Nature and Man. In Dimmesdale's midnight vigil we find that the entire night is pregnant with celestial, supernatural, social, political, psychological, and bodily signs that vibrate with meaning. Dimmesdale in his hallucination perceived the meteor as a giant red A while for the Puritans it appears as God's acceptance of Governor Winthrop as an angel. This definitely reflects Puritan chauvinism. Hawthorne's refusal to fix any definitive meaning is often playful because certain things in this world are beyond the boundary of human language, interpretations and articulations. The cosmic light of the meteor is actually an illumination in the dark mind of humanity. In Chapter 1, the wild rose is beautiful and fascinating but it refers to wilderness and primeval spirit of New England as well as it also suggests the primordial spirit within each of us, the Freudian 'id' that is repressed within us. The rose relates to Hester's blooming passion and love for Dimmesdale in the grey hinterland of New England. It is a complete contrast to the social world of man-made discipline and natural world of freedom. Unlike the rose that blossomed antithetically beside the prison gate, Hester's flowering of passion is seen as damnable and corrupt.

The flower as the symbol has been Hawthorne's fascinating area. The rose as a flower is of choice and not of necessity, it cannot be stigmatised or beautified as moral or immoral. In chapter seven, we see Pearl's fascination for the rose in the mansion of the Governor that indicates how the child is as pure and at her own whims like the rose. Hawthorne describes her as "that little creature, whose innocent life had sprung,....a lovely and immortal flower" (*SL*). In his short story, "The Snow Image", children are given names of flowers like Primrose, Sweet Fern, Cowslip and others and these children are presented to have a carefree life. In the other short story called "Edward Fane's Rosebud", Hawthorne shows how an aged widow recalls her youthful romance like a rose. Hawthorne suggests that like the Blakian world, innocence is bound to be destroyed by experience. The rose as an archetypal symbol is more significant for female beauty, passion and innocence. The brilliant colour of the rose with its beautiful texture, sensuous perfume and incurved shape also anticipates that Pearl will be equally 'desirable' like her mother. Rose in the ancient world has been attributed to Aphrodite or Venus, the goddess of love and sexuality. Thus Hawthorne's careful choice of this queen of flower is to signify that how Hester and her daughter are both cynosure in the Puritanical society because of their inherent beauty and passion. Apart from rose, Hawthorne also used other symbolical references to flowers especially in describing Pearl's frolicking in the forest when she attempts to imitate her mother's scarlet letter on her bosom with leaves and flowers. Apart from flowers, sunshine has been another essential symbolic use in Hawthorne's writings. Sunlight seems to be the hue of heaven, showering delight and joy in abundance. Hester is always presented far removed from sunshine. When Hester approaches Governor Bellingham's mansion, Pearl demands from her mother to grasp the sunlight to which Hester replies: "thou must gather thine own sunshine. I have none to give thee.! (*SL* 129)". When Hester Prynne enters the forest, the sunlight seems to be disappearing wherever she ventures in. Strangely in the opening scene, the sunlight is said to have cast a glistening glow on Hester's waves of hair highlighting her unfathomable passion. The sunshine also stands for truth and hence during the secret rendezvous of Dimmesdale and Hester in the forest, no sunlight pervaded in the darkest spot where they bathe in each other's emotions. It is only Pearl who seems to be shining and dandling in the warm sunlight even in the deep forest. Her spontaneous play with flickering sunlight suggests the radiance of innocence in the child.

Other natural components like birds, trees, grasshoppers, and butterflies who are little Pearl's companions remind eloquently the phenomenological world of nature and how Pearl's superabundant vitality is as pure and wild as nature. The flaming colour of the butterfly is the description of Pearl's passion and the secret of her heart. Like the butterfly or the falcon, Pearl is unbounded and untamed. This unforgettable intimacy is celebrated when the river casts Pearl's shadow.

The river functions as a mirror reflecting love of Dimmesdale and Hester in the form of the image of Pearl. The stream is also a boundary for the couple, a social division that sets them outside the laws of society. The stream for Pearl suggests the incessant rhythm of life. Pearl's reflection in the river suggests the synthesis between the subject and the object, between nature and humanity. The mirror image in the water may hint at Romantic Imagination, the casement of human mind and so Pearl creates her own story out of that reflection. The forest on the other hand is the 'uncanny' of human mind, complex, mysterious yet fascinating. The vignette details of the forest with its mossy path and rustling leaves is a journey into the unconscious. The forest is invested with duality of mind, it is pure as well as virile, violent yet peaceful, beautiful yet unnerving and above all soothing restive place and yet haunting. The forest is the place of epiphanies, enchantment, erotic exposure, nostalgia and confrontation with the id. It is untouched by human pretension, regulations and corruption; it is the repository of secret history and art. It is the forbidden place and is the Foucauldian heterotopia, standing at the outskirt of society and it is often seen as the place for repentance, guilt and retribution. The forest has been always fascinating for Hawthorne especially when he indulged in long walks and recorded about this wilderness in his *Notebook*:

> How very desolating looks the forest, when seen this way,—as if, should you venture one step within its wild, tangled, many stamped, and dark shadowed verge, you would inevitably be lost forever.

The forest therefore stands for the human mind; it can be perilous and also peaceful. The Puritans believed that Satan dwells in the forest and he lures forbidden souls. The forest is the primal landscape of romance. If the Puritans have seen the American forest as heathen and wild, the transcendentalists view the forest as the inspiring possibility and outlet of freedom of human mind. For Mistress Hibbins or Hester Prynne, the forest is like their secluded heart which nobody can venture while for Pearl it is the paradise of the world.The glimpse of hyper sexualized Hester Prynne with her lustrous black hair, burning passion and fascinating charm is revitalised in the forest:

> The stigma gone, Hester heaved a long, deep sigh, in which the burden of shame and anguish departed from her spirit. O exquisite relief!... By another impulse, she took off her formal cap that confined her hair; and down it fell upon her shoulders, dark and rich, with at once a shadow and a light in its abundance, and imparting the charm of softness to her features.
>
> There played around her mouth, and beamed out of her eyes, a radiant tender smile, that seemed gushing from the very heart of womanhood. A crimson flush was glowing on her cheek, that had been long so pale. Her sex, her youth, and the whole richness of her beauty, came back from what men call the irrevocable past, and clustered themselves, with her maiden hope, and a happiness unknown, within, the magic circle of this hour.... (*SL*)

Hawthorne's fascination with the forest is therefore pregnant with historical reality, biblical doctrine and classical mythology. Beside forest, Hawthorne has emphasised on the chiaroscuro of light and darkness. Infact, *The Scarlet Letter* is symbolically enriched with varied colours. Hawthorne's references to the play of light and darkness, sunshine and shadows, noon and midnight, are all representations of the various moods and themes in the author's mind. Colours like red, gray, and black—play a role in the symbolic role in denoting passions, sin, jealousy and death.In Chapter 16, Hester and Dimmesdale meet in the forest with a "gray expanse of cloud" and a narrow path hemmed in by the black and dense forest. The sun is the symbol of untroubled, guilt-free happiness, or perhaps the approval of God and nature. It also stands for the light of truth and grace. Darkness is always associated with Chillingworth. It is also part of the description of the jail in Chapter 1, the scene of sin and punishment. The Puritans in that scene are wearing grey hats, and the darkness of the jail is relieved by the sunshine from outside. The predominant repetitive colour is red, seen in the roses, the letter, Pearl's clothing, the"scarlet woman," Chillingworth's eyes, and the streak of the meteor. Hawthorne plays with the varied interpretations of the same colour. It can be associated with evil, part of nature, passion, lawlessness, and love. Between the forest and the town stands Hester's cottage, the uninhabitable derelict land where the haunted cottage seems like some deprived soul, "built by an earlier settler, and abandoned, because the soil about it was too sterile for cultivation." Surrounded by the wilderness and woods, the land cannot sustain life. It symbolises barrenness, lost Eden, transgression, sin, blighted memory, incapable to bear any fruit of civilisation.

The most significant symbol is definitely the scarlet alphabet 'A'. A can suggest adultery, Arthur, Abel, America, first man (Adam), first sin and first letter of the alphabet. It is therefore claimed to be the ur-letter. 'A' stands for alpha, the beginning and initiation of everything. *The Scarlet Letter* is an allegory of alphabetization. With golden embroidery it is beautifully embedded by Hester Prynne in the history of Puritan America but she has invisibly knitted in that letter about Hawthorne and his ancestors, story of several Hester, Pearl, Arthur, Chillingworth and the entire Salem community. The A is so powerful that it "gave her a sympathetic knowledge of the hidden sin in other hearts". It has the immense power to transcend the bodily limitation and read people as texts, to enter into them without their knowledge. Not only does Hester read others, but she must patiently endure being read by them. Pearl's uncontrollable desire for the 'A' on her mother's bosom shows also that the child is inclined to invest a new meaning to the letter.

Hawthorne's mystic symbols evoke subtle sensibilities, untold history, autobiographical elements, psychological dilemma and human complexity and above all nation and politics culminate in the birth of new literary style in American literature. Hawthorne's mysterious analogies of the world through symbols and deep psychological analysis undoubtedly prove that he is one of the greatest accomplished writers in world literature.

NOTES

1. Eco, Umberto. *The Limits of Interpretation.* Indiana University Press, 1994, p. 8.
2. Gougeon, Len. *Emerson and Eros: The Making of a Cultural Hero.* Suny Press, 2007, p. 116.
3. Bercovitch, Sacvan. *American Puritan Imagination: Essays in Revaluation.* Cambridge University Press, 1974, p. 10.
4. Feidelson, Charles. *Symbolism and American Literature.* University of Chicago Press, 1953, p. 14.
5. *The Collected Works of Ralph Waldo Emerson: Nature, Addresses, and Lectures.* Waldo Emerson, Ralph. Slater, Joseph. Ferguson Carr, Jean. Harvard University Press, 1971, p. 9.
6. Hawthorne, Nathaniel. *The American Notebooks.* Cambridge Scholars Publishing, 2009, p. 121.

Chapter 12

TEXTUAL NOTES AND ALLUSIONS

THE CUSTOM-HOUSE INTRODUCTORY TO "THE SCARLET LETTER"

America and Puritanism

The background of the novel is the American Puritanical world where the Puritans newly arrived and settled from England deviated from the influence of England's Crown and Catholic Church. The Puritanical Movement started in 1500. These Puritans escaped from England when Charles I in 1629 compelled the Puritans to conform. The Puritans unlike the Catholics believed that spiritual enlightenment need not be received from any particular representative of God like the Pope but one can gain spirituality by following the *Bible*. Salem has been one of those earliest Puritanical settlements where the president is being called as governor and the vice-president as deputy governor. John Winthrop has been the first governor of Massachusetts and a resident of Boston. As a leader of the first residents of the colony, he established a government of civil and religious ideals.

Anne Hutchinson when moved to Boston from Lincolnshire, for the first time protested against the Puritans and as an outspoken woman started raising question about morality and immorality in Puritanical sense. Hutchinson encouraged in multiple ways of worshipping god and as a result because of her daring protest, she was ostracised from the colony. Six years later, it is said that Hutchinson and one of her children were killed by the Indians on Long Islands. No doubt, Hawthorne supported Hutchinson and her impact is strongly revealed in the opening chapter of the book.

In her civil trial in 1637, the accusers claimed that Hutchinson claimed that her preacher John Cotton has taught the truth which is the covenant of grace while other preachers are false. Her words are manipulated and in reality she has said that John Cotton preaches better than many ministers. The charge is also that in this way she has dishonoured the elderly church personalities and insulted them. In 1837, after her first trial she was found guilty of treason and is sentenced to be banished from the Massachusetts Bay Colony. Her second trial done by the church took place four months later. Reverend Wilson thought that he can excommunicate her with the power of vote but then tells her pastor John Cotton to admonish her publicly and teach her the lesson. Cotton spoke to the women of the church who are being helped by Hutchinson and explains that Hutchinson has misled then and they should not support her. Hutchinson was charged for sexual immorality by falsely interpreting her meetings at her house with men and women regarding Puritanical anarchy.

Salem Custom House—The Salem Custom House, constructed in 1819 is a superb example of American Federalist public architecture. Hawthorne worked here as surveyor of the port from 1846-49; import duties collected here helped finance the federal government. Constructed on ground where the George Crowninshield house once stood, the Salem Custom House, says Bryant F. Tolles, Jr. in Architecture of Salem, "may be entered through a beautifully adorned front central doorway serviced by a sweeping flight of granite steps. Combining delicate restraint and rich detail in the best tradition of Salem Federal architecture are the balustraded front entrance, with its four attenuated Ionic composite columns and fully developed entablature, and the modified Palladian window above which the porch column entablature elements are repeated.

P.P. Clerk of the Parish—He is the author of "The Memories of P.P." collected in the book *Memoirs of Martinus Scriblerus*. His actual authorship is difficult to recognise. It may also refer to the talkative hero of a literary parody ascribed to the British author Alexander Pope (1688-1744) or his Scriblerus Club. Probably Hawthorne read it in the Works of Alexander Pope, as he checked out the 1808 edition from the Salem Athenaeum in 1828.

King Derby—The nick name given to Elias Hasket Derby (1739-99) who is a merchant and started trade with Oriental world. He developed trading links with India, China and Russia.

Old Manse—A manse is a residential house where inhabited ministesr, usually used in the context of Presbyterian, Methodist, Baptist, United Church and other traditions. The Old Manse is a historic manse famous for its American literary associations. It is now owned and operated as a non-profit museum by the Trustees of Reservations. It was built for Ralph Waldo Emerson's grandfather.

Nova Scotia—It is the second smallest province in Canada. The name Nova Scotia means New England.

Uncle Sam—It is a national personification of the American government. Samuel Wilson was the real man who inspired this expression and the iconographic image. He provided barrels of beef to the U.S. Army during the War of 1812. The barrels were stamped "U.S." to indicate that they were government property, but they came to be associated with Wilson's nickname, and eventually "Uncle Sam" became a nickname for the U.S. government. The most popular visual representation of Uncle Sam is a cartoon image drawn by James Montgomery Flagg in 1916 of a white-haired, bearded, Caucasian male dressed in a patriotic top hat and jacket for a U.S. Army recruitment poster with the words "I Want You." The term is commonly used by financial writers, often in conjunction with discussions of income taxes.

Yankee Aspect—The term "Yankee" and its contracted form "Yank" refers to any American, including Southerners and minorities. It is a derogatory term that signifies shrewdness, thrift, craftiness, rudeness, arrogance, and loudness.

Acts of Congress—An Act of Congress is a statute enacted by the United States Congress. It can either be a Public Law, relating to the general public, or a Private Law, relating to specific institutions or individuals.

Digest of the Revenue Laws—This revenue law was arranged under distinctive heads, naval officers and collectors which contains the forms and oaths in use at the custom house.

Locofoco Surveyor—A Locofoco is a member of a radical faction of the New York City Democrats, organized in 1835. The Locofocos were a radical wing of the Democratic party, named after a type of self-lighting match used to relight lamps extinguished as a prank at a Tammany Hall meeting. Hawthorne was accused of Locofoco activities by Salem Whigs regarding his removal from Custom House.

Quakers—The Quakers are the members of the religious movement popularly known as Religious Society of Friends. Valiant Sixty is the first Quaker. Their doctrine is derived from a verse in the *New Testament* and they believed themselves as a Christian denomination. Quakers aim to live simply and truthfully, working for a more just, equitable and peaceful world. Their commitment to non-violence in thought, word and deed is based on living out the word of God, as known in the life and teachings of Jesus, as well as from the word of God known in their own hearts and demonstrated in the lives of others.

Whigs and Democrats—After the election of 1842, factions of Democratic Republican party segregated as Whigs and Democrats. The first leader of the Democrats was Andrew Jackson. They did not like the Federal Government's involvement in social and economic affairs. They believed in individualism, supported the Mexican War and for them the ideal citizen is a living farmer. On the other hand, important members of the Whig party were Daniel Webster, Henry Clay, William Henry Harrison and Zachary Taylor. They supported Federal government in everything and more believed in strength of community rather than individualism. They supported gradual territorial expansion and consisted of members who are more nationalists and industrialists. The Whig Party finally branched off into the Free-Soil Party, the Know-Nothing Party and the modern Republican Party.

Assabeth—It is the name of a small river about 20 miles (30 km) west of Boston, Massachusetts, USA.

Ellery Channing—He was the Unitarian preacher in the early nineteenth century. His published sermons, lighting a path between orthodoxy and infidelity, were widely influential abroad as well as throughout the United States. His Christian humanism inspired both religious and literary features of the Transcendentalist movement. An exemplar of Christian piety and a champion of human rights and dignity, he effectively fostered social reform in areas of free speech, education, peace, relief for the poor, and anti-slavery. His pulpit orations made him, according to Emerson, "a kind of public Conscience."

Billy Gray—Billy Gray was the wealthiest man in Salem when he died. His mansion was one of the most admirable aspects of the town. Billy Gray's best known house during his life in Salem was undoubtedly the mansion he constructed at 176 Essex St., a building famous of years as the Essex House and which lasted, in much altered form, until torn down in the 1970s to make way for the construction of the East India Mall. In addition to the Essex House, the property housed many famous inns and taverns in its time.

General Taylor—Zachary Taylor (November 24, 1784 – July 9, 1850) was the 12th President of the United States (1849–1850) and an American military leader.

Governor Shirley—was a British colonial administrator who was the longest-serving governor of the Province of Massachusetts Bay. Politically well connected, Shirley began his career in Massachusetts as advocate general in the admiralty court, and quickly became an opponent of Governor Jonathan Belcher. Shirley strongly believed that the Acadians would form a fifth column against English forces in the region and perceived them to be a menace because of their proximity to New England.

Irving's Headless Horseman—The American author Washington Irving created the fictional character Headless Horseman in his short-story "The Legend of Sleepy Hollow". The headless horseman has appeared in many forms of literature throughout history and throughout the world. In the story, the character is a ghost who is being decapitated by a cannon ball during the American Revolution. His spirit haunts the town of Sleepy Hollow.

THE PRISON DOOR

Utopia—The term and the concept was first introduced by Sir Thomas More in his book *Utopia* (1515). Puritan Boston was meant to be a "city on the hill" or a good society in contrast to England—but of course More was Catholic and so the Puritans would have appreciated neither the book nor the reference to it. In some ways this book is similar to More's book—both authors use fiction to lament a world that was being lost, a warning against politics and modern life overwhelming the values of traditional society and individual rights. Hawthorne had lived at Brook Farm, meant to be a sort of Utopian community.

Anne Hutchinson—Ann Hutchinson is a real historical figure who was tried and punished for expressing her belief that humans should focus on their individual relationships to God rather than relying on the words of ministers. Born in England in a Puritanical family, she grew up with strong religious beliefs. She got married to William Hutchinson, who was a sheep farmer and a cloth seller. The couples were influenced by the preaching of John Cotton and soon made several visits to Boston. She was persecuted by the Puritans and banished from Massachusetts in 1638 for her beliefs. Hutchinson used to hold meetings to discuss about religion while the Puritanical authoritative figures believed only the male members of the church have the power and the authority to discuss on religious issues. Hutchinson was asked to apologise which she refused. Governor John Winthrop believed that she is a dangerous threat in misdirecting people. She was charged of dishonouring the ministers and religion. Steadfast in her decision she defended herself with quotes from Bible. When she claimed that God has directed her about the trial, it was declared that she was a misfit and disruption to the religious life of New England.

Isaac Johnson—Isaac Johnson (1601-30): One of the first settlers of the Boston area. He was an Officer of the Massachusetts Bay Commonwealth. He was one of the founders of Massachusetts. He was the largest shareholder of the Massachusetts Bay Company and was one of the twelve men to sign the Cambridge Agreement on 29 August 1629. In 1630 he sailed in the Winthrop Fleet to America, arriving at Salem on 12 June, and was one of the four who founded the first church at Charlestown on 30 July. The want of good water at Charlestown obliged them, on 7 September, to move to Shawmut, now Boston, which was settled under Johnson's supervision. He died at Boston on 30 September 1630, the richest man in the colony. He is believed to be buried in King's Chapel Burying Ground which is on part of his estate.

King's Chapel—Founded by Royal Governor Sir Edmund Andros in 1686, it is the first Anglican Church in New England during the reign of King James II. The church was designed by Peter Harrison when King James II ordered an Anglican parish to be built in Boston. Since none of the colonists were interested in selling suitable land for the Church, the King ordered Governor Andros to seize a corner of the burying ground for the Church of England.

THE MARKET-PLACE

Mistress Hibbins—The name is taken from the real life character of Ann Hibbins who was put to death as a witch in 1656. Her execution was the third for witchcraft in Boston and predated the Salem Witch Trials. Ann Hibbins had some supporters, among them selectman Joshua Scottow, who later apologized to the General Court for his support of Hibbins. Ann's first husband left her with three sons, all of whom lived in England at the time of her death. It appears that there was no one to defend her, save a few friends in her will who were not influential enough to change her fate. Her will shows that one of her sons came to Boston to be with her when she died.

Antinomian—The word has its root from Greek meaning lawless. After Protestant Reformation, this term referred to those who think that moral law is of no use. Although the term is 16th century, the topic has its roots in Christian views on the old covenant extending back to the 1st century. It can also be extended to any individual who rejects a socially established morality. Anne Hutchinson was considered to be an antinomian.

Beadle—A low level church officer having a variety of minor duties. His job is to keep order and maintain reports and organise religious functions.

Papist—It refers to a Roman Catholic and its preaching. The term was coined during the English Reformation to denote a person whose loyalties were to the Pope, rather than to the Church of England. This term is used by Protestants to show contempt for Roman Catholic practices and tenets. Jonathan Swift employed the term throughout in his satirical *A Modest Proposal.*

THE RECOGNITION

Bellingham, Governor Richard (1592-1672): He was initially a land owner in Linconshire. Elected governor of Massachusetts Bay Colony (1641, 1654, 1665-72); born in Boston, Lincolshire, England; came to Boston, Mass in 1634. In 1635, Richard Bellingham was elected Deputy Governor of the Massachusetts Bay Colony. This was the first of thirteen years he would serve in this position. In 1641, Richard Bellingham was elected for the first of ten various years as governor. He was appointed governor over adversary John Winthrop. Much of Bellingham's term of office was marked with disputes with other officials. Bellingham was prosecuted for a breach of law, but being a judge he refused to leave the bench instead trying and freeing himself of all charges.

Wilson, Reverend John (1588-1667): He was the Puritan clergyman who came to Boston in 1630. He was the chief prosecutor of Anne Hutchinson. Wilson came to New England along with his friend John Winthrop and the Winthrop Fleet in 1630. He was the first minister of the settlers, who established themselves in Charlestown, but soon crossed the Charles River into Boston. Wilson and Governor Winthrop always supported each other. When Anne Hutchinson started criticising Wilson, he played the crucial role of banishing Hutchinson.

Daniel—The word Daniel in Hebrew means "God is my judge". He is the eponymous protagonist of *The Book of Bible.*

Daniel was among the Israelites taken captive from Jerusalem when King Nebuchadnezzar of Babylon besieged it. Daniel was selected to be part of the king's court because he met certain criteria according to the king's request. Daniel's faith in God always kept him pure as a result God endowed him with the power to interpret dreams and visions.

THE INTERVIEW

Lethe: In Greek mythology, Lethe is the river of forgetfulness in Hades. The dead drank from Lethe upon their arrival in the underworld. It is one of the five rivers of the Greek underworld. The other four rivers are Styx (river of hate), Akheron (river of sorrow), Kokytos (river of lamentation) and Phlegethon (the river of fire). Lethe is also the name of the Greek spirit of oblivion with whom the river is identified.The River Lethe flowed through the plain of Lethe in Hades. Also known as the Ameles potamos (river of unmindfulness), the river flowed around the cave of Hypnos where its murmuring induces drowsiness. The shades of the dead were required to drink from its water in order to forget their earthly life. Poets frequently use Lethe as a metaphor for the underworld in general.

Nepenthe: In Greek mythology, Nepenthe is a drug taken to banish pain. Also known popularly as drug of forgetfulness, it is said to be a medicine for sorrow.

Paracelsus (1493-1541): He was a German-Swiss Renaissance alchemist, botanist and studied medieval chemistry that attempted to transform base metals into gold. Popularly known as "Father of toxicology", he challenged the traditional view that diseases are due to internal problems. Paracelsus claimed that illness was the result of being attacked by outside agents.

Black Man—The Black referred to the symbolical concept of an evil spirit or Devil. Blackness associated with evilness is the result of the racial difference and physician orientation of the white settlers and the Native Americans. White Puritans were acutely aware of physical differences with the Native Americans and hence they described Native Americans as "tawny," "copper," "tanned."

HESTER AT HER NEEDLE

Cain: Biblical character who is the son of Adam and Eve, brother of Abel. Cain is the first person to commit murder. Like his father Adam, he became a farmer and worked the soil. When Cain and his brother Abel brought offerings, God was happy with Abel's sacrifice and Cain became jealous and angry and thus committed murder. He was the first human child who was physically strong but his weakness was jealousy and anger.

Sumptuary Laws: Rules limiting personal expenditures that affected the way people dressed. These laws prevented extravagance in private life and emphasised on a life of control and balance. It also attempted to control certain human behaviour such as exhibitionism, drinking and living a life of luxury. The word sumptuary comes from the Latin word which means expenditure.This is due to the Reformation in the early 1500. The English Parliament restricted the number of courses for a meal to two, except on holidays. It also regulated the amount that members in each class of society could spend on clothes.

PEARL

Martin Luther (1483-1546): He was the German leader of the Protestant Reformation and was a Catholic priest. He was the first person to translate Bible in German language. He was an Augustinian monk whose Protestant views were condemned as heretical by Pope Leo X in the bull Exsurge Domine in 1520. He preached tolerance towards Jewish people but later called for the death of certain Jews. His last written words were, "Know that no one can have indulged in the Holy Writers sufficiently, unless he has governed churches for a hundred years with the prophets, such as Elijah and Elisha, John the Baptist, Christ and the apostles.... We are beggars: this is true."

THE GOVERNOR'S HALL

Seven Years' Slave: This is an allusion to indentured servants. This was the only way many people could afford to come to the New World. It referred to agreement and contract between servants and masters where the servants were bound to serve within the stipulated given period in the contract.

Chronicles of England: This was one of a uniform series of chronicles published under the superintendence of Sir Henry Ellis. In 1577, the edition was compiled by Holinshed, William Harrison and Richard Stanyhurst. It is a text that provided geographical description of each region of England, its history, prehistory and origin. It had been a great source to William Shakespeare.

Aladdin's Palace—It refers to the Middle Eastern romance "The Arabian Nights" where the story of Aladdin and his magical device is one of the most cherished in literature of all ages. Aladdin's palace is the imaginative supernatural castle made of gold and silver.

Pequot War: This was the first of the many wars between American settlers and the Native Americans. In 1633 the English Puritan settlements at Plimoth and Massachusetts Bay Colonies expanded across the Connecticut River Valley but one of the major obstacles was the powerful Pequot Indians of Southern Connecticut. It was the first serious armed conflict between indigenous people and settlers in New England. The Pequot War was significant because the defeat of the Pequots eliminated the possibility of strong armed resistance.

Sir Francis Bacon (1561-1626), **Sir Edward Coke** (1552-1634), **Sir William Noye** (1577-1634), **Sir John Finch** (1584-1660)—They are the authoritative figures or English lawyers of British Common Law. Bacon was philosopher, scientist and orator. He was the member of the parliament but ended his career in disgrace. A parliamentary committee on the administration of the law charged him with 23 separate counts of corruption. He was famous for his style of aphorism and didactism. Some of his famous books include *The Advancement of Learning Divine and Human* (1605) and *Novum Organum Scientiarum* ('New Method', 1620). Sir Edward Coke was known as "the Puritan Hero" and was famous for his work OnLittleton. The book was edited by William Prynne. He is heralded as the codifier and defender of moral law. Sir William Noye was the Attorney-General to King Charles the First. *His Treatise of the Principal Grounds* and Maxim of the *Laws of this Kingdom* have been very popular texts. Sir John Finch was the speaker of the house of the commons.

THE ELF-CHILD AND THE MINISTER

King James I (1566-1625): King James was the son of Mary Queen of Scots and her second husband Henry Stewart, Lord Darnley. He was descended through the Scottish kings from Robert the Bruce, and the English Tudors through his great-grandmother Margaret Tudor, sister of Henry VIII. He commissioned the Authorized King James Version of the Bible.

Lord of Misrule: Lord of Misrule refers to the master of the revels in medieval Christmas celebrations. He was also called Abbot Of Misrule, or King Of Misrule. He was appointed for management of Christmas festival in early Tudor period in England. During his reign, which lasted anywhere from 12 days to 3 months, the Lord of Misrule was responsible for arranging and directing all Christmas entertainment, including elaborate masques and processions, plays, and feasts. The lord himself usually presided over these affairs with a mock court and received comic homage from the revelers.

John the Baptist: A reference to the *Bible*, specifically the Gospels. John baptized Jesus. He was one of the famous biblical figures in The New Testament. He had an unusual flair for fashion, wearing wild-looking clothing made of camel's hair and a leather belt around his waist. He lived in the desert wilderness, ate locust and wild honey and preached a strange message. Unlike so many people, John the Baptist knew his mission in life. He clearly understood that he had been set apart by God for a purpose.

New England Primer: The most commonly used textbook in the United States for over 100 years. It was used to help teach children to read. It also includes religious references. It was the first designed premier for the American colonies and became very popular in 18th century America.It was first printed in Boston in 1690 by Benjamin Harris who had published a similar volume in London. It was used by students into the 19th century. Over five million copies of the book were sold.

Westminster Catechism: It refers to a series of questions and their prescribed answers used to teach children about Christianity. Children memorize the answers and recite them to exhibit their knowledge.

THE LEECH

Elixir of Life: A term derived from alchemy and used to denote the supposed liquid, a draught of which would give eternal life. It is a hypothetical belief of restoring life. It is equated with philosopher's stone and is also known as elixir of immortality. It is known by different names in different parts of the world like Aab-i-Hayat, Maha Ras, Aab-Haiwan, Dancing Water, Chasma-i-Kausar, Mansarover or the Pool of Nectar, Philosopher's stone, and Soma Ras.

Gobelin Looms: It refers to tapestry factory where a simple vertical loom produces rugs or tapestries.

David and Bathsheba: This is from the Bible, Kings 2:11-12. The tale is a story of adultery. Bathsheba was King David's most famous wife and their relationship is the result of an illicit affair during the reign of David. It is said that when David was having a war against the Ammonites, the king stayed behind in Jerusalem because he was secured with strong army to send his general. When King David was relaxing on a palace above the city, he spied a beautiful woman taking a bath. Soon he came to know that she was Bathsheba, wife of Uriah the Hittite, who had gone to battle for David. The eternal question remained whether Bathsheba trapped David in her sexuality or David's lust was uncontrollable. It is believed that David saw Bathsheba in her ritualistic bath of purification after her ovulation. They indulged in sexual relationship and Bathsheba conceived.

Nathan the Prophet: Nathan was a prophet in the times of David and Solomon. The word Nathan, in Hebrew meant 'God has given'. He was a prophet of God who served King David and his son and successor King Solomon. He was a wise and steadfast servant of God, and of the Israelite monarchy, who was often consulted by the kings. He was also fearless; it was Nathan who rebuked David after the incident with Bathsheba, and it was Nathan who intervened during the attempted palace coup by Adonijah.

Sir Thomas Overbury and Dr. Forman: Dr Simon Forman was an Elizabethan occultist, a quack physician who was imprisoned for occult practices and prescribing dangerous potions that resulted in death. Sir Thomas Overbury was the advisor of Robert Carr, a favourite in Court. He died in September 1613 whilst serving a jail sentence in the Tower of London for refusing the appointment of Ambassador to Russia. In 1615 the trial of Lady Frances Dr Simon Forman Howard (Lady Essex), and her good friend Anne Turner, insinuated that Dr Forman had somehow corrupted the women whilst they were his patients. Lady Essex was unhappily married and wanted to be with Robert Carr, but Overbury had spoken against this, and this had led to his murder. Anne Turner was hanged for the crime, Lady Essex was forgiven and Forman scandalised himself and his profession.

The European Pharmacopoeia—It is a pharmacopoeia of the Council of Europe, listing a wide range of active substances and excipients used to prepare pharmaceutical products in Europe.

Sir Kenelm Digby—He was a historical figure often known as "The Ornament of England". He was a Courtier, a Naval Commander, a Statesman, a Philosopher and a Scientist during the reign of Charles I. He played active role in private affairs and also explored the theological world. He was the member of the Royal society and he made contribution to alchemy. It is said that he is the first one to report on the existence of oxygen.

THE LEECH AND HIS PATIENT

John Bunyan (1628-88): He is the author of *Pilgrim's Progress*. He was an English preacher and writer, born in 1628 in Elstow. The most astounding event in his life which he described in his autobiographical *Grace Abounding to the Chief of Sinners* is about his religious conversion. When he was a member of the Church of England, he heard an inner voice "Wilt thou leave thy sins and go to heaven, or have thy sins and go to hell?" Bunyan was actually playing some game which in the Puritanical world is considered to be sinful. It is believed that Bunyan started having an inner conflict due to guilt conscience and self-doubt. More than the Puritanical orders, Bunyan wanted to follow the Bible and his internal turmoil was reflected in his physical weakness. But he soon found the answer not in his internal conflicts but the world outside. Once the Stuart monarchy had been reestablished in 1660, it was illegal for anyone to preach who was not an ordained clergyman in the Church of England, and Bunyan spent most of the next twelve years in Bedford Gaol because he would not undertake to give up preaching, although the confinement was not onerous and he was out on parole on several occasions.

Holy Writ: Although it refers to Bible, yet in general it means the holy scriptures in any religion. It also refers to canonical religious works and relates to divine revelation. The messages in these books are taken as unquestionable authority and people should follow them.

THE INTERIOR OF A HEART

Pentecost: In Jewish tradition the festival commemorates the giving of the law to Moses at Mt. Sinai. On the Pentecost after the resurrection of Jesus, the Holy Spirit descended on the disciples in the form of tongues of fire accompanied by the sound of a rush of wind, and gave them the power of speaking in such a way that people of different languages could understand them. Learn more about the Pentecost.

Sanctity of Enoch: This refers to the extra-Biblical literature. The theme of the *Book of Enoch* deals with the nature and deeds of the fallen angels.It supposed to have been written by the ancient patriarch, Enoch, seventh in line from Adam. The passages here deal with fallen angels cohabiting with women. Many scholars claim that the book is written even before the Great Flood and is preserved for nearly 6,000 years.

Tongue of Flame—It refers to the Biblical reference that details how on the holy day of Pentecost, the marvellous gift came from the Holy Spirit. The Spirit of God descended and soon the gift of the Spirit was accompanied by extraordinary manifestations or phenomena. The first effect was appeal to the ear. The disciples heard a "sound from heaven," which rushed with mighty force into the house and filled it even as the storm rushes, but there was no wind. Then the eye was arrested by the appearance of tongues of fire which rested on each of the gathered company. The result was the effect of a new strange power to speak in languages they had never learned.

THE MINISTER'S VIGIL

Mill-stone: These are paired stones used to grind wheat or other grains into flour.

Geneva Cloak: It refers to the black coat worn by Calvinist ministers. It was made of heavy wool to stay warm and was dark in colour. The name comes from its use in Geneva by the followers of the Protestant theologian Calvin.

Governor Winthrop (1588-1649): John Winthrop was the first Puritan leader of the Massachusetts Bay Colony. A very religious governor, he was the son of a wealthy cloth manufacturer in England. His first wife died after eleven years of marriage giving birth to six children, two of them died in the infancy. His second wife died during childbirth along with baby. This bereavement transformed Winthrop into a religious man. In 1639 when the religious and political world of England is in total doldrums, he moved to New England. He then served as the governor of the Massachusetts Bay Colony from 1630-33, 1637-39 and 1642-48.He then became Deputy Governor in 1636 and actively sought the banishment of Mrs Anne Hutchinson and her followers. He died on 26 March 1649.

HESTER AND PEARL

Horn-book: It refers to the tablet used to teach spelling. It consisted of a single page protected by a transparent sheet of horn, formerly used in teaching children to read. It originated in England around 1450. In United States, the horn book is also referred to the law book of a particular region that entailed the treatise and laws of that place.

A FOREST WALK

Apostle Eliot—Apostle Eliot known as John Eliot was born in Hertfordshire, England, in 1604 and graduated from Cambridge in 1622. After being influenced by the Puritans, he chose the career of becoming a minister. In 1631 he went to New

England and was ordained to preach at Roxbury. Apostle soon interested in Native American's language and culture and soon started preaching in the language of Algonkian. He published a catechism for them in 1654 and by 1658 translated the Bible into Algonkian, the first Bible to be printed in North America. Eliot also wrote *The Christian Commonwealth* (1659), *Up-bookum Psalmes* (1663), *The Communion of Churches* (1665), *The Indian Primer* (1669), and *The Harmony of the Gospels* (1678), and was a major contributor to the *Bay Psalm Book*.

THE PASTOR AND HIS PARISHIONER

Tongue of Pentecost—Pentecost is a feast in ancient Israel celebrating the giving of the Law on Sinai. Tongue of Pentecost refers to speech and eloquence. In the text it refers to Dimmesdale's power of oration which is hypocritical.

THE CHILD AT THE BROOK-SIDE

Hieroglyphic: Ancient form of writing using pictures instead of letters and words. It refers to designating or pertaining to a pictographic script, particularly that of the ancient Egyptians, in which many of the symbols are conventionalized, recognizable pictures of the things represented.

THE MINISTER IN A MAZE

Indian Wigwam—The word wigwam came from the Native Indian language Algonquian. The root of this word can be traced back to the word "wik" meaning to dwell. It refers a Native American dwelling commonly having an arched or conical framework overlaid with bark, hides, or mats.

The Spanish Main: In the days of the Spanish New World Empire, the mainland of the American continent enclosing the Caribbean Sea and the Gulf of Mexico was referred to as the Spanish Main. It encompasses the West Indies and has been famous for trade of gold and silver.

Election Sermon: Election Sermons referred to sermons preached on the mornings of the general elections of the colony or township. The purpose of these sermons was to instruct the people on the biblical foundations of social order. It was a common practice in eighteenth century New England. The Election Day in Massachusetts in the mid-18th century was a colony-wide holiday. It began with cannon firing, military exercises, and usually some form of procession of government officials from the seat of government to a nearby church. The audience of the Sermons included common people as well as most politically and socially important members of community. The Sermons on that day followed particular patterns. They asserted that civil government is founded based on agreement between God and citizens to establish political systems that promote the common good. The people were encouraged to have faith and believe in the minister elected.

Bristol: It is the famous British seaport. Most ships travelled between New England and England, and not directly to European ports.

Ann Turner and Sir Thomas Overbury murder: Anne Turner was involved in the adultery scandal with Sir Thomas Overbury and Dr. Forman. It was the greatest sensational scandal of seventeenth century and was famous for adultery, necromancy and murder. She was the beautiful widow of a respectable London physician Doctor George Turner who later became the mistress of Sir Arthur Mainwaring and was hanged at Tyburn for her role in the famous 1613 poisoning of Sir Thomas Overbury. Mrs Turner was also an independent businesswoman who ran her own "houses of ill-repute" at Paternoster Row and Hammersmith, where couples could indulge themselves together in secrecy. In the annals of crime, Anne Turner is a infamous, criminal but being the Countess of Somerset, received the king's pardon, and after undergoing an imprisonment for some years, was allowed to retire. Robert Carr or Ker was a young Scottish adventurer of the border-family of Ferniherst and became very popular by ascending influential posts in the kingdom of James I while Sir Thomas Overbury, as his best friend furnished him with most useful and judicious advice. Carr had his eyes on the Countess of Essex, the beautiful and fascinating daughter of the Earl of Suffolk, who was married at the age of thirteen to the Earl of Essex, son of Queen Elizabeth. Carr's illicit love was said to have developed under pernicious lessons of Mrs. Turner. Sir

Thomas Overbury opposed all these and the day a divorce had been instituted by the Countess of Essex against her husband, Sir Thomas Overbury, died in the Tower.

THE NEW ENGLAND HOLIDAY

Wampum Belts: The wampum belts are sign of peace and friendship. These belts are ceremoniously exchanged during serious occasions such as the signing of a peace treaty. They are made of beads which are of rectangular cutouts, with drilled holes, rolled smooth on sandstone and then woven into a shell-beaded fabric. The belt consisting of these several beads record agreements. Wampum was an Algonquian term meaning "white string of beads". These strings (or belts) could be used like currency and were considered sacred. They often contained pictograph designs that told a story or symbolised the unity of tribal confederations.

Wrestling in the Style of Cornwall and Devonshire: Cornwall and Devonshire are regions in England. Devon wrestling was a very popular distinctive style noted for kicking or tripping the opponent. Wrestling was an essential part of Devonshire men and though became extinct but along with Cornish Wrestling they are considered as earliest form of wrestling art. The unique wrestling 'costume' of both Devon and Cornwall comprised of breeches and a short. loose wrestling jacket. Devonshire wrestlers also wore hard shoes with which, as Vancouver noted, it was permissible to kick the opponent anywhere below the knee. Some of the 'noted' Dartmoor wrestlers were William Cann of Throwleigh, John Bolt of Cheriton Bishop, and a man called Heyler from Meavy.

Merry Andrew—It refers to a person who amuses others by ridiculous behaviour.

THE PROCESSION

College of Arms: The College of Arms is the official repository of the coats of arms and pedigrees of English, Welsh, Northern Irish and Commonwealth families and their descendants. It consisted of professional officers and was founded by royal charter in 1484 by King Richard II.

Knights Templar: The Knights Templar was founded during the First Crusade with the express intent of protecting pilgrims. They are modelled for their humble beginning and their founder was Hugh de Payens, a French nobleman from the Champagne region, along with eight of his companions, in Jerusalem around 1119. The Knights Templar consisted of a group of knights who protected Christian pilgrims travelling to the Holy Land against attack from brigands and Saracen pirates, after the crusaders captured Jerusalem in 1099. They were gradually transformed into a chivalric order of warrior-monks who fought with distinction in the Crusades.

Increase Mather (1639-1723): A prominent Boston minister who is an elected president of Harvard College. It is said that the rise of Increase Mather illustrates Puritanism's downfall. Mather was from the "first family" of New England Puritanism and its zealous defender for decades. But after King Charles II revoked the original charter for Massachusetts in 1684, effectively ending Puritan self-governance in that colony, Mather became the only representative of the older generation to sign the second royal charter in 1691. The new royal charter meant that Anglicanism was now the official faith of Massachusetts and that use of the Book of Common Prayer was mandatory. The simple Puritan meeting house came increasingly to be displaced by the spires and stained glass windows of Anglican parish churches. Voting rights extended to all male landowners, not merely those who had supported the Puritan clergy as before. For all practical purposes, the new charter entailed that "the New England national covenant scheme was broken." That someone of the stature of Increase Mather would resign himself to this change amounted to a concession of Puritanism's defeat.

Chapter 13

NATHANIEL HAWTHORNE: BIOGRAPHY

In the American literary canon, Nathaniel Hawthorne is one such ineffaceable name that stands for moral ambiguity, controversial position in politics, sacrilegious criticism of Puritan ancestors and quintessentially American Literary spirit. From critical studies, postcolonialism to feminism and psychoanalytic perspectives, Hawthorne is still a subject of critical debate. He stands as one of those modern American writers whose writings reflect that denying the past, one cannot exist in the present. His literary overture reflects the entire gamut of American history ranging from Puritanism, millennialism, transcendentalism, associationism, mesmerism, spiritualism, vegetarianism, temperance, and abolitionism. Henry James, in his reflection upon Hawthorne's life in the book entitled *Hawthorne*, has best eulogised about this artist and his artistic genius when he compared his art to a rare flower that blossomed in the granite crevices of American bed rock:

> ...the flower of art blooms only where the soil is deep, that it takes a great deal of history to produce a little literature, that it needs a complex social machinery to set a writer in motion. American civilization has hitherto had other things to do than to produce flowers, and before giving birth to writers it has wisely occupied itself with providing something for them to write about. Three or four beautiful talents of trans-Atlantic growth are the sum of what the world usually recognizes, and in this modest

nosegay the genius of Hawthorne is admitted to have the rarest and sweetest fragrance.[1]

Born in Salem on the Independence Day, 1804, Hawthorne could have easily boasted his proud ancestors whose contribution in the settlement of America and Puritanical world is undeniable. However, that he is a deviant in the family is evident when he added 'w' to his surname in order to make the spelling conform to the pronunciation of the name. Although this is a coincidence, yet this symbolical act separated him as the man with a difference. His earliest ancestor William Hathorne has been "steeple-crowned progenitor" who arrived to Massachusetts with Governor Winthrop in 1630 and played a prominent role in colonisation. He has been famous for his notoriety especially for persecuting the Quakers. Williams's son, John Hathorne, who is known as "the hanging judge" became a lawyer and judge of the special court and is popularly famous for passing the death sentence of nineteen witches in the famous trials held in Salem in 1692.

Hawthorne's mother, Elizabeth Hathorne, like Hester Prynne of *The Scarlet Letter* faced 'unwanted' premarital pregnancy as a result of which she was ostracized by the Puritanical society. In 1849, when *The Scarlet Letter* is written, Hawthorne's mother expired. Hawthorne's relationships with various women in his life made tremendous impact on the fictional characters and inflamed the conundrum of criticisms regarding his controversial fictional female characters. He has seen the struggle of his widowed mother and spinster sisters afflicted with pain and subjugation and finally eclipsed from the important decisions in the family. His admiration for his wife's purity in love and devotion is also reflected in his personal letters and writings. At the same time he also shared contentious relationships with women like his sister-in-law Elizabeth Peabody and Margaret Fuller. The widows in the Puritanical New England are expected to cherish the memory of their dead husbands and live a life of self-abnegation. Hawthorne's mother is a strong willed lady, far removed from sentimentalism and blind customs. Unlike other widows, Mrs. Hathorne participated in family rituals and she spent the first Thanksgiving Day of her granddaughter's life enjoying and sharing joys and affection. Mark Van Doren writes that "It appears on the contrary that she was an excellent cook, an attentive mother, and an interesting talker about things past and present."[2] Thus, Hawthorne has always been provoked by women who attempted to deviate from the traditions and restrictions.

The blue-eyed attractive lad Nathaniel, known for his legendary shyness and introvert nature, has spent the early part of his life in aloofness. With innumerable illness and injuries in his childhood, the only male heir of the family was always the subject of attention and care. The inhibitions of a lame-footed child filled with anger and anguish is later reflected in his character of "The Gentle Boy" in his short story. In such forlorn world, he witnessed dreadful struggle of his widowed mother combatting against contemptuous society to survive with her children. The image of his father lingered as the sea captain who died of yellow fever in Surinam when he was only four years old, leaving his widow with three small children. When Captain Nathaniel Hathorne died, he could hardly bequeath little to his family and as a result his widow was forced to seek her own fortune. Hawthorne was always introvert by nature since his childhood and biographers have attributed this shyness to feminine influence. Biographer Bronson Alcott described him "as coy as a maiden" and queried "Was he some damsel imprisoned in that manly form?"[3] Hawthorne's Puritan forefathers have been pragmatic men of action who were courageous explorers ruling over lawless wild lands in the new found land. The men in his family have either been courageous sea-captains, farmers, soldiers, magistrates who dominated the world with full gusto. In contrast, Hawthorne stands as an opposition to this family legacy with his soft spoken shy sobriety and grace. In his childhood, Hawthorne's literary world consisted of classic literature and his favourite authors and their works ranged from Edmund Spenser's The Faerie Queene, John Bunyan's Pilgrim's Progress, William Shakespeare's tragedies, Walter Scott's works, and endless gothic romances. He immersed himself in the world of romance and classicism which had an impressible impact on his writings.

Nathaniel Hawthorne's maternal grandfather Manning left some inheritance for his grandson, with which Hawthorne began a life of struggle in his mother's attic. In the absence of a father figure, the entire Hawthorne family is economically dependent upon his uncle Robert Manning until he published anonymously his first novel Fanshawe in 1828. In 1818, Hawthorne moved with his family to Raymond, Maine. Here he attended school for a short time and spent almost an idyllic life of freedom, hunting, fishing and reading in the wilderness. In a short autobiographical account written for his friend Richard Henry Stoddard, Hawthorne has described those beautiful days of his life:

> When I was eight or nine years old, my mother, with her three children, took up her residence on the banks of the Sebago Lake, in Maine, where my family owned a large tract of land; and here I ran quite wild, and would, I doubt not, have willingly run wild till this time, fishing all day long, or shooting with an old fowling-piece.... Those were delightful days; for that part of the country was wild then, with only scattered clearings, and nine tenths of it primeval woods.[4]

Many critics and biographers overlook this phase of Hawthorne's life but Hawthorne's son, Julian Hawthorne, in the biography about his father *Nathaniel Hawthorne and His Wife* has described this phase as "half-wild Raymond life". Julian has elucidated how wilderness and proximity to nature enlivened his life. He explained various exciting boyhood adventures of his fathers and how shy adolescent Hawthorne experienced wild America. Julian also elucidated that Hawthorne underwent an almost aboriginal transformation in "the primeval forests of Maine,...he became a hunter and a fisherman; he consorted with Indians, and he learned the craft of the woods".[5] In *The Scarlet Letter*, Pearl's intimacy with nature and the effervescent romanticism with wilderness reflect Hawthorne's own childhood in the moonlit night and his refuge in the pure primeval nature. Hawthorne's sister Elizabeth, or "Ebe," would frequently accompany him on his evening treks. At one point, they reached into the deep jungle and ran the risk of being attacked by wild animals. The reminiscent of such adventurous life is also found in Hawthorne's diary. His diaries also reflected Hawthorne's thoughts about the Native Americans and their lives in the wilderness. Hawthorne wondered how the Indians were the extension of raw Nature and reveal an inherent bond with this wild sagacious spirit of Nature. For the Native Indians, landscape with its distinctiveness, variation of colour and shape of the foliage, the luminosity of sunlight appeared to be an intertwined part of their living and inner sensibilities. The land's body sometimes resonated in its breath the native spirit of the Indians. Hawthorne envied his sister Louisa, who still enjoyed the idylls at Raymond:

> How often do I long for my gun, and wish that I could again savagize with you. But I shall never again run wild in Raymond, and I shall never be so happy as when I did.[6]

At the same time Hawthorne has also been aware of the haunting past of Manning estate and southern Maine where mass killing of the natives took place. He remembered often the atrocious English explorer Sir William Phips who was infamous for practising genocide. Hawthorne is one of those rare Anglo American writers whose writings occasionally reflected the guilt conscience due to the cruelty of his forefathers over the Indians. However, this short yet impressive phase in his life has made him realise the intricate relationship between man and nature and also the significance of solitude. It is no doubt that at this point, the writer's imagination is wildly stimulated as he started contemplating the true essence of primitivism. This can be best understood in the words of his biographer Robert Cantwell:

> There was something moving in the picture of the children's vanishing into the wilderness that reached in an almost unbroken expanse of green for three thousand miles to the west. They would never have returned to civilization if the choice had been left to them.[7]

After attending Salem School, he attended Bowdoi College, in the far-off woods of New Brunswick, Maine, where he has come across eminent classmates and fellows like, Henry Wadsworth Longfellow, the then future American celebrated poet and distinguished professor of modern languages and Franklin Pierce, the future President of the United States. At this time, Hawthorne joined the Athenean Literary Society and started writing short stories. During this period, he also involved himself and turned out to be an ardent supporter of the Democratic Party in which his friend Franklin Pierce took active part. At the time of his graduation, Nathaniel Hawthorne received degree in rhetoric and composition. His academic career forewarned about future and hence he decided to return back to Salem. After he returned back to Salem, Hawthorne has chosen the most difficult and challenging troublesome career option, he aimed to become a writer. Concentrating rigorously on perfection in craft and style, and focusing primarily on maturity of mind, Hawthorne anonymously produced his first novel *Fanshawe: A Tale* (1828). This first novel in his life is published at his own expense based primarily on his ecstatic college life. It is believed that *Fanshawe* is influenced by Sir Walter Scott's writings tinged with romantic love, heroism and villainy. *Fanshawe* is a short gothic novel and lacked Hawthorne's mature style and architecture. Dissatisfied with this novel, Hawthorne attempted to buy all the copies so that no one could read it. Although Hawthorne is ashamed of his own creation and construed low opinion about the novel because of its failure to draw reader's attention, yet critics like William Leggett identified the shooting talent of the writer when he ascertained in *Critics: A Weekly Review of Literature, Fine Arts, and the Drama* that the "mind that produced this little, interesting volume, is capable of making great and rich additions to our native literature."[8]

For the next twelve years, Hawthorne secluded himself in upstairs chamber at his mother's house, where he worked hard to achieve lofty style and elevated concepts. He also maintained notebooks and journals, a habit which he continued throughout his life. He often jotted down ideas and descriptions which became the source of his writings. He has not published another novel for almost 25 years after *Fanshawe*. Ambivalence and concealment go hand in hand for Hawthorne. He appreciated the exquisite elegance of a tea service from China but strangely remained a lifelong, cigar smoking Democrat who has never hesitated taking political favour. Throughout his life he detested 'ugly' looks like his intolerance of cracked crockery on the dining table. Elitism and aristocracy are unassailable in him and they are reflected in his fictional characters.

By 1838, he has been writing two-thirds of the short stories that he produced throughout his life. None of these stories gained him much attention of any publishers until 1837, when his college friend Horatio Bridge backed the publishing of *Twice-Told Tales*, a collection of Hawthorne's stories that has been published separately in magazines. His schoolmate and friend, Longfellow, reviewed the book in golden words. Edgar Allan Poe, known for his excoriating reviews of writers, chose to comment warmly about Hawthorne's book and also took the opportunity to define the short story *Twice-Told Tales* which is considered as one of the American literary masterpieces. Some of the short stories are destroyed and burnt by Hawthorne out of extreme frustration as his manuscripts are being rejected innumerable times.

In this interim juncture of life when resentment about his own artistic output has grown too intensive, he often indulged in evening strolls along the seashore only to discover that the world is too dark and benumbed to inflame the creative frenzy in him. Around the age of twenty three Hawthorne gradually started gaining creative acumen as reflected in his several masterpieces but the final conquest occurred in 1837. It is believed that during those days of failure and frustration, Hawthorne like Dimmesdale has spent sleepless solitary nights wandering and peregrinating the deserted streets and shorelines of Salem. In his *Notebook* he has most poignantly commented about his gradual renunciation from the world. Hawthorne indulged in extensive summer tours to the New England Mountains and Niagara Falls. Like a vagabond he sauntered in the midst of nature and explored local taverns. Though Hawthorne claimed this phase as the useless phase in his life yet at this point Hawthorne's exploration of nature and humanity has stimulated him to wonder about the origin of guilt, love, hatred, repentance and revenge. In 1837, Hawthorne was invited to contribute to a new journal, founded by Louis O'Sullivan, the *United States Magazine and Democratic Review*. O'Sullivan believed that this journal designed is "to be of the highest rank of magazine literature," modelled on first class magazines in England. When the first issue appeared in October 1837, Hawthorne's short story "The Toll-Gatherer's Day" was included. During this phase, Hawthorne started becoming too critical about the Puritanical regime in his short stories.

In 1837, the year when *Twice-Told Tales* appeared, Hawthorne developed soft inclination for Marianne Silsbee, daughter of a wealthy merchant of Salem. Although there was a big difference in terms of class and social status, but due to personal and political interests Hawthorne was attracted towards Silsbee. On 11th November in the same year, when Elizabeth Peabody, daughter of Dr. Nathaniel Peabody and Elizabeth Palmer Peabody invited Hawthorne, he never knew that his visit to the Peabody family will usher a new chapter of romance and love in his life. Hawthorne and his sisters, Elizabeth and Louisa, are invited by the Peabodys at their home on Charter St. in Salem. He first developed a confused relationship with elder Peabody daughter, Elizabeth Peabody who seems to be bursting with ambition, passion and energy and at the same time an avant-garde woman taking active part in the major nationalist movements of the time. Undeniably, Elizabeth applauded and encouraged Hawthorne's art especially his historical works like *Grandfather's Chair, Liberty Tree* and *Biographical Sketches*. But in the secret chamber of his heart, he fell in love with the younger daughter, Sophia Amelia Peabody and soon the entire Salem seemed to be gossiping about the furtive love affair of Salem. The charm of Elizabeth Peabody has been her independent, vivacious defiant nature while Sophia's sublime delicacy appeared adorable to him. Sophia had a disturbing childhood due to her ill health. Due to the ill-treatment of her aunt, she used to have strange nightmares and developed bizarre temperaments. From her childhood, Sophia is given strong drugs and opium. Eventually Sophia's artistic talent is revealed when she started learning painting under the guidance of Thomas Daughty. Her parents have been apprehensive that Sophia is incapable of marriage and conjugal life because of affliction, poor health and jittery temperament. She was sent to Cuba for recovery of her health and to rejuvenate her melancholic mind. When Sophia returned from Cuba, she met Hawthorne and the presence of another artistic soul ignited the life force in her. Apart from being a talented budding painter, she also learnt classical languages like Greek, Latin, Italian, Hebrew and French and also took active part in transcendentalist Movement. It is interesting to note Sophia's observation about her husband at her initial observation. In her letter to Mrs. Caleb Foote, she writes:

> One afternoon Mr. Emerson and Mr. Thoreau went with him down the river. Henry Thoreau is an experienced skater, and was figuring dithyrambic dances and Bacchic leaps on the ice—very remarkable, but very ugly, me thought. Next him followed Mr. Hawthorne who, wrapped in his cloak, moved like a self impelled Greek statue, stately and grave. Mr. Emerson closed the line, evidently too weary to hold himself erect, pitching headforemost, half lying on the air.[9]

While Marianne married a much older Harvard professor and a widower named Jared Sparks, Hawthorne and Sophia got secretly engaged the following year. About Sophia's engagement Margaret Fuller commented "I think there will be a great happiness; for it ever I saw a man who combined delicate tenderness to understand the heart of a woman, it is Mr. Hawthorne."[10]

It is at this time that Hawthorne invested a thousand dollars of his meagre capital in the Brook Farm Community at West Roxbury. There he has become acquainted with Ralph Waldo Emerson and the naturalist Henry David Thoreau. These transcendentalist thinkers influenced Hawthornein realizing that intuition than intellect is more important in uncovering the truths about human life. Ralph Waldo Emerson, Margaret Fuller, Henry David Thoreau, Horatio Bridge, Henry Wadsworth Longfellow, Herman Melville, Ellery Channing and Beonson Alcott are some of the intellectuals who made a strong impact in Hawthorne's life. His fictional character Zenobia in *The Blithedale Romance* is constructed under the shadow of Fuller's feminism. In the same book the character of Hollingsworth reflects some traits of Emerson. Hawthorne left this transcendental experiment in November 1841, disillusioned by the community's viewpoint, exhausted from the work, and without financial hope to support his family. From this experience, however, he gained the setting for the novel, *The Blithedale Romance*. Philosophically, Hawthorne has been strongly influenced by the transcendentalists who emphasised on human conscience. They believed that if human conscience is at work as the ultimate determining element of all rights and wrongs, then social laws and regulations are not required and man can become his own moral judge. In a trip to Boston after leaving Brook Farm, Hawthorne realised pragmatically that a fixed salary is essential and hence he soon becomes inclined towards the *Democratic Review*. He married Sophia in Boston on July 9, 1842, and left for Concord, Massachusetts, where they resided in the famous "Old Manse."

Hawthorne's life at the "Old Manse" has been extremely jovial and productive, and can be counted as the happiest phase of his life. From the day of his marriage till the year 1985, he relished an idyllic honeymoon in paradise. Surrounded by the transcendentalists like Ralph Waldo Emerson, Henry David Thoreau, Margaret Fuller, Bronson Alcott and above all the angelic "Dove" of his life, as Hawthorne addressed Sophia; Hawthorne produced some of the brilliant tales that would be published in 1846 in *Mosses from an Old Manse*.

Among the intellectual transcendentalists, Hawthorne shared strange infatuation-repulsion relationship with the woman born before her time, Margaret Fuller. She has been the editor, journalist, translator, and charismatic polemicist who openly voiced about the desire and ambitions of women. She finds no sin if women desired to become a sea-captain of a ship. This independent bold activist used to hold "conversations," in order to uplift women from the social evils and patriarchal domination. Hawthorne's wife Sophia even dedicated a self-composed sonnet addressing Fuller as the "Priestess" while she imagines herself standing in adoration near the shrine of the priestess. Hawthorne enjoyed Fuller's companionship especially when both of them were immersed in the transcendental and esoteric discussion about American wilderness, fascinating memories of childhood and about mysteries of nature. But Hawthorne has been equally detesting that Fuller who seems to be too 'outrageous', independent and self-reliant regarding women's freedom and authority. The series of rebellious characters from Hawthorne's "The Birthmark," "The Artist of the Beautiful," "Rappaccini's

Daughter," "Egotism," "Bosom Serpent," and "Drowne's Wooden Image" no doubt reflect Fuller's inexorable shadow.

However, financial problems continued to plague Hawthorne and his family and the birth of their first child, Una, worried Hawthorne as he felt the necessity of a secured job. In order to mitigate economic crisis, Sophia has been desperately accepting donations from friends, including Ann Hooper and Francis and Anna Shaw. Sometimes these donations are in form of cash and sometimes in the form of clothes. She started selling the lampshades which she has painstakingly decorated with paintings of mythological scenes based on illustrations by John Flaxman. Hawthorne on the other hand is reluctant to take assistance and donation from friends as he explained: "It is something else besides pride that teaches me that ill-success in life is really and justly a matter of shame."[11] With the help of his old friends, Hawthorne secured appointment in the role of a surveyor for the port of Salem. In 1846, his son Julian is born but though the new job mitigated the financial problems, Hawthorne was dissatisfied because of repression and denial of his creative self. In the same year Hawthorne published *Mosses for an Old Manse*, a collection of sketches and tales reprinted from a variety of periodicals. This obviously ensured his financial security for next three years with a salary of $1,200 per annum. When the Whigs were victorious the 1848 election over the Democrats, Hawthorne was being dismissed from Salem Custom House. This is an unacceptable shock to the family although it later proved to be a blessing in disguise since it fortuitously propelled him to write *The Scarlet Letter*.

1849 is considered to be the gloomiest phase in Hawthorne's life. The Whigs ascended to power and fired Hawthorne and at the same time Hawthorne lost his mother in the summer of 1849. Hawthorne is shocked to witness the scene when he found his desolate sisters hovered over their mother's bedside. They are shrunken and lost and Hawthorne in his journal expressed: "I tried to keep them down...but it would not be—I kept filling up, till, for a few moments, I shook with sobs." Later he added, "Surely it is the darkest hour I ever lived."[12] He shared a strong love-fear relationship typical of mother-sonbond and always maintained a strange distance from her. Sophia has been aware about Hawthorne's psychological turmoil in his relationship with his mother but also knew there is a strong affection between them: "There was the deepest sentiment of love & reverence on both sides," she observed. Just two days before his mother died, Hawthorne look outside the window and saw his daughter playing and at this point he wrote: "And then I looked at my poor dying mother; and seemed to see the whole of human existence at once, standing in the dusty midst of it".[13]

In 1850, when *The Scarlet Letter* is produced, Hawthorne achieved universal prominence in the world of literature. The first edition, of 2,500 copies is published in March 1850 by Ticknor, Reed, and Fields, Boston, and is sold out within 10 days. The second edition, of 2,500 copies, is published in April 1850, and a third edition of 1,000 copies is published in September 1850. The Salem Gazette termed the book "thrilling." Edwin Whipple suggested that the introductory essay is like the work of Joseph Addison and Charles Lamb, and added that the novel pierced "directly through all externals to the core of things."[14] In 1851, the year in which his daughter Rose is born, Hawthorne published his second novel, *The House of the Seven Gables*, a story of ancestral guilt partially based on his own family history. In *The House of the Seven Gables*, Hawthorne aimed to "connect a bygone time" with the present that is continually disappearing. Also that year, a third collection of shorter pieces, *The Snow-Image* and *Other Twice-Told Tales*, appeared. Sophia Peabody's sister Elizabeth reviewed the book in the New-Yorker in March 1838 and recommended it to her many Boston and Concord friends, including Ralph Waldo Emerson. She encouraged Hawthorne to focus on writing historical accounts of New England's past for children. As a result, he wrote *Grandfather's Chair: A History for Youth* (1841), *Famous Old People: Being the Second Epoch of Grandfather's Chair* (1841), and *Liberty Tree: With the Last Words of Grandfather's Chair* (1841). All of these books were published by Elizabeth Peabody and sold in her bookshop. Another volume by Hawthorne, *Biographical Stories for Children* (1842), provided accounts of the colonial American painter Benjamin West, Benjamin Franklin, Sir Isaac

Newton, Oliver Cromwell, Samuel Johnson, and Queen Christina of Sweden. Though Hawthorne's reputation is said to be primarily depended on *The Scarlet Letter* but his other works especially his fictions are rich with intertexuality of American history. Regarding his creative and literary style, his daughter Rose has commented:

> His manner was philosophy, his style forgiveness. And for this temperate and logical and laconic work—giving nothing to the world for its mere enjoyment, but going beyond all that to ennoble each reader by his perfect renunciation of artistic clap-trap and artistic license—for this aim he needed a mental method that could entirely command itself, and when necessary, weigh and gauge with the laborious fidelity of a tool surveyor, before the account was rendered with pen and ink upon paper.[15]

In 1850, when Hawthorne is forty-six, he met Herman Melville in a picnic arranged by David Dudley Field. In their initial conversation, they discovered intellectual stimulation and growing bond of mutual sympathy. As if they found soul mate, both exasperated in pouring into each other the greatest passion for literary creation. Melville's intense friendship and respect for Hawthorne is reflected when he famously dedicated his most challenging novel, *Moby-Dick* (1851), to Hawthorne. The two writers lived with their families within six miles of each other in Berkshire County, Massachusetts, and they shared warm friendship and correspondence. According to Melville, Hawthorne seems to have emerged out of his social shell. Because of their intellectual equilibrium critics have called them "brothers in despair" but in reality Hawthorne is a "fatalist," while Melville is a "rebel." Some of the burning intellectual debate and discourses that these two men indulged in are time and eternity which Melville called "ontological heroics". It has been such an intense relationship that at later point Melville burnt the letters he received from Hawthorne. It is believed that Melville represented Hawthorne in his novel as *The Confidence Man* in the guise of huckster Frank Goodman and as the shy pilgrim Vine in his epic poem "Clarel."

In Concord, the Hawthornes managed to establish a permanent house, which they purchased from the transcendentalist writer and father of Louisa May Alcott. Bronson Alcott. Hawthorne renamed the house The Wayside, and in May, 1852, he and his family moved in. Here, Hawthorne is to write only two of his works: *Tanglewood Tales*, another collection designed for young readers, and *A Life of Pierce*, a campaign biography for his old friend Franklin Pierce from college. As a result of the biography, President Pierce awarded Hawthorne by appointing him to United States consul in Liverpool, England. The Hawthornes spent the next seven years in Europe. Although Hawthorne has not written any additional fiction while serving as consul, he used to maintain a journal that later served as a source of material for *Our Old Home*, a collection of sketches dealing with English scenery, life, and manners published in 1863. While in Italy, Hawthorne kept a notebook that provided material for his final, complete work of fiction, which is published in England as *Transformation* and, in America, as *The Marble Faun*. *The Blithedale Romance* is followed by two works for children, *A Wonder-Book for Girls and Boys* (1852) and *Tanglewood Tales* (1853), both based on Greek mythology. From 1853 till 1857, Hawthorne is appointed by President Franklin Pierce to serve U.S. consul. In 1858, Hawthorne started his journey from England to Italy by sea from Marseilles to Civita Vecchia. After such prolong journey, he appeared exhausted and homesick. His health deteriorated immensely and it became difficult for him to adjust in such inclement weather.

He soon travelled to Florence to spend the summer. During these days he interacted with artists and painters like the sculptor Mr. Powers to know about the essence of art. He has been more fascinated by Rome as it influenced him to write about Marble Faun. In 1863, he published *Our Old Home*, a series of essays on England and Anglo-American relations. He visited New Hampshire for betterment of his health. By now, he started becoming frequently ill and physically and psychologically distressed by the looming Civil War that threatened to tear the country apart. Despite having a happy family, he suffered from an unnerving sense of loneliness. On May 19 of that year he died at Plymouth, leaving four unfinished works. After his death, Sophia Hawthorne edited his English, American, and European notebooks, and also his collection of letters. Hawthorne's daughter Rose has recalled the last cherished memory about her philosopher father:

> In the afternoon my father went, if practicable, into the open spaces of nature, or at least into the fresh air, to gather inspiration for his work. I have sometimes had the pleasure of being present, always out-of-doors, while he was smoking a cigar, of which the fragrance was so exquisite that it has been a symbol of elegance to me all my life. He never, I think, smoked but one cigar a day, but it was of a quality to make up for this self-denial, and I am sure that he reserved his most puzzling literary involutions for the delicious half hour of this dainty rite. In Lenox he walked the "stately woods," as my mother calls them in a letter of that period, or lay upon his back under the trees beside the lake intervening between the "little red cottage" and Monument Mountain. Also, in Concord, a year afterward, my mother writes: "My husband at full length presented no hindrance to the tides of divine life that are ready to flow through us, if we will." She further says: "He cannot write deeply in midsummer at any rate. He can only seize the shirts of ideas, and pin them down for further investigation."[16]

Hawthorne is buried in Sleepy Hollow Cemetery in Concord on a hilltop under the pines. Emerson, the Alcotts, Elizabeth Peabody, Henry David Thoreau, and many other literary figures are also buried there.

When Hawthorne emerged as one of the literary figures of the U.S.A., the American literary world is suffering from the 'anxiety of influence'. Great writer like Benjamin Franklin has been writing under the strong shadow of Addison. At that point, American culture is still groping for its own national identity and trying to forge and shape national literature by discarding the predominant influence of British writers and their styles.Against such background, Hawthorne emerged with his own individuality that reflected a perfect confluence of fantasy and reality, gothic and supernatural, reason and emotion, didactic and personal and above all passionate and religious. Hawthorne's writing repeatedly reflects upon most sensitive and forbidden issues like the credibility of Puritans and Calvinism, manipulation of history and repressed guilt conscience for unlawful settlement and the fascinating arena of human psychology and its tendency to transcend the boundaries of rationality. His fidelity with poetry is seen in his inexhaustible vestry of imagination swarming with fantastic tinges, hues, passions and emotions. Brilliance of symbolism, variety of structural patterns and Hawthornian narrative techniques are undeniable. Apart from his personal and professional ambivalence, Hawthorne's contribution to American literary independence from England is immeasurable. That the enigma of this American prodigy is inexhaustible is evident when critics even today find inscrutable contentions behind the veil of Hawthorne's life and works.

NOTES

1. James, Henry. *The Art of Criticism: Henry James on the Theory and Practice of Fiction*. U.S.A: University of Chicago, 1986, p. 102.
2. Baym, Nina. *Feminism and American Literary Essays*. U.S.A: Rutgers University Press, 1992, p. 37.
3. Conte, F. Joseph. *The Notorious Nietzsche*. U.S.A.: Author House, 2004, p. 124.
4. Iles, George. (Ed) *Little Masterpieces of Autobiography: Writers Part Three*. U.S.A: Kessinger Publisher, 2005, p. 75.
5. Hawthorne, Julian. *Hawthorne Reading: An Essay*. Princeton University: Rowfant Club, 1902, p. 63.
6. Hawthorne, Nathaniel. Woodson, L. Thomas. Smith, Neal. Pearson, Holmes Norman. *The Letters 1813-1843*. Ohio State University Press, 1984, p. 119.
7. Cantwell, Robert. *Nathaniel Hawthorne: The American Years*. New York: Rinehart, 1948, p. 36.
8. Faust, Bertha. *Hawthorne's Contemporaneous Reputation: A Study of Literary Opinion in America and England, 1828-1864*. University of Michigan: Octagon Books, 1968, p. 11.
9. Hawthorne Lathrop, Rose. *Memories of Hawthorne*. Boston: Echo Library, 1897, p. 53.

10. Hudspeth, N. Robert. (Ed) *My Heart is a Large Kingdom: Selected Letters of Margaret Fuller*. U.S.A: Cornell University Press, 2001, p. 156.
11. Hawthorne, Nathaniel. *Selected Letters of Nathaniel Hawthorne*. U.S.A: The Ohio State University Press, 2002, p. 143.
12. Baym, Nina. *Feminism and American Literary Essays*. U.S.A: Rutgers University Press, 1992, p. 50.
13. *Nathaniel Hawthorne and His Wife: A Biography Part One*. U.S.A: Kessinger Publishing, 2004, p. 343.
14. Wineapple, Brenda. *Hawthorne: A Life*. U.S.A: Random House Trade Paperbacks, 2004, p. 217.
15. Lathrop Hawthorne, Rose. "My Father's Literary Methods", *The Ladies Home Journal,* Vol 11. University of Michigan: Downe Pub., 1894, p. 41.
16. *Ibid.*, p. 42.

Chapter 14

CHRONOLOGY OF HAWTHORNE'S LIFE

1804 On 4th July, he was born in Salem, Massachusetts. He was the second child of an American navy captain named also Nathaniel Hathorne. His mother was Elizabeth Manning Hathorne who belonged to an enterprising Salem family. His paternal side was stringent Puritan colonists. The 'w' in the surname of the author is added by himself. His two sisters are Elizabeth (1802-83) and Louisa (1808-52).

1808 His father died due to yellow fever in Surinam (Dutch Guiana) while the family returns and joins Manning household. During this time, he was admitted to school.

1809 On September 21, in Salem Sophia Amelia Peabody whom Hawthorne married was born.

1813 Hawthorne got terribly injured while playing football and he suffered lameness. For fourteen months, he remained confined at home and was tutored at home.

1818 He moved along with his family to Raymond, Maine. Here he attends school for a short time and spent a beautiful childhood of freedom, hunting, fishing and reading among the wilderness.

1819-20 Hawthorne Returns to Salem and started living with his Manning relatives while his mother and sisters stay back in Raymond. After attending school, he prepares for college under the tutelage of a Salem lawyer. Along with sister Louisa, he published a neighbourhood paper called the *Spectator*.

1821-25 He joins Bowdoin College in Brunswick, Maine, where he develops eternal friendships with Horatio Bridge, Jonathan Cilley and Franklin Pierce (who became the fourteenth President of the United States). During this time he came across Henry Wadsworth Longfellow who soon became a good friend.

1825 After completion of college graduation, he returns back to Salem. He started living there with his mother and sister for next ten years. At this point he started to establish himself as a professional writer. Simultaneously he started visiting various tourist destinations in New England and New York and his writings reflect his observations about these places. Some of his best short stories were written during this period. At the same time, his struggle in the literary world begins as Hawthorne was immature and green horn in the unremunerative literary enterprise. He was so frustrated at this point that he completely abandoned his ambition of publication and burnt one complete manuscript.

1828 Hawthorne published his first novel *Fanshawe* at his own expense. The novel was based on his experiences at Bowdoin. The novel was published anonymously keeping his identity undisclosed. In later part, he destroyed his own copy and burnt the unsold copies in Boston Bookstore fire in 1831.

1830 His first tale "The Hollow of the Three Hills," is published in the *Salem Gazette*. Sketches including "Mrs Hutchinson" were also published.

1830-33 His other anonymous publications like "Sights from a Steeple" appeared in *The Token*. It also included "The Gentle Boy," "My Kinsman, Major Molineux" and "Roger Malvin's Burial."

1834 Proposed a collection of tales and sketches, "The Story Teller," to Samuel Goodrich who finally refused it.

1835 Hawthorne further contributed stories and sketches like "The Minister's Black Veil" and "the May-Pole of Merry Mounth" to The Token. "Young Goodman Brown" appeared in *New England Magazine*.

1836 He became the editor of the *American Magazine of Useful and Entertaining Knowledge* when he moved to Boston. He was aided by his talented sister Elizabeth in his work.

But the publisher goes bankrupt and he resigns from the editorship. He then returns to Salem again. He started working with his sister on Peter Parley's Universal History, on the Basis of Geography which appeared in 1837.

1837 *Twice-told Tales*, a collection of his earlier eighteen tales is successfully published by The American Stationary Company of Boston. Horatio Bridge agrees to help in the publication. Moreover, Longfellow gives a favourable review of the text and acknowledges Hawthorne as a promising American writer. Franklin Pierce tried to appoint Hawthorne as historiographer on the South Seas Expedition commanded by Charles Wilkes. During this phase he also came across Sophia Peabody, his future wife. Sophia had a strong impact in the intellectual circle of Emerson. Sophia also started supporting Hawthorne and became his source of encouragement.

1838 Hawthorne befriended John L.O. Sullivan who was the editor of the *United States Magazine and Democratic Review*. He also promoted the idea of 'manifest destiny'. Hawthorne in his later life became associated with the Democratic Party and started publishing frequently in this magazine. One significant contribution at this point is his memorial essay on his college friend Jonathan Cilley who was killed in a fight. At this point in his life, he became romantically inclined to Mary Silsbee.

1839 Hawthorne is appointed as measurer in the Boston Custom House at an annual salary of $ 1100. During this time he got secretly engaged to Sophia Peabody as reflected in his series of love letters. He also published *The Gentle Boy: A Thrice-Told Tale*, featuring an engraving by Sophia.

1840 *Grandfather's Chair*, the first book for children is published which consisted of a collection of historical sketches. He leaves Boston Custom House and joins Brook Farm Community which later became the model for the utopian community depicted in the *Blithedale Romance*. Here he becomes a trustee and director of finance. With a future plan to settle down with Sophia, he purchases two $ 500 shares in project but soon leaves the community in late October.

1841 Published two more children's books namely *Famous Old People and Liberty Tree.*

1842 Hawthorne and Sophia became husband and wife on 9th July and settled down at the "Old Manse" in Concord, Massachusetts, adjacent to the field where the first battle of the Revolutionary War was fought. At this time, the second edition of *Twice-told Tales* came out in an expanded version.

1842-45 Hawthorne came across the Transcendentalist circle that consisted of Ralph Waldo Emerson; Henry David Thoreau, Margaret Fuller, and Ellery Channing. This is called the "Old Manse" period. Thoreau planted vegetable garden for the newly wedded couple. Some of the masterpieces and tales are also produced like "The Birth-Mark," "Rappaccini's Daughter," "The Artist of the Beautiful" and "The Celestial Rail-road". All these were later collected in *Mosses from an Old Manse.*

1844 His first child, daughter Una (1844-77) was born on 3rd March. She was named after Edmund Spenser's heroine from *Faerie Queene.*

1845 Horatio Bridge's *Journal of an African Cruiser* is edited. It contained account of his Bowdoin friend Horatio Bridge's journey to Africa. His family including mother and sister returned back to Salem due to economic crunch. His influential friends like Bridge and Franklin Pierce help him to seek political appointment. Hawthorne was nominated for position of surveyor of custom house by Salem Democrats.

1846 Hawthorne was appointed as surveyor in the Salem Custom House at an annual salary of $ 1,200. At this time he published *Mosses from an Old Manse*. It included tales like "Young Goodman Brown," "The Birth-mark," "The Artist of the Beautiful," "Rappaccini's Daughter," and "Roger Malvin's Burial." His second baby, son Julian (1846-1939) was born on 22nd June.

1849 When the new Whig administration came into power, Hawthorne was removed from surveyorship in June. This became considerably public controversial issue. During this year on July 31st, his mother also passed away. He also started writing *The Scarlet Letter*.

1850 The masterpiece *The Scarlet Letter* is published on March 16th by Ticknor and Fields. It had three editions within nine months. Ticknor and Fieldsare the main eminent publisher who published most of his works for the rest of his life. The family moves to Lenox in the Berkshire Mountains of Western Massachusetts after he leaves Salem. This year is also crucial in terms of his great academic friendship developed when he met Herman Melville. Melville published "Hawthorne and His Mosses," which is a distinctive manifesto in American Literature, in *The Literary World*.

1851 Published *The House of the Seven Gables, A Wonder-Book for Girls and Boys*. Besides, a new edition of *Twice-told Tales*, and *The Snow-Image*, and *Other Twice-told Tales* are also published. It contained uncollected tales and sketches like "Ethan Brand," "The Wives of the Dead," and "My Kinsman, Major Molineux". This year is also economically successful when for the first time he earns enough from writing to support his family. His daughter Rose (1851-1926) was also born on 20th May. In this significant year Melville dedicated his Moby Dick to the "Genius" of Nathaniel Hawthorne.

1852 *The Blithedale Romance* and *The Life of Franklin Pierce* are published. The second one consisted of the presidential candidate hid old friend Franklin Pierce's campaign biography. He returned to Concord, Massachusetts and purchased Bronson Alcott's former house which he renamed as "The Wayside". This year also marked the tragic death of his sister Louisa who died in a steamboat accident on 27th July on the Hudson River.

1853 While his family leaves for England, President Pierce appointed him as American Consul at Liverpool. *Tanglewood Tales for Girls and Boys* is also published.

1853-57 By this time he has started living in England performing his consular duties and travelling simultaneously in the British Isles. He started recording his impressions about English life in his notebooks. The second edition of

Mosses from an Old Manse is published in 1854. During 1856 and 1857 spring, he made last visit to Melville.

1858-59 Hawthorne started travelling to France and Italy, living in Rome and Florence. During this time he developed friendship with British and American expatriate artistic community like Robert Browning, Harriet Hosmer, Louisa Lander and William Wetmore. From July 1858, he started writing *The Marble Faun* and finished the rough draft by January in 1859. His daughter Una was attacked with malaria known as "Roman fever" in October 1858. In 1859, the family returned to England where Hawthorne finished revising *The Marble Faun.*

1860 *The Marble Faun* is published in England under the title of *Transformation.* After seven years, the family again sailed for America and finally returned to Wayside in Concord. He started writing three new romances *The American Claimant*, *The Elixir of Life*, and the *The Dolliver Romance.* However, Hawthorne abandoned these romances within the next four years before his death.

1862 Hawthorne visited Horatio Bridge in Washington, D.C with publisher William Ticknor and met Abraham Lincoln. His essay based on Civil War was published, called "Chiefly About War Matters," in the *Atlantic Monthly.*

1863 *Our Old Home* is published which was based on his reminiscences about England in Atlantic Monthly sketches. It was dedicated to Franklin Pierce.

1864 Hawthorne's health started deteriorating. With Franklin Pierce he left for northern England tour. On 19th May, he died in his sleep at Playmouth, near Hampshire. He was buried on 23rd May in Sleepy Hollow Cemetery, Concord, Massachusetts. His last work appeared in July in Atlantic Monthly under the title "Scenes from 'The Dolliver Romance.'"

Chapter 15

CHRONOLOGY OF HAWTHORNE'S Works

1828 *Fanshawe*. His first novel anonymously published at his own expense. It consisted of ten chapters and Hawthorne was so disappointed that he burnt almost all copies. It is difficult to get a copy.

1830 "The Hollow of the Three Hills"

1831 "Dr. Bullivant"

1833 "The Seven Vagabonds"

1835 "The Ambitious Guest," "The Canal Boat," "Alice Doane's Appeal," "The Vision of the Fountain,""The Devil in Manuscript"

1836 (Editor) *The American Magazine of Useful and Entertaining Knowledge*, "Thomas Green Fessenden"(January 1836) and "Old Ticonderoga. A Picture of the Past"

1837 Contributes to *Peter Parley Series for Children; writes Peter Parley's Universal History* with his sister Elizabeth; publishes *Twice-told Tales*; "A Bell's Biography," "The Minister's Black Veil," "Dr. Heidegger's Experiment," "Edward Fane's Rosebud," "Sylph Etherege," "David Swan—A Fantasy," "Mrs. Bullfrog"

1838 "Chippings with a Chisel," "Roger Malvin's Burial," "Snow-Flakes," "Howe's Masquerade," "Edward Randolph's Portrait," "Lady Eleanore's Mantle"

1839 "Night Sketches under an Umbrella," "Old Esther Dudley," "The Lily's Quest: An Apologue"

1840 "John Inglefield's Thanksgiving"

1841 Grandfather's Chair, "The Provincial Muster," "Famous Old People"

1842 *Biographical Stories for Children*, "The Village Uncle"

1843 "The Birth-Mark," "Little Daffydowndilly," "Buds and Bird-Voices," "The Antique Ring"

1844 "The Artist of the Beautiful," "Rappaccini's Daughter," "Earth's Holocaust," "The Intelligence Office," "A Book of Autographs," "The Celestial Rail-road" (1844-46), "Drowne's Wooden Image"

1846 *Mosses from an Old Manse*

1847 *American Notebooks*

1850 *The Scarlet Letter*

1851 *The House of the Seven Gables*, *The Snow-Image and Other Twice-told Tales*, *True Stories from History and Biography*

1852 *The Blithedale Romance, A Wonder Book for Girls* and Boys, "The Canterbury Pilgrims," The Life of Franklin Pierce (campaign biography), "The Dragon's Teeth"

1853 *Tanglewood Tales for Girls and Boys*

1860 *The Marble Faun*

1861 "Near Oxford"

1862 "Chiefly About War-Matters," "Leamington Spa," "Pilgrimage to Old Boston"

1863 *Our Old Home*, "A London Suburb," "Outside Glimpses of English Poverty," "Consular Experiences"

1864 [Hawthorne dies at Plymouth, New Hampshire]

1876 *The Dolliver Romance* (published posthumously)

Bibliography

Baym, Nina. "The Blithedale Romance: A Radical Reading." *Journal of English and Germanic Philology*, 67 (1968): 545-69.

Beauchamp, Gorman. "Hawthorne and the Universal Reformers." *Utopian Studies: Journal of the Society for Utopian Studies*, 13, no. 2 (2002): 38-52.

Bell, Michael Davitt. *Hawthorne and the Historical Romance of New England*. Princeton, N.J.: Princeton University Press, 1971.

Bercovitch, Sacvan. "The A-Politics of Ambiguity in The Scarlet Letter." *New Literary History*, 19 (1988): 629-54.

Blythe, Hal, and Charlie Sweet. "Hawthorne's Dating Problem in *The Scarlet Letter*." ANQ: *A Quarterly Journal of Short Articles, Notes, and Reviews*, 16, no. 3 (summer 2003): 35-37.

Clark, Michael. "Another Look at the Scaffold Scenes in Hawthorne's *The Scarlet Letter*." *American Transcendental Quarterly* n.s., 1 (1987): 135-44.

Crowley, J. Donald, ed. *Nathaniel Hawthorne: The Critical Heritage*. London and New York: Routledge, 1970.

Donoghue, Denis. "Hawthorne and Sin." *Christianity and Literature*, 52 (winter 2003): 215-34.

Elbert, Monika. "Hester on the Scaffold, Dimmesdale in the Closet: Hawthorne's *Seven Year Itch*." *Essays in Literature*, 16 (1989): 234-55.

Hawthorne, Julian. *Hawthorne and His Circle*. New York: Harder, 1903.

Hawthorne, Sophia. *Notes in England and Italy*. Italy: Putnam and Sons, 1869.

Hoeltje, Hubert H. *Inward Sky: The Mind and Heart of Nathaniel Hawthorne*. Durham, N.C.: Duke University Press, 1962.

Loebel, Thomas. "'A' Confession: How to Avoid Speaking the Name of the Father." *Arizona Quarterly: A Journal of American Literature, Culture, and Theory*, 59, no. 1 (spring 2003): 1-29.

Matsusaka, Hitoshi. "Hawthorne's 'Egotism' and the Ambiguous Snake." *Chu-Shikoku Studies in American Literature*, 26 (June 1990): 1-9.

Matthiessen, F.O. *American Renaissance: Art and Expression in the Age of Emerson and Whitman*. New York: Oxford University Press, 1941.

Mellow, James R. *Nathaniel Hawthorne in His Times*. Boston: Houghton Mifflin, 1980.

Millington, H. Richard. Ed. *The Cambridge Companion to Nathaniel Hawthorne*. Cambridge: Cambridge University of Press, 2004.

Monteiro, George. "A Nonliterary Source for Hawthorne's 'Egotism: or the Bosom Serpent,'" *American Literature*, 41 (1970): 575-77.

Morsberger, Robert E. "Hawthorne: The Civil War as the Unpardonable Sin." *Nathaniel Hawthorne Journal* (1977): 111-22.

Newberry, Frederick. "The Artist of the Beautiful: Crossing the Transcendent Divide in Hawthorne's Fiction." *Nineteenth-Century Literature*, 50 (June 1995), 78-96.

Normand, Jean. *Nathaniel Hawthorne: An Approach to an Analysis of Artistic Creation*. Cleveland: Case Western Reserve, 1970.

Pearce, Roy Harvey. Ed. *Hawthorne Centenary Essays*. Ohio State University Press, 1964.

Pennell, Melissa. *Student Companion to Nathaniel Hawthorne.* Westport, Conn.: Greenwood Press, 1999.

Person, Leland S. *The Cambridge Introduction to Nathaniel Hawthorne.* Cambridge University Press, 2007.

Reid, Bethany. "Narrative of the Captivity and Redemption of Roger Prynne: Rereading *The Scarlet Letter.*" *Studies in the Novel,* 33 (Fall 2001): 247-68.

Reynolds, Larry J. (Ed) *A Historical Guide to Nathaniel Hawthorne.* Oxford University Press, 2001.

Tharp, Louise Hall. *The Peabody Sisters of Salem.* Boston: Little, Brown, 1953.

Wagenknecht, Edward. *Nathaniel Hawthorne: Man and Writer.* New York: Oxford University Press, 1961.

Waggoner, Hyatt. *Hawthorne: A Critical Study.* Cambridge, Mass.: Belknap Press of Harvard University Press, 1963.

Wineapple, Brenda. "The Biographical Imperative; or, Hawthorne Family Values." *Biography and Source Studies*, Vol. 6, edited by Frederick Karl. New York: AMS Press, 1998.

Wright, Sarah Bird. *Critical Companion to Nathaniel Hawthorne: A Literary Reference to His Life and Work.* New York: An imprint of Infobase Publishing, 2007.

Yokozawa, Shiro. "Nathaniel Hawthorne's Mental Attitude toward the Civil War." *Journal of the English Institute,* 11 (1980): 27-41.